FROM THE FLIGHTDECK

More stories from

'the sharp end'

By James McBride

an imprint of

flightsofpassion.com

Published by: flightsofpassion.com

www.flightsofpassion.com

🐦 @flightsopassion

First published 2016

Copyright © James McBride 2016

PAPERBACK ISBN: 978-0-9931368-2-5

Front Cover Photo by Gianluca Onnis

(Author with VIP B737 - finals into Cagliari from Moscow)

Some of these stories first appeared in *Flight Training News*

The author has written a regular monthly column in this publication since 2006

This is the first time these stories have been published together

*

Also by James McBride

The Flightdeck Survival Manual – 2014

Cooking on the Piste – 2015 (with Mark Chetham)

"Oh! I have slipped the surly bonds of earth,
And danced the skies on laughter-silvered wings;
Sunward I've climbed, and joined the tumbling mirth
Of sun-split clouds, --and done a hundred things..."

August 1941

John Gillespie Magee, Jnr.

FOREWORD BY JOHN PETERS

"I went through flying training with James. He was a natural pilot with charm and a warm wit. Add 30+ years of flying experience, both military and civilian, and this book exudes an innate understanding of how pilots think.

This book is an invaluable font of knowledge for any aspiring or experienced pilot, who wants to better appreciate the nuances of the aviator's mindset, the joy in the challenges that aviation presents, particularly with the evolution of the digital cockpit, and how the human element is challenged when things go wrong.

Every pilot appreciates that the real key to becoming a good pilot is 'airmanship', particularly in the unforgiving environment where bad weather, technological complexities and the limitations of human capacity meet. When it comes to airmanship, good decisions are a product of experience; experience is a product of bad decisions.

With his natural empathy, James recounts a lifetime of collective learning. Learning from our own experience is the best learning, but so, so slow; so don't wait for those pivotal moments – learn from others' experiences. If you are a pilot, buy this book, read with care, share with fellow aviators and learn from the shared wisdom within.

Each story in this book will be of benefit; one may just save you".

John Peters

16th December 2016

Former Squadron Leader John Peters RAF came to the world's attention in January 1991 – the first Gulf War.

A Tornado GR1 pilot, he was shot down and his bruised and battered face flashed onto television screens around the world as a prisoner of war.

He was joint author of bestseller "TORNADO DOWN".

During the remainder of his 16-year RAF career, he became a Tornado Instructor and then later, at the Inspectorate of Flight Safety, was involved in Human Factors and was responsible for the dissemination of shared learning within RAF aviation.

In John's own words; *"By definition, a good pilot has the same number of takeoffs as landings, so unfortunately I failed to meet that criteria!!"*

(He also still has a great sense of humour ☺)

CONTENTS

ACKNOWLEDGMENTS

I would like to acknowledge the help, guidance, training input, humour and wisdom of all the other pilots with whom I have flown aeroplanes. Their names are recorded in my flying logbooks as mine is in theirs. In the words of John Gillespie Magee, together we did "a hundred things"... in fact many more than a hundred. The following pages tell the stories of just some of them.

James McBride, December 2016

1 - THUNDER ROAD

That skid mark was not ours....

The clock ticks on...and the tension builds imperceptibly... "How much longer is it going to be?" asks the First Officer on my right-hand side. What he's referring to of course is 'takeoff clearance'. We've been given a hold short instruction and have been here waiting for quite some minutes at the holding point of runway 09. Our destination is Nice in the South of France and the F/O is keen to get underway, especially as today is one of his Command Assessment flights and 1 am his assessor. In addition of course, I am also the Captain of the Boeing 737 in which we sit – today I have a dual role and one with which I am pretty familiar. He needn't worry about his assessment, I know him well, we have operated airliners together several times before and I already have a fair idea of his potential as an aircraft Commander.

Possibly he senses this (at least he should do if he ponders on it) even though I have given him no direct cause for thinking today's assessment flight is a foregone conclusion. From his position, the runway to our left is partly obscured and he doesn't have such a good view as I do from my side of the flightdeck. At the other end of the runway a Spanish registered airliner is making an approach and we have to wait until his landing is complete prior to being allowed onto the runway. I listen to the voice of the ATCO in the tower, "Surface wind 090 at 10 knots, Spanair 3203 clear to land Runway 27" – *hmm*, I wonder; that will be an interesting approach with plenty of tailwind – quite a high rate of descent too I imagine.

"Why the hell is he landing with such a tailwind?" asks my colleague from the right-hand seat. "Well... they've only just changed runways and he was probably set up for two seven, add to that the fact it's more track miles for him to make the approach to zero nine and maybe he's running late..." Our speculation was prompted by the fact that clearly the airport was now operating on the Easterly runway and it just didn't make a lot of sense to permit aircraft to approach for a Westerly landing – but then I have long since ceased wondering about some of the more esoteric decisions of Air Traffic Control. We continued to wait patiently for our turn to use the runway. We were careful not to allow our verbal exchanges to deteriorate into non-operational chatting – this is always a risk when circumstances give us too much time – yes the devil makes work for idle tongues. If we start to chat at times like this, then we become distracted and the integrity of the operation will suffer. The taxi out and takeoff phases of flight in an airliner are usually times of high workload and when all of a sudden the workload decreases, having too much time can be a problem. Where is he? I thought, as I looked out of the flightdeck window again along the runway, *ah here he comes, still airborne and just about to flare.*

In the offices just to the north of the east-west runway, they said afterwards that they thought it was the sound of thunder. But the source of the noise seemed to move too rapidly and they realised it was coming from the runway itself. As the MD83 touched down hard with what was a good 10 knots of tailwind (possibly 15), the pilot deployed maximum reverse thrust – no wonder they thought it sounded like thunder! Those old style Pratt and Whitney JT8s don't half make some noise when they are in full reverse. The sound of thunder however was augmented by the scream of tortured metal as the right main gear collapsed and the starboard wing took the weight of several tonnes while scraping along the concrete at a hundred plus knots...

A big sigh from my right and again the words, "How much *longer* is it going to be...?" I replied in a matter of fact tone, "Well it's going to be a flippin' sight longer NOW, LOOK AT THIS!" He leaned forward in his seat harness so he could see past me to the left. From our vantage point we could see smoke, sparks and clouds of debris from the starboard wing, with large chunks of the flaps coming off as the white coloured airliner careered and slewed along the runway towards us – *will it stop in time?* Was my first thought, as it was difficult to judge its speed or rate of deceleration from the head-on angle which was my view. I knew it would be too late to try to get our 737 moving if it didn't stop before it hit us – the problem is that it takes a finite amount of time to overcome 50 tonnes of inertia even with plenty of thrust and our CFM56s take time to wind up – "Ah good; it's going to stop short, phew that's lucky because he was heading straight for us". The experience had been slightly surreal up to this time as it had been silent, due to the Doppler effect of the sound waves as the jet slid towards us and also the attenuating effect of the thick glass flightdeck windows, but now we heard the muted roar – *will there be a fire?* No, there was thankfully no fire; however the subsequent R/T exchanges on the tower frequency were interesting.

"Spanair 3203 do you have a landing gear problem?"

"No ees hokay, all ees hokay, ees NORMAL...we have... erm, technical problem..." Bearing in mind that at this point the aircraft was at an angle of 20° of bank, with the right-hand side of the flightdeck much closer to the ground, than the left, this statement was clearly going to take some believing. As we continued to watch the saga unfold, the two forward doors just aft of the flightdeck opened, the inflatable escape slides deployed and passengers started jumping out, quickly followed by the cabin crew. "Spanair 3203 are you going to EVACUATE?" the reply came back, "Negateev, we no EEVacuate, all ees OHKAY".

I remarked that I thought the Captain had a problem with situational awareness, "I guess he doesn't know what's going on just a few feet behind the cockpit, look they've blown the slides!" At this point there were now passengers and crew on the tarmac and it was clear we were going nowhere in a hurry as the runway was blocked, probably for hours. "Ladies and gentlemen, I apologise for this, however it is obvious that we are not going to be able to takeoff in the immediate future, so we're going back to the terminal, your patience would be appreciated". We taxied slowly back to the stand and shutdown. Little did we know that the runway would be out of service until the next morning.

Interestingly, when the airport emergency services arrived at the empty aircraft a few minutes later, they found that the overwing exits had been opened and the hatches thrown out, however none of the passengers had used this means of escape. Due to the close proximity of the engine intakes just aft of the wing and the fact that they were only finally shutdown by the fire crews, it is hardly surprising that the passengers were not keen on exiting this way. It was fortunate too that there were only 45 people onboard in addition to the crew.

There were a couple of major learning points for me from this accident. Firstly, effective communication with the cabin crew is essential in that short time period after a sudden stop on the runway and I was lucky to work for a company which had a short PA announcement written into their SOPs, "Passengers and Cabin Crew remain seated" to use on just such an occasion. Secondly and most important of all, we should ensure that the full drills are complete; engines shutdown, before we leave the flightdeck in an evacuation. Specifically referring to the aircraft QRH (or equivalent) to crosscheck the actions is one way of doing this.

If nothing else, the whole episode served to remind me of the importance of that huge, slim, rectangular piece of concrete to our world. It is often referred to by pilots in quite derogatory terms, such as, "Yeah, one runway's just like any other". On the other hand, occasionally you will hear respect being paid when the runway at a particular aerodrome is described as "Two miles of booming concrete!" – And here is the key. The connection is made between the physical and audible aspect of aircraft operations. This really is *Thunder Road!* The rolling boom of jet engines at high power settings produces a sound just like thunder as aircraft carry out their takeoff roll – the noise is both evocative and distinctive. The high pitched whistling whoosh from narrow intake JT8s, contrasting with the quieter, growling, roar from Rolls Royce RB211s is easily distinguishable to the enthusiast's ear.

.....where man actually demonstrates the defeat of gravity

The runway is a very special place. It is the place where man actually demonstrates the defeat of gravity. It is where he proves time and again that the laws of physics hold true and Leonardo was right. Sufficient Thrust produces Lift which overcomes Drag and Weight - the result is the magic of flight... All of us still experience a rush when we are sat in the cockpit of a powered flying machine at the threshold of a long runway which we know we're going to use most of to get airborne. We look down the length of the hard surface and see the perspective of the runway edges as they head towards the vanishing point just below the horizon. The sight is impressive and few people get to see it for real. That's the view, straight down Thunder Road.

There are times even now when I fly as a passenger and I sit in the cabin next to the window and I marvel at man's achievement. I will watch absent-mindedly as the runway blurs, feel the cabin deck angle tilt and then see the ground fall smoothly away – I smile to myself and think, *'Wow...that's such a cool trick!'*

Spanair MD83 accident Liverpool

--0--

2 - SEAT NEXT TO THE WINDOW SIR?

('Competency Based Interview' as used to assess airline pilots)

Initial approach towards Urumqi Diwopu airport, China B767F

Here's a good question for you. In October 2002 the result of research to find the world's funniest joke was published. This project, which was run by Dr Wiseman (ironic name don't you think), determined that statistically the jokes thought especially funny contained 103 words. Significantly, THE FUNNIEST joke however, contained only 102... The question is why was that? Another good question is; why do some otherwise competent, effective, professional pilots perform poorly in a formal recruitment interview?

*

The answer to the first question is difficult, however the second one is easier to solve. Basically the main reason many pilots fail to score well in this situation is not lack of knowledge, poor communicating skills or stress, it is good old fashioned lack of preparation. It is vital that you prepare yourself and your answers in advance.

Back in the good old days, the applicant would be asked straight forward questions such as "Why do want to work for us?", "What do you think your strengths and weaknesses are?" etc. But now the world has changed and in a similar way to the effect of the bean-counting fraternity on commercial activities, so the HR Specialists and Recruitment Consultants have made a real difference to the way in which personnel are assessed for employment.

Interviews are now streamlined and carefully designed to fit with the type of occupation. The appliance of science has made a dramatic impact on the way in which people are assessed for all sorts of jobs. However there is nothing to be afraid of here, quite simply you should prepare for a Competency Based Interview in the same meticulous manner that you prepare yourself to go flying. Take the same attitude to the C.B.I. and you'll perform much better on the day.

I have carried out many pilot recruitment interviews over a period of several years and therefore have a fair knowledge of the subject. Also, the study of psychology played a big part of my training in a former life so I think I am qualified to advise potential candidates on the do's and don'ts when facing the Competency Based Interview. You will know that it is a CBI because all of the questions ask for specific **examples** of your past performance.

This technique is also referred to as 'Behavioural Interviewing' and as the name suggests the interviewers (normally two of them) want to hear real examples of actual behaviour from you - the candidate. The interview takes normally 45 minutes or so and the questions are the same as given to all the other applicants before you to ensure the quality/standard of interviewing is maintained.

As one of the interviewers asks the questions, the other one scores your answers, marking down notes to remind him/her later of the quality of your responses. In addition to the questions in front of them, they will have examples of what constitutes positive scoring replies and negative also.

The scoring is based on the amount of 'evidence' which you provide. For example if you are asked a question and your mind goes blank and cannot give them an answer, this will be marked as 'nil evidence' which is the same score as the poorest response. The important point to get across here is you MUST say something.

If you feel that you need more time to think about it, then you can suggest "Can we move on to the next question please and come back to that one so I can think of a good example for you?" Normally the assessors will do this for you (it would be unfair if they did not in our enlightened PC age); however you WILL have to find an answer or example to give them when you return to the question at the end of the interview.

There are strategies you can practice prior to the interview day to ensure your performance does credit to your abilities. These strategies are aimed specifically at ensuring your answers match the competency they are trying to assess. One of these is called *the PAR Approach* – no seriously, it's true, stop laughing. The letters PAR in this context stand for **P**roblem, **A**ctions, **and Result**. The way you use it is this. Describe the Problem which *you* faced, go through the Actions which *you* took and detail the Result which *you* achieved.

Note the emphasis on **YOU**; it's all about **YOU** and **your** role in the situation which **YOU** encountered. Sounds easy doesn't it?

Well it needs practise to get it right. Paradoxically you will have to practise the technique aloud, to ensure that the answers which you give are articulate and convincing, yet <u>unrehearsed</u>.

It is not cheating to prepare in advance like this, because quite frankly many of your contemporaries are already doing so and your performance will be judged against theirs on the day. You should make up questions and answers then practise them with a colleague, friend or family member.

The point of this is so that you get into the interview mindset in advance. Practising speaking aloud in a formal setting so that when you have to do it for real, means there will be less tension and you have spare mental capacity to be able to think on your feet.

Different airlines will have a slightly altered structure to their recruitment day, but as they are all looking to assess for the same qualities, there will be much common ground. Remember the type of person they are looking for will be essentially a 'rule following professional', who can demonstrate a capacity for initiative and creative thought. They must be a 'good team player' who works well and in a 'cooperative manner' when under stress. Given these basic desirable qualities, you could design the interview questions yourself if you sat down and thought about it. Help is at hand however because you don't have to, try these for size.

"Can you give me an example of when you had to act quickly in a situation, where you had to think for yourself because there were no set procedures?" A tricky one this. It is obviously a CBI question, because they are asking for an example of what **YOU** did and for **YOU** to tell the tale of what happened.

Think of each answer as being a short story, based upon the PAR principle above so it's nice and neat. Don't drag it on too long, but at the same time keep in mind they want the 'evidence' to write down to satisfy the score that this will achieve. In the question above, they want evidence of YOU using YOUR initiative and thinking 'outside the box', but at the same time, you must be careful that the example you give does not imply YOU to be a 'rule breaker'.

"Can you give me an example of when YOU found it difficult to get your point across to another member of the crew? What did YOU do to solve this problem?" Again it is a CBI question, directly relating to airline operations. Here they are looking for evidence of you being a good communicator. What they don't want to hear is that you had a "blazing row with the Captain" on the flightdeck in flight during the descent into Dublin with your last airline!

No joke - this was one answer we heard to this question during the CBI. No prizes for guessing they did not get the job. The only saving grace for the chap in this story is that he was very honest, when perhaps a little more discretion would have been appropriate.

"Can you tell me about a time when you had to finish something in a rush when you felt you could have done it better with a little more time?" Here they are probing your commitment to excellence and therefore your attitude to quality/attention to detail. You know that there are times when quality has to be sacrificed for getting an *acceptable* result and you will have done so yourself on occasions in the past – tell it how it was and make sure that the R in PAR is/was *positive!*

It is important also to understand that not all of your examples have to be from within the world of aviation. One ex-serviceman we spoke to, gave a perfect example of his ability to continue being effective in a stressful situation. He literally demonstrated 'coolness under fire' while acting in command of a Royal Navy Minesweeper while docking in Belfast harbour many years ago.

The sound of the glass in the bridge windows being shattered by machine gun fire preceded his dive to the deck, but still clutching the microphone he screamed the Executive Command *"FULL ASTERN!"*

The rapid response from the rest of the crew ensured the safety of the vessel and all those onboard. He told the story in such a way as to score top marks. The *Problem* was acute and easy to visualise, his *Action* was exemplary and the *Result* was entirely positive.

Although the example he gave was not from an aviation setting, it fitted nicely - operating with other crewmembers and the whole philosophy which surrounds that concept. In fact the machine gun was not being fired at the ship, but was an unrelated dispute in the dockyard between rival terrorist factions.

So when you are thinking about your answers to the questions which will be posed, do bear in mind former careers and the situations you faced at those times. These examples can be used just as effectively to convince the interview team they're looking at the right man/woman for the job.

As part of the process, once the CBI is over you can expect some technical questions to give the assessors some idea of your technical awareness/competence. These may be along the lines of recent CAA AICs (Aeronautical Information Circulars) and perhaps some questions about the aircraft type you currently fly.

If you are not currently employed as an airline pilot, then you should anticipate questions of a more general nature with an ATPL exam type flavour to them. What is the formula for working out Local Speed of Sound for example? How does the CofG affect Stalling Speed? What do aircraft wing Spoilers do? What is the function of a Yaw Damper? What are the pros and cons of 'podded engines'?

Describe the lighting of an 'Instrument Runway'. What timing should be used for an instrument procedure turn? How would you define 'wake turbulence'? And how many minutes behind a heavy aircraft takeoff must a medium type wait? What gas is used to inflate aircraft tyres and why? Define Vmcg and when is it a factor in a takeoff calculation?

Remember that if you hold an ATPL and current Instrument Rating, then none of the above questions should faze you. If they do, it's time to get the books out again and refresh your knowledge base or you will impress no-one.

I hope the above has been of use if you are preparing for that all important airline interview and remember there is much more information out there to be accumulated. Try Googling 'Competency Based Interview' for a start and you will see what I mean. After you have surfed enough, sit down and design some questions then practise your answers with an 'interviewer'.

Get them to give you an honest appraisal of your performance and seek their advice on how to improve your delivery. Don't ever think, *"Oh I'll just Wing-It!"* Those days are gone and in the same way that the companies have applied psychology to the assessment process, you must structure your approach to the CBI.

So now it's time to consider again the first question which started this article. You will notice that as an Alpha personality type with a strong affinity for factual data, I picked up on the numerical anomaly from the original story.

Having considered the question carefully, noting there is one digit difference between the number of words in the majority of the best jokes and *THE FUNNIEST* joke in the world, I would say the answer is...

...it really doesn't matter! It's still the world's funniest joke and if you want to read it I suggest a brief browse on the internet will

provide the answer, simply Google 'world's funniest joke'.

*

**Your friendly Pilot Recruitment Team may look like this one –
seen here in Oslo recruiting for easyJet back in the day**

L-R: Roddy, Sarah, Self, Laure, James & Neil

--0--

3 - THE WRONG TROUSERS!

The Sim Assessor can usually tell within 5 minutes.

There is an old saying which states; *"you only get one chance to make a first impression"* and when it comes to the selection process for professional aviators never a truer word was said. The alternate school of thought goes along the lines of, *"why should it matter what I look like or even how I behave, surely it's my ability as a pilot that matters?"* Let's be clear. The occupation of professional pilot, whether it be military or commercial falls into the bracket of 'their lives in your hands' which is why so much emphasis is put upon selecting the right pair of hands in the first place. Both the armed services and the airlines are looking to recruit pilots who are conformist, responsible people who operate well in a disciplined environment. For the aspiring aviator, this means a barrage of tests, both mental and physical, which will have to be passed to achieve the ultimate goal of being paid to fly.

In the commercial world, one of the most important stages of the process is the dreaded 'Sim Ride'. Not all airlines test their applicants with a simulator assessment, but most do and this is often accomplished with the same aircraft type Sim which the company operates on the line. The candidates will normally receive a written brief in advance which explains the elements of the assessment and indicates what is required of them. The brief is almost certain to include the profile of the flight and reassurance that the pilot is not expected to fly the airliner as if they were an expert.

Wording in the brief such as "...purpose of the simulator assessment is not for you to demonstrate that you can fly a B757 without the need for any training...." serves to prove the point here. Of course the Sim Ride is not the be all and end all of Airline Recruitment as any airline worth its salt will have a multi-stage process in place to be able to view their applicants in the round. The Simulator assessment is weighted so highly however, it should be considered one of the key elements. As such, it is important to get it right first time if you are a candidate and in this respect, prior preparation and research are vital.

It must be established what type of aircraft is going to be used for the Sim – for example, British Airways used to use their trusty BAC 1-11 for assessing their applicants. This machine was legendary for the challenge which it presented any pilot that had not experienced a Smiths Flight-Director presentation before. In essence, when you look at the primary flight instruments of the BAC 1-11 and the accompanying (Smiths) flight director, it appears to react in the opposite sense when bank is applied – you can imagine how distracting this can be to the uninitiated, it feels as if the control wheel has been fitted upside down. Add to this the fact that the flap settings are all weird (British) and you had to make calls such as "Flap 11 please" or "Flap 16 please" and you build the impression that this machine was going to be a real test.

Naturally from the company's viewpoint, this is fine as they are reassured that if you can fly this, you can fly ANYTHING! Another idiosyncrasy of the BAC 1-11 flight instrumentation was the blue and yellow ILS display. No, really! Back in the 1950s when it was designed, this British masterpiece was considered to be the pinnacle of flight instrumentation – mind you this has to be kept in perspective, remember we also built aircraft such as the Brabazon, so maybe it wasn't such a smart idea after all. On a smaller scale and going back in time even further, the Smith's instruments as fitted to the venerable (and venerated) de Havilland Chipmunk had some peculiarities which are worthy of note, if only to cause some head-scratching these days.

Both the Altimeter and the engine RPM gauge in the Chippy are almost identical in both size and shape, but to increase the potential for confusion, some genius decided that all the odd numbers should be painted on the face in green and all of the even ones in white – on both instruments! Many is the time when I have been instructing from the back seat in times gone by and found that the student in the front has tried to set the engine speed while looking at the altimeter – a quite understandable error, but let's get back to business.

Chipmunk Altimeter and RPM gauge easily confused

There are several computer flight simulator programmes on the market which feature airliners and any candidate who is facing their own Sim Ride, would be well advised to practice flying the same type to get used to the presentation. (The Boeing Attitude Indicator display on the EADI for example can be misread when you first convert on to the type as the bank angle is indicated by the sky-pointer at the top of the instrument. Prior to flying with EFIS, it is likely that all of your attitude indicators displayed bank angle at the bottom of the display). Be careful how far you take this though, as it must be borne in mind that there is no motion present and therefore any inputs on the controls cannot be felt. Most airline Sim Rides will be full motion simulators, as this really is the only way you can properly assess a pilot's true ability and potential. Just as important as preparing yourself for what instrumentation you will be required to 'scan' during the assessment, is to research what manoeuvres will be given to you.

The brief should include the profile of the flight and will also have a section on Standard Operating Procedures. SOPs, as they are universally referred to in the airline industry, are essentially the bedrock upon which safe commercial operations are based. Proper adherence to and observance of the SOPs cannot be overemphasised and this will come as something of a culture shock to many pilots who have never operated aircraft in such a disciplined manner. Of course it's easy to see why SOPs are so important in commercial ops, because it means that any of an airline's pilots can fly together, (never having met each other before) and the quality of their operation will be assured. The written SOP includes the standard 'calls' – these are the spoken words/phrases which are used at the various phases of flight and are the precise words used by the pilots to communicate to each other.

At critical phases, these words alone and no other should be used to ensure that cross cockpit communications are not misunderstood. There have been too many occasions in the past when non-standard and/or inappropriate phraseology has lead to unfortunate situations. One such time was the Captain who noticed that his First Officer had been quiet and preoccupied during their pre-flight preparations and thought that he would have to try and improve his mood during the flight. The well meaning Captain chose the wrong moment to do so however when on the takeoff roll and with the aircraft barely airborne, he merrily called, "Oh... CHEER UP!" – the First Officer misheard him and thought he had said "GEAR Up!" with predictable consequences......

It is worth spending plenty of time revising these SOP calls as they are given to you and being prepared to use them in the simulator – your knowledge and use of them will be assessed. Any candidate, who comes into the Sim and demonstrates their lack of knowledge of the SOP calls, will provide the assessor with evidence that their attitude to the job of professional aviation is poor and be marked accordingly. Hence time spent learning the

SOPs is never wasted. Additionally, the standard calls, although probably a bastardised version of the company's own SOPs will most likely be similar to all other carriers in the same market place. In the final analysis, the SOPs are based upon what the manufacturer recommends to be used and all airlines will mostly conform fairly closely to that.

Another important consideration is appearance. I well recall the story a friend of mine told me about his son who went for his driving test at age 17 and returned very crestfallen having failed to pass it. His father made enquiries into how the test had been conducted − after all there was always a chance that an improperly conducted test could have been appealed against. His son assured him that the test had been done absolutely fairly and he accepted that it was his driving that was at fault, although he stated that he felt the examiner was biased against him.

My friend probed a little deeper to see if he could determine if there was a reason for this, but nothing seemed to be forthcoming. Then he noticed how his son was dressed, slashed denims, cool tee-shirt and ultra modern dark shades...... *"Did you go dressed like that for your test?"* he asked, *"Yeah, why?"* came the response. *"What, did you even wear the sunglasses, when it wasn't sunny?"* he couldn't believe it was true. *"Yeah too right I did, and I had my new black leather driving gloves on too!"*

In the words of one disappointed parent, when Anthony told me this story he said, *"D'ya'know the examiner probably took one look at him and thought, you'd better be good son! It's no surprise he failed".* Well of course you could say that an examiner should only judge performance and should do so in a completely objective manner, however an examiner's 'judgement' may be coloured by all sorts of things, even when they concentrate on trying to ignore other elements of the presentation.

As a simulator recruitment assessor myself, I had an interesting example of this some time back. Remember that the assessment itself starts from the moment the candidate is introduced to the examiner – there is no going back from this point. While I was making the introductions to the group of applicants who I had been tasked with assessing on the Boeing 757, I noticed that nearly all of them were wearing formal collar and tie except one who was casually dressed. In fact he had on a pair of what I assumed were his skateboarding jeans, along with a casual sweatshirt and the predictable trainers on his feet...... oh dear.

While I completed the brief I tried not to allow myself to be influenced by this young gentleman's appearance, however the words of my friend Anthony came to mind, "*.....you'd better be good son!*" Of course in reality, it's all numbers – either the pilot can fly the aircraft level on instruments and steady on a heading or not. If not, there is a quantifiable error which can be recorded and I am trained to note the numbers for future reference. We decided upon the batting order and then set off for the Sim. The casually dressed young man was number three for the assessment and he was wearing the 'wrong trousers' – no his real name wasn't Wallis!

The first two candidates had performed quite well and now it was Wallis's turn – this would be interesting. Although he received exactly the same briefing as the other pilots, Wallis quickly displayed a lack of Selective Radial Scan – in fact on occasions his instrument scan broke down completely at times during the flight. His entry to the hold was disastrous (lost several hundred feet in the turn) and the subsequent ILS was a real struggle for him. He was constantly flying behind the aircraft and appeared poorly prepared in all respects.

His was the sort of performance where you would seriously advise him to think of another career, because he was a poor fit for the occupation of professional aviator. After he landed halfway down the runway, (Gatwick) at well below Vref for Flap 30, he forgot to use reverse thrust and was slow to use the brakes, so we only just stopped by the upwind threshold! He made a flippant comment about it and did not seem unduly concerned with the apparent lack of retardation – I just breathed a sigh of relief and informed him that the Sim Ride was completed now and I was switching the motion off. He was fully debriefed by the company's Flight Training Manager later on with his report (written by me) as to why he had not achieved the standard required.

Was it the trousers? No of course not, but they were a clear indicator of someone who had not given the Sim Ride a great deal of thought. It was also a warning sign, that here was a pilot who had only ever flown in light aircraft in a flying club environment. His attitude therefore was that flying is a recreational activity, thus his approach to it was casual.

If his Instrument Flying had been smooth, accurate and professional (including knowledge of SOPs), then he would have passed the check, no doubt about it – after all, it's not a beauty contest. The moral of the tale is, spend some time thinking about how you are going to present yourself if your Sim Ride is coming up. Consider the way you are going to dress and how you wish to be perceived.

Even though your appearance should not be a factor, it could cause an assessor's judgement to be coloured and their decision could be the difference between a job offer or not.

--O--

4 - TRAINING BONDS – A THORNY ISSUE?

What is it with us pilots? Many of us seem to think we are instant experts on Contract Law regarding Training Bonds, when we are being asked to comply wlth the contract which we signed up for. You could see this whimsically as a variation of the cooking programme on TV, only in this instance it is entitled *"Can't Pay, Won't Pay!"* I suppose realistically, most commercial pilots have made huge sacrifices to get to where they are, so once they achieve their ambition, they are keen to extract as much financial reward as possible. Could this be the origin of the Cabin Crew's branding of us as *"Those tight Flightdeck"?* Probably, but I digress. In my case I have a clear vision of things – they're either black or they're white! For sure when we are talking about owing money I hark back to hearing my dear old Dad's voice when we were kids, solemnly intoning, *"A gentleman ALWAYS pays his debts!"*

For the uninitiated, a Training Bond consists of a legal contract between one party (the trainee) and another party, the training provider. The training provider (usually an airline) offers to pay for a pilot's training (normally the Type Rating) and in return expects a return of service by the individual. The pilot thereafter is known as "bonded" to the employer for the agreed period. Most bonds are reasonable, for example to be asked to sign for a £17,000 bond for a Boeing type rating, decreasing over a three year period to nil owed at the end is quite usual – especially when the actual cost to the airline is £25k plus.

Where the bond decreases over time, this is known as 'amortising' and is quite common. A more restrictive contract and one that could be seen as harsh from the pilot's viewpoint, is one where the bond does not amortise over time and therefore if the pilot leaves the employer even one day before the end of the bonded period, they become liable for the whole debt immediately! A well known airline based in the South of the UK, used to have such a bond in place for turboprop ratings and it used to cause a lot of angst among its pilots.

In an airline where I worked as a Pilot Manager, the issue of Training Bonds used to be very topical. The bond was basically a set amount of money (£17,000) over a three year period, which commenced from the date of the Pilot's Final Line Check. Thus after one years' service the pilot owes the company £11,322 (reducing at the rate of £472 per month). The amount outstanding only really raised its head when the pilot decided to leave the company before the end of the bonded period.

In most cases, all that was necessary was for the Line Manager, to work out how much of the bond was owed at the date of leaving the company and inform the pilot by letter. The departing pilot would then give the company a cheque for the amount and all would be well. Bearing in mind that there were no secretaries at the company working for managers and all their correspondence had to be written in person, the bond issue was yet another task which needed to be added to an already heavy workload.

When a pilot resigned, I normally liked to see him/her in person as their Line Manager and discuss their leaving arrangements on a one to one basis with them. Quite often they would be apologetic about leaving the company, but I would assure them that no offence was taken and at the end of the day, movement of pilots within the industry is actually good news for all of us. It keeps the management teams of airlines keenly aware of what a vital and expensive resource they are managing. This in turn, is no bad thing where our own terms and conditions are concerned, since those airlines who fail to attract and keep their pilots with sufficiently generous packages will pay more to replace them over the long term.

I have known pilot managers in the past who take it personally when one of their employees wants to leave the company and I was always at pains to point out that it is NOT an emotive issue – it's just business. Then came the part about the repayment of the outstanding bond money. As indicated above, for the most part the pilot was quite clear about their responsibility in this regard and there was little to be said other than to work out how much the settlement cheque needed to be written out for. In a few cases however, it was not so easy...

I would normally get the vibes along the lines of, "Do you think the company would be happy to accept instalment payment terms to clear the amount?" At which point I would clearly reiterate the terms of the training bond and ensure that the original agreement document was available for them to see. I used to ask them to think of it this way. "If I borrowed your car for a day or two and then had a major accident in it for which I was not insured, would it be reasonable for me to ask you for terms to repay the debt? No, I think we agree that I would owe you a car and you would be right to ask for all the money back to replace it ASAP. You have to think in terms of the bond repayment in the same way".

The discussion would often take the turn then of, "I haven't got the money and cannot afford to pay!" ("Can't Pay, Won't Pay!") At which point I would retrieve their salary figures for the period they had worked for the company - typically £35,000 per annum in the case of a First Officer. I would point out that such a salary gives a person an extremely good credit rating and even if they could not raise the money from their savings, they could easily obtain a loan to repay the company.

Additionally, most pilots were leaving the company to further their career and this often meant a pay-rise as they entered the employment of the next airline. After all this, most of them would agree and we would reach an amicable settlement, although a few would persist and these would end up in my "Troublesome

Parishioners" file on my desktop. Someone once said that 90% of a manager's workload is generated by 5% of their people and this is not far from the truth.

The next stage would be as their leaving date was getting closer and I would have to start chasing the bond money. I recall one particular case when the departing F/O was quite insistent that he had been given legal advice which indicated that, *"I've got a very good case in law and the bond agreement is not worth the paper it's written on, it won't stand up in court. My solicitor says I should fight this all the way and if necessary you can take me to court for it, because it's not fair to make me pay it all back in one lump sum".*

We had a long meeting about it and tossed it back and forth. I stressed that the agreement did not make any provision for instalment repayments and also that I too had taken legal advice – this from our company solicitor who said the opposite of what the pilot was being told. In fact I highlighted the fact that his solicitor was almost bound to encourage him to go to court over it, because even if he lost (I was certain he would) then the legal teams would still get paid! At least he could see the logic of this.

The story had a happy ending however, because finally he responded to my last letter, which was written with reference to the company Legal Eagle and resulted in the production of a cheque for several thousand pounds as if from nowhere from the man who could "not afford to pay". He was then able to further his career with a longhaul airline based in the Far East and he had our blessing to do so.

On another occasion, a casualty from 9/11 who had been made redundant as a result of that catastrophe, declined to repay his bond on leaving the company even though we had taken him in when he was unemployed, yet experienced. He appeared to be quite insistent about the matter until it came to the time for him to obtain a written reference from his former employer (us) which would enable him to gain an airside security pass. I called him to remind him about the outstanding bond situation and the response was pretty blank until I also informed him that we had received the reference request which had to be completed by his Line Manager (me). The reference asked the question; *do you believe this person to be an honest, responsible and trustworthy employee who can be recommended for an airside security pass?* The important point about this form is that it is a legal document and to make a false statement is a criminal offence.

I stated that it would be easier for me to answer this question in the knowledge that the former employee had repaid their debt to the company in full, because he had already indicated a lack of willingness to pay and therefore I couldn't honestly say that I could vouch for his integrity… Funny thing was, he popped into the office the very next day with his cheque.

Now throughout all of this, there were many of our company pilots who thought I was being overly harsh, or "enforcer" like in my approach to the training bond, however what I sincerely wished to avoid, was for them to end up in court in a legal battle with our airline. I was convinced that on a scale of one to ten of 'bad things to happen in your career' this would be a definite 9+.

I know that one of my old mates from many years previously couldn't see it, when I insisted that he too should cough up before he departed for the Middle East. He even tried to circumvent the system by going directly to HR at the company headquarters to try to avoid paying the bond – asking them to provide a fax which he could show to his new employer, stating that he had no outstanding debt with us. Very naughty of him really and I admonished him in a friendly way when I found out – but still made him pay.

In other bases however, things were not done in quite the same way. We had a case where a First Officer who had only recently finished his B737 course, but decided that for "family reasons" he needed to be working at an airport nearer home. His Line Manager indicated to him in a written reply, that 'There might be some way to get round the "thorny issue of the bond" in such circumstances and that he would speak to head office for clarification........' I advised the Line Manager directly that there was no way round it and sad though we were to lose the services of a pilot and although we wished him well with his next employer, the bond MUST be paid – it was £12,750. Unfortunately, that initial advice of his Line Manager probably coloured the way in which he approached the situation, even though successive levels of management thereafter were quite firm on the issue of the bond.

Afterwards an old friend and former colleague in that base who still works for the company, called me with some news on the case. It did go to court finally in Scotland and after all the legal wrangling was over, (summer 2005), the Judge found in favour of the company.

The poorly advised pilot was ordered to repay the bond £12,750 plus 8% interest for the time the amount had been owing and additionally he was ordered to pay ALL the costs of the case – in round figures £100,000! I was very sad when I read this, because if only this pilot had been managed in a proper manner and given quality advice on the subject from the word go, he would not be in such a financially parlous state now.

For me the moral of the story is, *a gentleman (or woman) ALWAYS repays their debts.*

--0--

5 - THE AIRLINE THAT CAME IN FROM THE COLD

Air Astana are modernising that's for sure!

With only 500 feet to go on finals and still in thick cloud we were now being buffeted by really heavy turbulence. It was then that ATC kindly informed us that the surface wind had increased to "45 knots with Blowing Snow". 'Great,' I thought. 'This is Gander all over again.' I was starting to doubt ever so slightly whether accepting the invitation by Air Astana had been the right idea...

*

Let me explain. Everyone likes to enjoy hospitality while travelling to foreign parts of the world and I am no exception. When I received an invitation in 2008 to visit Kazakhstan as a guest of Air Astana, I relished the prospect, but little did I know that I would be heading for a reprise of one of my most difficult landings ever. This time it would be in unfamiliar territory, a very long way from home, close to the border with China.

It is important to put this all into context. As a Pilot Trainer of Boeing 757 and 767 flightdeck crews, some of my work in previous years brought me into contact with Air Astana pilots whom I was training and checking in the simulator in the UK. Generally the standard of their operation was quite high and even though there are language challenges at times, the level of communication was good. On several occasions the pilots asked if I had ever been to Kazakhstan, to which I replied in the negative. Upon hearing this, they would become very animated and I soon lost count of the number of offers of hospitality. In February 2008, my diary had a window in it that required to be filled, so with a few telephone calls and emails to my colleagues in Air Astana, the arrangements for a five day visit were made.

I joined the Air Astana flight from London Heathrow's Terminal 2 on the evening of February 19, 2008. Flight KC902 is scheduled to depart at 1715 local time with the destination being Almaty, one of the major cities in the country. Almaty used to be the capital of Kazakhstan until about 11 years before, when it was decided to move the capital city to Astana, a more central location; however it is still an important financial focus for the nation. My colleagues in Air Astana asked me to travel in uniform, with my airline ID card, so that I would be allowed access to the flightdeck jumpseat with the permission of the Captain. In these days of stringent security restrictions, such an invitation is rare indeed and I was delighted to accept.

The Air Astana B757-200 has a total seating capacity of 170 passengers. 20 of these are Business (J) class in the forward part of the cabin ahead of doors 2 (left and right) and the remainder 150 seats are Economy (Y) class. In fact, even the economy seating has generous pitch and legroom, with handsome dark blue leather upholstery throughout. Bearing in mind that charter company configuration 757s in the UK used to fit in 235 seats and you get a feeling of the extra space inside the Air Astana version.

The London scheduled service KC901/2 is no stranger to carrying VIPs to and from Almaty and this evening was no exception. In addition to some Commercially Important Passengers (CIPs), we were carrying the airline President's wife, Mrs Carmelita Foster. The crew were all very aware that she was onboard the flight, as only the previous week the flight carrying her husband (Peter Foster) had been required to make a diversion to an alternate airport due to poor weather. Although rare, diversions due to weather are a normal part of commercial airline operations, but when it happens with the President of the airline onboard, it can be embarrassing.

As I was made welcome in the flightdeck by the pilots, Captain Nurlan Kanatbayez and First Officer Alexei Litvinov, they were obviously concerned about the forecast of freezing fog in Almaty for our arrival time of 0625 local the next morning. The Terminal Airfield Forecast (TAF) for Almaty (ALA/UAAA) for the period included Freezing Fog (FZFG) 1100m Runway Visual Range (RVR). It was obvious that all the crew were thinking, *'Oh no! NOT AGAIN!?'*

This was emphasised by Martin Craggs the London Heathrow Station Manager for the company, who told me, "We REALLY want to avoid another weather diversion so soon if we can. It was bad enough having the President onboard last week, but to do the same to his wife will look like incompetence..." There was a twenty minute delay to pushback which was introduced by ATC on the Delivery frequency due to departure traffic congestion from runway 09R.   In the flightdeck, I was listening on the spare headset and could hear the Station Manager calling the Captain, "We're nearly ready down here Skipper, just closing the cargo holds now, please call for push and start". It was obvious that Craggs was keen to see an ontime departure.

While we waited for the push and start release to come through on the R/T, I noted that the flightplan time showed a little over 7 hours flying time with an average tailwind component of +37 knots overall.   Once airborne from Heathrow, the Flight Management Computer (FMC) predicted ETA was 0045z.   As Almaty is 6 hours ahead of London, this translated to 0645 local time, only 20 minutes behind schedule, assuming that we were able to land off the first instrument approach...

The pilots flew at Economical (ECON) cruise speed, Mach .802 for the most part. The B757 has effectively a Mach .80 wing, in other words the most efficient cruising speed is M.80, which is virtually 94% of the maximum speed the aircraft can fly at — very clever of the Boeing engineers when you think about it. The maximum speed for the aircraft is Mach .84, beyond which the overspeed clacker will sound. For the most part, the journey was uneventful and our routing took us at Flight Level 370 (37,000 feet with 1013 HPa set on the altimeters) across Germany, Poland and the Ukraine, entering Kazakhstan airspace just north of the Caspian Sea.

Kazakhstan is the 9th largest country on the globe. It is bigger in actual landmass than all of Western Europe put together. Even after crossing the western border, we still had the best part of 3 hours flying time to go to destination, which is in the far east of the country close to the Chinese border.

Fortunately luck was with us, as the visibility for arrival was much better than the forecast and permitted an expeditious Instrument Landing System (ILS) approach and landing onto runway 05 at 0640 local time in freezing conditions Outside Air Temperature (OAT) -5^{0}C with very light winds. All the radar vectoring was done in English and all the briefings and checklists by the pilots were completed in English also, which was very much appreciated by me as my Russian is pretty thin and my knowledge of Kazakh even less! FO Litvinov made a good night landing, switching off the automatics at around 1000 feet on finals and then the Captain took control of the aircraft for a very careful taxy to the terminal. Due to the extreme weather conditions that Air Astana pilots are called to operate in, they get used to being very, very cautious when taxying, as not only the runway, but also the taxiways can be very slippery in winter.

The engines were shutdown at the gate only 25 minutes behind schedule with 10,600 kgs of fuel onboard. This shutdown fuel included the reserves necessary to hold for a long period of time and then to fly to the alternate of Astana (TSE/UACC) should it have been required by the weather. I was very grateful to my hosts and was met airside by the Air Astana meet and greet girl who kindly organised the crewbus to the Hyatt Regency Hotel, some 40 minutes away from the airport. As we waited outside the airport, I was introduced to a couple of the contract pilots working for Air Astana, including Capt Jack Vandsworth an ex Continental Airlines 757 skipper. With the temperature hovering at a chilly -10 Celsius while we waited for the bus outside the terminal building in the snow, I was reminded by Jack that I should have brought a proper coat.

"Jeez fella! Is that all ya got with you, that little jacket and nuthin' else?" He remarked, looking with pity at me in my lightweight uniform, I shrugged it off with a
"Don't worry about me I'll be fine, we'll soon be inside again!"
'Brrrr, but it WAS cold here' I thought. Mental note to self; *'check the forecast next time you dummy'.*

*

Two days later I had the pleasure of joining another crew on a flight from Almaty; it was a domestic flight to and from the capital city called Astana. The Captain for this flight was Alexey Trofimov (Chief Instructor B757/767) and his co-pilot was Senior First Officer Viktor Schmidt, who was only 6 months away from getting an upgrade to Commander. I met both pilots at the briefing room in the base of Air Astana Centre Number One building which is located very close to the main airport terminal and was again invited to shadow the crew throughout their working day.

Capt Alexey Trofimov & Senior FO Viktor Schmidt KC853

This time in addition to being in uniform and possessing my own crew ID pass, I was required to have a special "Flightdeck Clearance" security pass too. The flight numbers were KC853 and 854 and the aircraft in use was another B757. The pilots received their initial weather and airport information briefing from the company at the briefing office and were given their flightplans too. An initial fuel figure was requested and this was passed onto the fuelling department out on the ramp.

It was then time for us to walk over to the terminal, pass through multiple crew security checks before exiting airside and climbing the stairs to the airport's own briefing centre. Once inside, the pilots in common with all airline crew had to undergo a medical check with a doctor to ensure fitness to fly. This procedure was certainly strange to me as the western pilots only see their Aviation Medical Examiner once every 12 months, but it is a hangover from the former Soviet way of operating. It was explained to me that there had been historical issues with airline crews and alcohol abuse in the former USSR. The only way the authorities had found to control the practice had been to make all crew see the Doctor prior to flight. If the Doc detected alcohol, then the crew would be subjected to breathalyser and blood tests – all very foreign to those of us who had grown up in the West.

Naturally my curiosity was aroused and I asked the question, "But what happens after an overnight stop downroute...?" To which I was told that it was the aircraft Commander's duty at crew report time, to look each crew-member in the eye, face to face and ask "Have you been drinking...?" To which I had a further query; "But what - hypothetically speaking - if they were ALL at the same crew party the night before...?"

Once the medical was completed, they proceeded firstly to the weather (Meteo) briefing office where a lady meteorologist showed the Captain all the weather data including satellite pictures from her screens. After this came another office which dealt solely with the Notices To Airmen (NOTAMs) and from here the Captain increased the fuel figure and requested new flight plans. The first alternate airport Qaraghandy (KGF/UAKK) was closed due to a huge snowstorm and was not due to reopen for the rest of the day, which meant that the Captain had decided to carry much more fuel than usual to ensure other alternates were available.

The TAF for our destination was pretty bad with very strong winds gusting to 50 knots (25m/s) with poor Vis and low cloud base, 'Blowing Snow' (BLSN) and an OAT of -6 Celsius. I laughed when I saw the weather and joked with Viktor the First Officer that I was going to go back to the hotel; after all I was just a passenger and not part of the required crew. Thinking back, the last time I saw real 'blowing snow' was in the early '90s during a night approach in a B757 to Gander in Canada.

I remember the visual illusion was that the runway was drifting sideways - very disconcerting while you try to land in a crosswind in the dark! On that occasion we were pursued down the runway by the fleet of snowploughs, who were desperately trying to keep the airport open, all very exciting. Today's flight looked like it was going to be similarly afflicted by the weather; however, apart from putting on more fuel and talking about de-icing, Alexey and Viktor did not seem to be in the least bit alarmed. 'We shall see how they react a little bit later', I thought to myself, when they get the actual weather inflight and have to shoot the approach or hold off until it improves.

On arrival at the aircraft I was introduced to the rest of the crew, 6 female Flight Attendants and one male – this is an exaggerated representation of the population demographic of this part of the world where there appears to be a surplus of females to males. The crew were very welcoming and quite cheerful, including Anna the attractive Senior Flight Attendant, but when she saw my camera her reaction was quite sharp. In a very stern voice with echoes of the old Soviet Union mentality she barked at me, "Photography Is PROHIBITED!" I replied,
"Prohibited by whom? By Anna?" Then she burst out laughing, much to my relief and said, "Yes by Anna!"

Anna – Senior Cabin Crew Member KC853

I was extra polite about taking photos after this, but the crew were all very keen to oblige. Not so long ago, Anna's stern warning would have been for real and under the previous regime, stiff penalties would apply. Passengers are still not allowed to take photographs without consent, especially out of the windows on the ground. Only a year or so before, one of the Air Astana airliners was ordered to return to the gate, when a security officer on the ramp spotted a passenger taking photos out of the window towards the VIP terminal where the President's private jet was parked.

The Captain gave his welcome onboard Public Address announcement (PA) in both Russian and English, telling the passengers, "Ladies and gentlemen, welcome onboard, the flight time is a little over one and a half hours and the weather in Astana is snow showers with windy conditions and the outside temperature there is minus 6 degrees Celsius". 'Holy Shemoly' I thought to myself, 'Minus 6 with a 40 knot wind...? WHOA! That's going to be REALLY FLIPPIN' COLD!'

```
Дата   21-02-2008        Время:  08:55  UTC

UACC 210558Z 210716 20020G25MPS 2000 -SN BLSN OVC010
TEMPO 0710 0400 +SN BLSN OVC015 BECMG 1012 26020G25MPS
1500 SN BLSN OVC006 TEMPO 1216 0400 SHSN BLSN BKN005CB=
```

Not often you will see a Forecast as 'sporting' as this one

Passenger boarding was completed without a hitch, 12 in J class and 100 in Economy. There are four flights per day between the two major cities in Kazakhstan and this was the lunchtime rotation. The aircraft pushed back from the gate right on schedule at 1255 local time. Soon we were airborne and heading for Astana, as we took off from Almaty, I noted that the rain was turning to snow – not a good sign for our return later.

It is strange to see odd numbers in the autopilot mode control panel (MCP) for the altitude, but in this part of the world all of the flight levels are in metres as opposed to feet. Conversion tables are stuck to the instrument panels to enable crosschecks to be made before setting the Altitude window.

CRUISING LEVEL KAZAKHSTAN, MONGOLIA, RUSSIA	
WEST (180 - 359)	**EAST** (360 - 179)
← 13.100 = **43000**	
← 11.600 = **38100**	12.100 = 39700 →
← 10.600 = **34800**	11.100 = 36400 →
← 9.600 = **31500**	10.100 = 33100 →
← 8.600 = **28200**	9.100 = 29900 →
← 7.800 = **25600**	8.100 = 26600 →
← 7.200 = **23600**	7.500 = 24600 →
← 6.600 = **21700**	6.900 = 22600 →
← 6.000 = **19700**	6.300 = 20700 →
← 5.400 = **17700**	5.700 = 18700 →
← 4.800 = **15700**	5.100 = 16700 →
← 4.200 = **13800**	4.500 = 14800 →
← 3.600 = **11800**	3.900 = 12800 →
← 3.000 = **9800**	3.300 = 10800 →
← 2.400 = **7900**	2.700 = 8900 →
← 1.800 = **5900**	2.100 = 6900 →
← 1.200 = **3900**	1.500 = 4900 →
← 800 = **2600**	900 = 3000 →
← 600 = **2000**	700 = 2300 →
← 400 = **1300**	500 = 1600 →
← 200 = **660**	300 = 1000 →
	100 = 330 →
FOTL-0129 (R.0)	(B757)

Altimeter metric conversion chart Metres=Feet

Autopilot MCP cruise ALT set for 10,600 metres (34,800ft)

So the instruction "Climb Flight Level 10 Thousand 600 Metres" from Air Traffic Control (ATC) becomes 34,800 feet set in the ALT window – very strange when you are used to seeing only whole thousands in there.

As we climbed out of Almaty into thick cloud, the 'Terrain' function on the Ground Proximity Warning System (GPWS) which was indicating on the lower Electronic Flight Instrumentation System (EFIS) screen showed mountains to the side of us up to 15,200 feet – they were depicted in red.

This was more than a salutary reminder of the Minimum Safe Altitude (MSA) to the south and east of Almaty which goes up to 17,900 feet inside 25 nautical miles (NM) of the airport, in fact there is also an MSA of 16,700 within 15 NM to the southeast – not to be taken lightly especially at night or in cloud.

Lat & Long on the IRS – here showing 73° <u>EAST</u> of Greenwich

Close to the top of climb we actually broke out of cloud and had blue skies above, a very pleasant sight. However, due to the short cruise segment, it was soon time to commence the descent. Captain Alexey and Viktor had checked the weather and another complication had now come into play – the runway braking action was reported as 0.35 which reduced the possible crosswind acceptable for landing. The crew checked the braking action table to be sure and then crosschecked the autoland table for wind limits.

It would not be possible to make an autoland because the surface wind was now in excess of 25 knots... 'Hmmm', I thought, 'rather sporting flying conditions in Astana today!'

Capt Alexey consults the Boeing Adverse Weather section

The final Automated Terminal Information System (ATIS) weather report just before they commenced the instrument approach to runway 22 gave a surface wind of 36 knots with gusts up to 46 knots, there was blowing snow and the current Runway Visual Range (RVR) was 450metres.

During the briefing for the approach, there was a moment of light relief when Captain Alexey pointed out that our final turn towards the extended centreline of the runway must not infringe the no-fly zone around the President's Palace! This was depicted on the Jeppesen approach plate. 'Just one more little thing to worry about then chaps, eh?'

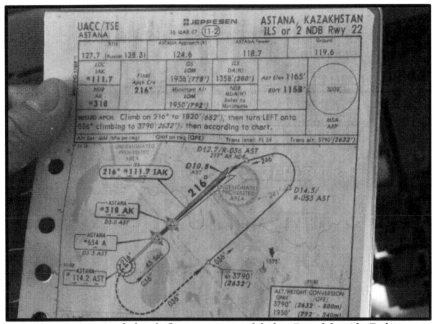

And don't forget to avoid the President's Palace...

Coming onto long finals, with the Engine Thermal Anti-Ice going strong, and with moderate turbulence, we received "Visibility now 1700 metres, in Blowing Snow, continue approach..." The final approach speed carried all the extra 20 knots permitted by the manufacturer on top of the standard threshold speed so we were now flying at 146 knots in the landing configuration, passing 500 feet on the Radio Altimeter and still no sight of the ground. The wind at this point was indicating 200 degrees at 45 knots on the EFIS Map. Captain Alexey had been following through all the way on the flight controls as the automatics had locked on to the ILS beams and now took the autopilot out, its customary bleep, bleep warning seeming louder than usual.

"VISUAL!" The yell from both pilots was a shock and a relief at the same time, 'now all he has to do is land the damn thing' I thought, tensing myself up on the jumpseat. Just like I remembered from Gander, the runway appeared to be moving sideways as the snow blew in white streaks diagonally from left to right, nearly blizzard conditions. To complicate matters the strong gusts of wind were making Captain Alexey work really hard to keep the wings level as we got closer to the ground. The synthetic voice of the automated Radalt callouts sounded really quite loud.

"VISUAL!" The yell from both pilots was a shock...

"FIFTY..." We were rocking and rolling towards the runway. "THIRTY..." 'Here it comes; now for the flare manoeuvre'. Then in quick succession, "TWENTY...TEN!" And Alexey raised the nose, closed the thrust levers and committed us to the landing. Thump! The aircraft made a firm touchdown on the centreline and very little braking was required.

In common with all Air Astana pilots he did not immediately engage reverse thrust, just in case the aircraft started to slide to the downwind side of the runway, but the braking action was better than reported and the 757 stuck like glue. What a great aeroplane and a very good landing! It is always better to make a firm touchdown in difficult conditions like these, rather than try to "grease it on". In the trade it's known colloquially as a "Standard Boeing Landing" and is the recommended technique.

'Blowing Snow' for real – B757 landing in Astana

Futuristic main passenger terminal building

Captain Alexey taxied very cautiously towards the ramp, behind the follow-me truck on the frozen taxiways and as we came onto stand, nose in to the terminal, it was clear that part of the terminal roof was being lifted off by the strong south-westerly winds. Just after parking several pieces of roofing material got airborne and started heading northeast doing around 40 knots – most impressive.

Terminal roof parts heading northeast doing around 40 knots

After the checklists were all completed and the passengers were disembarking, with the aircraft rocking from side to side and the OAT indicating -6, I asked if it was going to be the First Officer's walkround.

They both laughed heartily and said that in these conditions normally it is left to the ground engineers. The Captain did have to visit the Air Traffic Control tower though and sign for the briefing of the return flight. As all I had with me was my "little jacket" so I was spared this duty - instead I was served with a business class lunch in row one by the lovely Zlata, who was the forward galley Purser.

The starter was Caviar with a main course of Roast Chicken and vegetables with a delicious dessert to follow. The only menu item lacking was a glass of chilled white wine, but as I was in uniform and sort of on duty, this was not to be. The cabin service is well up to western standards, with 7 hard working and enthusiastic cabin crew on every flight. On flights exceeding 5 hours duration there are two meal services, but today there would be only one.

Cabin Crew of KC853

I took the opportunity to chat with the cabin crew during the turnround and discovered that they were looking forward to receiving their new uniforms; I asked them "What is wrong with the one you have already, it looks great to me?" The immaculately dressed stewardess said, "Look", pulling at the cloth, "ees too cold in winter and ees too warm in summer" She paused for half a second while she put her thoughts into English, "ees only good in September!" She laughed and I did too. She had very neatly described the climate in Kazakhstan which has extremes of temperature common to all central continental areas.

Once the cabin was cleaned and boarding nearly completed, Anna arrived in the flightdeck and asked us all if we would like a hot drink. The two pilots ask for coffee, I had already had one with lunch, but Anna was keen to serve so she asked if I would like anything else at all. I thought for a moment and then used one of my few Russian words, "Hmmm... Morozhennoe please?" I looked pleadingly at her. She threw her head back and laughed, "Okay just two minutes Captain, and I will go into the terminal for you". We all laughed at the thought of poor Anna who was already so busy with boarding passengers, going into the terminal to buy ice-cream for me. Before she went back from the flightdeck I did make sure she knew it was only a joke.

Minus 6C with a 40KT wind = Very Cold

The dispatcher entered the flightdeck then and asked for the key to the safe in the cargo hold. When I enquired why with Captain Alexey, he waved a piece of paper and said airily, "Oh, it's just for a gun that one of the passengers is carrying". Surprised, I asked, "What sort of gun is it? Maybe it's a sporting rifle or shotgun?" I knew that the Kazakhs are keen hunters.

"No. Is automatic pistol, Bang, Bang, Bye, Bye!" He indicated a pistol shape with his fingers and a big smile, to assure me that this was an entirely normal occurrence. Either the passenger was a bodyguard, a soldier on duty, or it could even have been a VIP – I never did find out. It is commonplace in Kazakhstan, although guns are no longer carried in the cabin fortunately.

The return flight was similar in that by the time we had returned to Almaty it had been snowing quite heavily and the 757 was making tracks in the snow on the taxiways again as we parked up. The RVRs for the approach to runway 23 were 650/500/650 metres, so again it was pretty close to minimums, although one of the big advantages with Almaty's climatology is that there is rarely any strong wind. For me, one of the most impressive things which I picked up on was that the pilots appeared completely relaxed yet professional. All the radio transmissions were very polite and calm and the standard of English by Kazakh ATC was very good indeed. A good example of this was Alexey's reply for a frequency change to the approach controller.

"Roger, one two zero decimal eight; have a good day, Astana 854".   And this was just before they commenced the final approach to land at Almaty airport, in poor weather and where the MSA is higher than that for Mont Blanc in Western Europe. These guys have obviously been doing this sort of flying for years in this part of the world in all kinds of ex Soviet machines (Tupolev 134s and 154s for example), but I got the feeling now that they are much safer in the modern day airliners from the West.

Back in Almaty the rain had turned to snow...

Saying goodbye to all the cabin crew, we three pilots boarded the crewbus for the terminal and it really did feel that we had done a full day's work, although both my companions seemed fresh and cheerful.   These Kazakhs are tough guys I realised.   Not only tough, but professional too and they have been doing this sort of flying day in, day out for years.   Less than 24 hours later I arrived back in Heathrow, only a day older, but very much wiser about the operating challenges facing one of the youngest national carriers in the world.

*

My grateful thanks to my hosts Capt Patrick Rotsaert (VP Flight Ops Air Astana), Capt Tom Nichols, (Flight Ops Manager Air Astana) and Capt Alexey Trofimov, (Chief Instructor B757&767 Air Astana).

Patrick Rotsaert – Vice President Flight Ops Air Astana 2008

Capt Tom Nichols – Flight Ops Manager Air Astana 2008

--0--

6 - THE CLASS OF 1990

Group Selfie long before the word was invented.

Of the thousand or so Chipmunks manufactured at the De Havilland factory (Hawarden airfield) near Chester, two of them didn't get very far. G-BARS and G-BBRV were still resident in 1990, when I was working at Hawarden as a part-time flying instructor. Both aircraft were civilianised examples of the DHC1 finished in an attractive (de Havilland house?) colour scheme of cream with dark green coach lines.

Although they had been resident for many years at Hawarden Flying Club, the amount of use by the members had fallen to a very low level, partly due to the fact that the HFC Instructors did not like the idea of instructing on them. As a result bookings had died off and the aeroplanes spent most of their time on terra firma. I was asked by the CFI to start encouraging the newer PPL holders and even some of the older ones to fly the aircraft and was instantly promoted to CTI (Chief Tailwheel Instructor).

I put an advert up in the clubhouse with a photo of a pretty young maiden smiling coquettishly from the front seat of 'RV, with the slogan "Perhaps you too could find something pleasing in the front seat of a Chipmunk...?" The bookings for Tailwheel conversions started almost immediately! On each flight we always managed to get a few 'Aeros' in prior to coming back to the circuit and I think it was this which acted as a catalyst for the growth in popularity of the type, most of the pilots had never been upside down before.

Before long the clubhouse was alive with "Chipmunk speak" and lots of the boys took to wearing their flying suits while lounging around waiting their turn to fly. *"Bloody Hell! It's like chuffin' 633 Squadron in here!"* remarked one of the older members who had come in to fly as he walked through the door. Unfortunately he wanted to fly the Chippy and we had it pre-booked all day long for tailwheel conversions – he was not amused. Funnily enough the 'real 633 Squadron' was not far away, as the last airworthy example of the Mosquito was hangared behind the ochre coloured doors, sharing the space with the flying club aeroplanes. Many was the time that we had a sit in the cockpit of this wonderful machine once we had put the club fleet to bed.

Not only PPL holders were learning to fly the classic taildragger, but we even had a couple of student pilots who wanted to go all the way through to gain their PPL on the type. One of these was a really nice young chap called Steve Watson. Steve was a technician who worked for British Aerospace at Hawarden – in the same factory premises which had once been Hawker Siddeley and prior to that de Havilland. I did some of Steve's PPL training flights and sadly I was also there on the day he died.

This was to be six years later at Barton Airshow in Manchester on 21st July 1996 when the Mosquito crashed during its display. At the time Steve was flying as Pilot's Assistant in the right-hand seat, even though technically speaking the Mossie was a single pilot aeroplane.

Meanwhile back in 1990, as we went into the summer, we had to start earlier and earlier on the weekend to get all the flying in by the newbie taildragger pilots. As there were no cartridges for the Coffman starter anymore, we had to hand swing the aircraft to start it and therefore to minimise the risks we used to carry out running crew changes. The main challenge from the instructor's point of view was the lack of vision from the rear cockpit with the canopy closed. This lead to more than a slight nervous twitch on finals especially if the front seat trainee was not exactly a star performer...

I lost count of the number of times I banged my head against the Plexiglas as I swapped it from side to side trying to judge the height above the runway on short finals. Of course even once the aircraft was on the ground the landing wasn't over as the potential for ground looping loomed large on the rollout. I didn't actually have any ground loop incidents, but it was a damned close run thing on occasions. It didn't help that the intercom was less than sparkling either, but when required, my shout from the back of *"I HAVE CONTROL!!"* could be heard in the clubhouse, so that solved that problem.

Of course the major challenge of instructing from the rear cockpit was that it was difficult to get feedback on what was going on up front. Add to the lack of visual cues, the dodgy intercom, loud engine noise and very basic instrumentation, you can see that the instructor often felt quite detached. A trick I did discover was that there was an awful lot of feedback available through the rudder pedals, but to gain full advantage of this required a very light touch in the rear cockpit with the softest footwear. While wearing lightweight training shoes and using a delicate follow through on the pedals in the back, I was able to sense when 'things' were not going right in the front seat and was able to offer, or take, corrective action before they went truly awry. During the summer of 1990, I was perfecting my 'soft-shoe shuffle'.

One of the really fortunate aspects of carrying out flying training from Hawarden was the almost complete lack of other Air Traffic movements. There was the occasional corporate jet test flight; one or two Bizjets through the day, but that was about it. This made for an easy training environment indeed. Often we used to rejoin the circuit in the Chipmunk and carry out a run-in and break to land (with Air Traffic's blessing). With practice, it was possible to get quite good at these from the rear cockpit and as the clubhouse was quite close to the threshold of runway 32 it was also an excellent method of signalling our return so the next Chipmunk pilots could meet the aircraft as we taxied in.

The sound of Romeo Victor whizzing over the rooftop close to VNE before pulling up for the break used to do the trick! As we pulled up, I used to smoothly close the throttle, simultaneously putting in lots of aileron to bank into the final turn, while pushing nearly full-opposite rudder to get the speed off. BUMFFHH checks in the turn, 90 knots, first stage of flap, 70 knots, second stage of flap, roll out on short finals, carb heat to cold and...... touchdown. Mmmm... Bliss!

It was after one of these arrivals that I was met by an irate Mr Garston. Although his first name was Jack, no-one ever called him anything except "Mister Garston" - at one time he was known as Black Jack among the factory employees. He was an autocrat of the old school and had just the one style of management. At de Havilland's, then Hawker Siddeley's (as it used to be in the days before BAe) he ruled the factory as if it were his personal fiefdom.

An example of this was when he was instructed by head office to "destroy all remaining Mosquito aircraft" that were in storage there in the 1950s. He did so, all except one. RR299 remained the only flying example of the marque until July 1996, simply because Jack Garston had decided that one should survive. There were some great stories of how the aircraft was moved to different parts of the site under cover of darkness when various factory inspections were carried out by senior managers from headquarters. It was hidden under tarpaulins behind hangars and then moved again when the coast was clear for years.

RR299's existence finally came to light in the 1970s and fortunately the company had the good sense to see what a unique piece of aviation history was in their possession. She was made airworthy again and put on the airshow circuit. By 1990, Jack Garston's domain had shrunk to the size of the flying club as he had retired from the factory management some years before.

Meanwhile as we taxied back in, I was unaware of Black Jack's presence in the clubhouse and unprepared for the sight of him as I bounded in through the door in my flying suit. Another mission accomplished and another crew on their way skywards in 'RV.

"MISTER MCBRIDE! Was that YOU I observed maltreating one of our beloved Chipmunks just now?" His words boomed out of the office door at the end of the clubroom and I was quite startled. Thinking quickly, I shot back with.

"Nonsense Mister Garston, you know a run and break is the fastest way to get a fighter on the ground, there could have been a Jerry hanging about!" He was so taken aback, it was as if we had briefly entered a time warp and I was one of the squadron pilots of the old RAF unit that had been based there five decades before. Time stood still for one beautiful moment and I waited for the onslaught, but his mood had changed.

"Aye...well get yourself some coffee, you've got more students waiting to fly it". And that was it. I was amazed and relieved at the same time and I suppose looking back, he knew it was a special time too. This was to be the last swansong of a summer for the HFC Chipmunks and big corporate British Aerospace was just about to call "Time" on the whole operation.

Many of the pilots from that period went on to fly much bigger aeroplanes and I know several that are now successful commercial aviators. I think they will share the same memories with me.

The majesty of those summer dawns, the sticking hangar doors, the smell of grease, oil and Avgas, the hushed quiet of the hangar (Black Jack's secret Chipmunk spares stash locked in the storeroom at the back) and the omnipotent presence of Mosquito RR299 standing guard over it all.......

Ahhhh... halcyon days indeed.

More enthusiasm than technique!

--0--

7 - HEAD TRIP

RAF Dishforth 1984 – JP3A first time round

I noted the line-up of smart cars outside the flying club as I parked my aging BMW among them. 'Smart' is not a reference to the currently fashionable eco-friendly two-seater which is not much bigger than a roller skate by the way, but rather defines the row of Bentleys, Ferraris, Lambos and sprinkling of classy SUVs outside the clubhouse.

Bear in mind this was 1993 well before we all knew the term Global Economic Crisis, so thirsty cars were all the rage. It also defined the type of membership of this particular flying club... wealthy! I was not here to join as a recreational member however; I had been called for a specific job. A group of ten PPLs had formed to own and operate an ex-military jet trainer, a Jet Provost.

They needed an experienced QFI (preferably ex-military) to help them become familiar with the machine, so my job was to train them up so they could fly the aircraft safely. A JP3A has substantial performance compared to the usual single engine flying club aeroplanes, so making provision for specialist training was a wise move.

Whether I would be the right fit for this role was yet to be established. Sure, I had flown the JP3A and the cooking version the 5A some 10 years earlier, but now I had a commercial airline career to look after and risking my life with amateurs, especially of the 'gung-ho' variety was not an attractive prospect.

Still I mused as I entered the building with my mini-flightbag - *perhaps they have the right mental attitude and it is worth being here...* As I walked into the main clubroom and approached the coffee bar my trainee greeted me with, "Hello. Nice to meet you James, my name's Dick. I am the BEST PILOT in our group!" No doubt about it, these boys had certainly got the confidence, but then owning a medium sized manufacturing company while driving a hundred grand car probably helped a bit.

I smiled and returned the greeting as we shook hands firmly. Looking him steadily in the eyes, I said slowly, "Hello Dick, good to meet you... I'm the best pilot I've ever met!"

*

...the same smell of the cockpit, it's so tiny in here, seems more cramped than before... I had a good lookout ahead and above through the Plexiglas canopy and was glad to have given it a thorough polish before we started the session – a beautiful blue-sky day.

With HASELL checks completed and after ensuring that the sky was clear, I called to him on the intercom, "Right, pulling up for a wingover". Gently does it. Not too much 'G' *just a couple* and then check forward with the nose at about 30 degrees above the horizon and ro-o-o-o-o-o-ll smoothly to 90 degrees angle of bank while again increasing back pressure on the stick.

As my head swiveled through all axes, encased in the khaki bonedome I noted at the side of me, that his appeared to be frozen in one position. *Great to be wearing proper flying gear again* I thought to myself as I listened to his panting over the intercom. "How are you feeling Dick? All okay mate? Uhh! Just clearing the area for a few Aeros, like we briefed before..."

"YEAH...! I'm fine...URR, yep NO PROBS... erm... mate" He didn't sound quite so sure, but I was hearing the right words anyway. I kept it lighthearted as I said,

"Oh, GOOD! It's a shame not fly a few loops and rolls while we're up here..." As I exited the second part of the big wingover clearing turn, I continued cheerfully, "...this first one's a loop so we'll need plenty of speed eh? Follow me through...!" and at that point I allowed the nose to slice through the horizon a long way below it before rolling hard to the right. The ASI displayed the rapidly increasing airspeed and I waited until the magic number was on the clock...

"Looking UP...and... PULLING UP!" I shouted above the noise of the slipstream over the canopy as I applied back pressure on the stick. With the increased airspeed, the controls were now nice and firm with plenty of feedback from the airframe – lovely!

His reply was a muffled, "WAAYHAAAAYY!... OH GOD!" and a slightly muffled, "OH FURCK...!" as his oxygen mask slipped down his face with the increasing gravitational forces, now reading 4G. I kept talking through the loop, slow and clear to reassure him, "looking up and... BACK for the next horizon...and here she comes, checking WINGS LEVEL over the top...

...maintaining POSITIVE GEE, not pulling so hard now, see the speed – dropped right off as we go inverted... trying to be SMOOOOTH with the pullout here, aiming for our own slipstream... looking to feel a bump, ah there it is, that was good, now... nose high above the horizon again, barrel roll this time..."

"WHOAHH! WAAYHAAAAYY!..... URGGH!!" came through the intercom and I realised that he was not enjoying this as much as I was. He had also stopped following me through on the stick and throttle and as we pulled out of the barrel roll I thought *it is time to stop*. Nose on the horizon and power back, trimmed for straight and level flight, I gave him control.

I said "Are you feeling okay mate?" to which he replied in the affirmative, so I said "Let's call up RAF XXX and see if we can get a run-and-break for a low approach and go-around, I bet it's a few years since they've had a JP in the circuit".

With R/T contact established and ATC permission, we flew in for the run and break. I took control again and pointed the nose down with throttle wide open. Checking T's and P's, accelerating in the dive, our little jet really started to show its owner what it could do.

Now running level at just a few hundred feet AGL along the axis of the main runway and maintaining its thunderous progress, I warned him to brace himself for the imminent 'G' loading and then counted down, "...three, two, one, NOW!" and flung the stick hard-over, while pulling back hard and closing the throttle. Wham! She responded like a thoroughbred as we whacked into a 75 degree banked turn with 4G+ on the clock.

Again there was an unseemly grunting, gurgling, squealing noise through the intercom from the other seat which was a little distracting as I started to lower the undercarriage and extend the flaps in the final curving approach to the runway. On short finals and "cleared for the low approach and overshoot", I applied full power, retracted flaps and gear and we started to climb away.

The owner flew the aeroplane after that, all the way back to our airfield of departure where I talked him through the approach and landing. By the time we walked back into the clubhouse and the main lounge, it was clear that he had recovered his composure. As I followed him in, I thought *swaggering doesn't really cover it!* Naturally there were some pilots there who were looking forward to hearing all about our 'Sortie' and I found it hard to believe it was the same guy who started telling them all about OUR flying manoeuvres.

"YEAH! Well we did a few aeros, ya'know, loops and rolls like. Then we beat up RAF XXX, it was just like Maverick in the film and we was pullin' loadsa Gee ya'know..." While 'Biggles' was entertaining some of the PPLs with tales of how brave we were, I was introduced to another wealthy middle-aged member of the group who proceeded to tell me how he planned to "...go home and take wife t'bed for't'afternoon, 'cos me girlfriend's workin'. So that'll gi'mme brownie points won't it?" with a big lecherous wink. I smiled, rinsed my coffee mug, said my goodbyes, gathered my flying stuff and headed for the door. Outside the air was a lot fresher it seemed, probably because I couldn't smell any Bullshit.

*

I don't know what happened to the aircraft and the group of owners because I never returned; they must have found a replacement instructor with a higher nausea threshold. Later, when I related this story to a senior QFI who was acquainted with Richard, he roared laughing and said, "Yes, he TALKS A GOOD FLIGHT doesn't he?!"

Regardless of all the foregoing, having confidence in your own abilities while operating powered flying machines is still very important. Let's face it, ours is only the second generation of humans to have successfully defied gravity and we have been around for a million years or so.

I have often tried to imbue in my trainees the philosophy that flying is really 'all in the head'. It is that mental confidence to "hack it" which provides us with our positive attitude to learning our craft. Every day's a school day? Yes, most definitely true throughout the life of any pilot. The day you stop learning, it is time to give up.

Fast forward many years from the Jet Provost flying group and I was operating a foreign registered VIP Jet with fellow pilot, Captain Stefan – my teenage daughter sat behind us on the jumpseat for an empty ferry flight. It was a nice perk of the job, there are not many left.

She took lots of photos and seemed to thoroughly enjoy the experience. Two days later, we all flew again, this time on another empty flight. Stefan was in the driving seat with another pilot acting as FO and my inquisitive daughter was observing again from the jumpseat while I travelled in the VIP cabin, a rare treat.

After the flight was over and when we were alone together, I asked her how she had enjoyed her second trip on the jumpseat in only a few days. She turned to me, smiled and said, "He's better than you, ya'know..." there was a pause before I replied, aghast;

"WHO IS? What do you mean by that? I am your father, darling you cannot be serious!" but she was not to be put off, as I heard the words, "You told me that YOU were the best pilot in the world Dad. But he is better than you; Stefan. He's SOOOO SMOOTH when he's flying and dead relaxed when he moves the switches and controls, it's dead cool to watch!"

So that is how my good mate for many years, Capt Stefan Kondak became "possibly the best pilot in the world – according to my daughter". I never fail to remind him whenever we meet and we always have a good laugh about it; although the funny thing is... inside, deep down, I don't really believe it...

With "possibly the best pilot in the world

– according to my daughter" (Capt Stefan Kondak)

--0--

8 - COINCIDENCE DOES NOT EXIST

In reality it was an unlucky event that the airliner which was shot down by Russian backed militia in Eastern Ukraine belonged to the same company which had already suffered such a tragic loss only a matter of weeks before. The similarities were extraordinary. Same company, same fleet, total sudden loss of life and aircraft; similar flight number - nothing lucky about the number seven here. In truth if the missile had been launched a few minutes earlier it would have downed an Air India and if it had been a few minutes later, then Singapore Airlines would have lost one.

For those of us in the industry observing the horrifying news reports, there was nothing surprising about the way in which the media, on behalf of the various governments involved were attempting to manipulate the 'story' to satisfy political ends. The big search for and eventual handing over of the Flight Data Recorder and Cockpit Voice Recorder (FDR/CVR the famous black boxes, coloured orange) was part of it of course. But nobody needed an FDR to tell what happened here.

An airliner exploding in mid air at 33,000 feet while cruising along a recognised airway above a war zone... and above armed forces who had already shot down several other aircraft very recently... You could say that this was an accident waiting to happen, but you would be wrong. In essence it will prove to have been a result of inadequate risk assessment by those airlines which continued to overfly Ukraine's eastern territory while there was a war going on. More specifically those same companies failed to recognise the potential dangers of the surface to air missile systems which had been brought into the conflict.

They say hindsight is 20/20 of course, but it has become apparent that several agencies from other governments were aware of the existence (and risk) from the BUK missile system, but this intelligence was not widely shared. For example, British Airways had not been overflying that particular area for some time and they were not alone. It is likely that the fundamental failings in management at Malaysian Airlines after these two terrible losses will see the demise of the company. Whether that is a fair outcome is a moot point, for they were operating flights just like their contemporaries, but then on the other side of the coin there is a view that there is 'no such thing as coincidence'. Only those people inside the upper echelons of the management of the airline will be able to answer if there were deficiencies in the safety management system.

Over the years we have flown at cruise altitude over many warzones and areas of conflict, at least safe in the knowledge that "Up here, they can't reach us..." I recall overflying former Yugoslavia in the 1990's during the bitter fighting which was happening there, taking our holiday passengers to and from their vacations. From time to time on a clear night you could see the glow from fires on the ground and could only imagine what was happening 6 miles below our aircraft. One of the things which we always used to do as a matter of Standard Operating Procedure was to keep the 'Weather Radar' switched on even when there were no clouds in the sky.

The reasoning behind this was that the weather radar beam from a civilian airliner is very powerful and shines a huge electronic transmission forwards for hundreds of miles, from the nose Radome which can be seen by military electronic warfare detection systems which are looking for electromagnetic radiation. It says quite clearly "we are a civilian airliner, don't shoot!" Many times we would see a bright 'spike' coming back directly towards us from what was assumed to be a fire control radar... anxious thoughts would then occupy our minds until it went away again after a few more sweeps from our radar. We had these thoughts even though we believed that the troops on the ground of either side had no weapons system that could harm us.

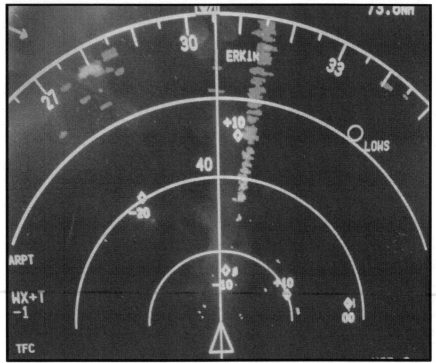

Illuminated by a ground based military radar

The plain truth of it all is that people make mistakes and accidents do happen. Like the time in 2003 when terrorists with a portable surface to air missile system (SAM) managed to hit a DHL Cargo Airbus A300 climbing out of Baghdad airport. According to reports from the media, the mistake was that the terrorists were hoping to hit a military transport aircraft instead of a civil machine and at the time of the hit, they were celebrating a strike on a USAF transport.

The heat-seeking SA7 shoulder launched Manpad which they used then actually has an effective range of 18,000 feet, more than enough to achieve the aim of shooting down a large target from close to an airport. The good news part of the DHL shootdown was that the crew actually managed to land the aircraft back at Baghdad even though they had lost ALL of the hydraulic systems and they walked away from it.

There is an incredible photo of the three of them standing there in uniform under the wing just after they had got out of the freighter. By happy chance I did meet the Flight Engineer (Mario) some years later and was able to ask him about some of the details of this heroic incident. In common with many real life heroes, quietly spoken Mario was very modest in his description of the events and played down his part in the affair, although I knew from other sources that HE played a key role in their survival. Was our meeting a coincidence or was it pre-ordained? I had made a full study of the accident for another project in which I had been involved so was very familiar with all the facts. I never felt that our meeting was coincidental.

Anecdotally there are two definitions of a "successful landing" one of which states that you manage to "walk away from it" (and in this case that was certainly true), but another definition states that the "company is able to reuse the aeroplane..." The second one was not possible as can be evidenced from the shocking photos on the internet – have a look and you will see what I mean. This one really was a wing and a prayer.

*

It is a fact that aviation security and airline safety are constantly shifting and interconnected environments. Only a few years ago, it seemed that the Libyan revolution had seen a successful transition to democracy which would lead to stabilisation of the country and return to normality. I was asked by one company to research the security situation with a view to operating an EU registered corporate airliner in-country on behalf of the nascent elected government. Although all of the mainstream news was positive (and this still in the light of the sacking of the US Embassy with the murder of the US ambassador), my request for security analysis from contacts at a major aviation insurance company resulted in a prognosis which has been very nearly borne out exactly by recent events.

The country is descending into civil war with an extremely dangerous and unpredictable environment for civil aircraft operations. I remember at the time when I offered the security analysis to the aforementioned European aviation company, they appeared to question it in great detail, as the commercial terms of the contract on offer was very attractive to them. Now I should imagine they are relieved that they took the prudent course of action, deciding not to go ahead with the contract.

*

So where does the recent tragedy leave us all in regard to aviation safety? I suggest that contrary to what it looks like, the terrible loss of life and destruction of property as a result of what is essentially state sponsored terrorism will actually make our industry much safer. As a modern invention, aviation is a very safety lead form of transportation and therefore the lessons will be learned by all parties involved.

Airline companies worldwide will take their duty of care very seriously towards assessment of the risks of overflying warzones and this should filter out into increased awareness of the importance of risk analyses for all areas of the operation. The potential risks of making highly sophisticated and capable weapons systems available to ill-disciplined forces/terrorists who then proceed to make mistakes with their targeting are all too clear. For sure it has been a Russian own-goal in diplomatic terms.

The grossly offensive spectacle of the Russian separatist armed militia group, which treated the corpses of the innocent victims in such an appalling manner, was in complete contrast to the dignity and respect accorded to them all by the government and people of the Netherlands as most of the bodies were delivered "home".

--0--

9 - LET'S HAVE A PROPER BREW

Good asymmetric airliner flying requires plenty of focus

The Captain was PF (Pilot Flying) and the First Officer was PM (Pilot Monitoring). As a crew, it was their fourth takeoff of the day and up to then everything had gone quite well. The First Officer called, "Vee-One, Rotate..." and as he did so there was an almighty bang and a shudder through the airframe. The left-hand engine had suffered severe damage and there was a dramatic loss of thrust just at the point of getting airborne. The airliner was close to maximum takeoff weight which did not make the controlling of the aircraft any easier, but the Captain did well to hold the heading with an application of a large input of right rudder and some right aileron also.

At the sight of two indications of positive climb, the First Officer called, *"Positive Rate!"* with some urgency and the Captain responded with a clear call of "Gear UP!" As the major amount of drag retracted, the aircraft started to accelerate and climb better simultaneously. There was a slight pause in proceedings as they climbed away from the runway and they were both aware that there was nothing they should do before they reached 400 feet above the ground.

The First Officer (whose first language was not English), decided then to call ATC to advise them of the situation... "Mayday, Mayday, Mayday, JetAir 123 Mayday... we lost engine after we takeoff..." he released the transmit switch and the Air Traffic controller very efficiently replied with, "Roger your Mayday JetAir - call radar NOW, frequency wun, wun, niner, decimal four!" The First Officer switched frequency and gave the same Mayday transmission again, now the altimeter was through 400 feet and the flying pilot opened his mouth to speak, but he was interrupted, so he cancelled the Fire Warning Master Caution instead.

The radar controller had responded immediately with, "Roger, JetAir 123, your Mayday is acknowledged, climb on runway heading to minimum 3000 feet altitude. When able, please advise souls on board, fuel endurance and intentions". The First Officer now started thinking about how many passengers were in the cabin and adding that number to the cabin crew, then he turned towards the Captain, "What our intentions Commander...?"

The Captain had other ideas, exasperated he blurted out – "CONFIRM THE MALFUNCTION!" to which the First Officer responded with, "YES, left engine is problem Commander... Ahh, we got 240 passengers isn't it?" Then from the left hand seat a direct instruction, "TAKE ACTION! MEMORY ITEMS...! ENGINE FIRE and SEVERE DAMAGE – NOW!" You could tell he was exasperated by the despair in his voice. The point had been made, so I hit the freeze button in the back of the Simulator. I leaned forward, they were completely still for the moment and I said to them, "Gentlemen, we do need to talk about this..."

*

The recent IFALPA report on MPL training (17th June, 2014), makes depressing reading. Even those of us who had our doubts about the proposals to train the next generation of airline pilots mostly in the simulator some years ago, still had hopes that when the time came the training would actually be driven by quality not price. If the IFALPA study is a fair presentation of the state of MPL training as it stands now, unfortunately our worst fears have been realised.

Without going through all the details consider the conclusions of the document. It states quite clearly and with supporting evidence that the latest trainees demonstrated sub-standard 'Basic Flying Skills' inadequate 'Airmanship', ineffective/underdeveloped 'CRM' skills and finally they were judged to be lacking in 'ATC Situational Awareness'. Well, there is not a lot left is there?

Surely it cannot be true that all trainees are suffering from the same training quality deficit globally, but the IFALPA report is fairly conclusive regarding widespread (and worldwide) gaps and poor standards. It does seem to be as though when the original course specifications were set out, there was perhaps a naive assumption on the part of the authorities that the MPL ATOs would set higher limits in their syllabi than the minimums described. Not so, it appears to have been quite frankly 'a race to the bottom' not in standards initially, but in the defined hours on the courses. Of course where training is delivered to just the box-ticking basic minimum level, we should not be surprised where standards fall to as a result.

It is such a disappointment in many ways as the training of professional aviators had been steadily improving over the previous decades. No seriously, think about it; from the post-war 1940's, through the birth of the jet age (1950's and 60's) and into glass-cockpit and fly-by-wire, (70's and 80's) the training had been steadily getting better. The application of technological marvels such as CBT (Computer Based Training) in the 1980s and then innovative CRM training in the early 90s contributed overall to a much improved quality of standard airline pilot.

I suggest it is possible to define where the quality peaked and that was the end of the 90s with the advent of the Low Cost Carrier. No matter how much they try to reinvent themselves as Low FARES Carriers, we KNOW there is only one way to offer lower fares and that is by cutting the baseline costs of the airline operation. Pilots funding their own type-ratings was an early win for the airlines, then along came the MPL which would deliver great numbers of First Officers at a much reduced cost.

The prime concern for all of us involved in the business is the safety margin of flying airliners and this has been steadily improving over the years too. Again, technology has played a big part in this as the manufacturing of aircraft has become so good as to eradicate many of the technical malfunctions of the early generation of jets.

Before anyone mentions it, yes the B787 did have major technical issues with regard to the Lithium-Ion batteries, but it still remains (along with its predecessor, the triple seven) one of the most technologically superior and reliable aircraft ever built. Modern airliner dispatch reliability (i.e. the percentage of times that the machines on the 'line can launch without a serious fault which prevents them departing on schedule) is in the region of 97 to 99%. Incredible when you consider all of the parts which could fail and don't - they just keep on trucking.

The days of being able to support pilot training programmes as intensive and costly as the military (and major airline sponsored) flying courses of the 1960's, 70's and 80's are over and will never come back. During that time nobody even considered the price of training. Which is why the generation just before mine produced the best stick and rudder merchants the industry has ever seen.

When the superior flying skills and airmanship of these pilots was mixed with modern CRM training as they became middle aged, then we witnessed a gold age indeed. For me as a youthful First Officer on new Boeing 757s in the early 90's flying the line with these guys... well; every trip was like a day out with Yoda, Master of the Jedi. I am not kidding. Even then I realised that frequently I was 'in the presence of greatness' although I admit to not understanding why; I was spending most of my time trying not to accidentally cut myself with my light-sabre!

It was just that the 'mix' was so right. If you talk in terms of the analogy for making a good cup of tea, the 'brew' had been perfected. Not only the aviators on the line demonstrated quality at every turn, but also the airline managers were top of the range too. Sadly these days we often don't see the same calibre of managers anywhere in the airlines. Without going into detail there are too many politicians and 'yes-men' and not enough of them with the right-stuff in my opinion. Of course, it is cheaper to have 'yes-men'... until something goes horribly wrong.

Back to the training and in my own case I well remember the basic propeller and jet courses which I went through in the 1980's, mostly as it happens in Yorkshire. The quality of the instruction and checking on these courses was world class and like it or not, myself and my contemporaries all received very thorough training in every discipline whether it was navigation, formation, aerobatics, instruments; either we were good enough to pass the course or we were chopped. So staying with Yorkshire and considering the essence of the IFALPA concerns, what they are really saying in tea making terms is, "Let's have a Proper Brew!"

--0--

10 - LOSING YOUR FIRST COMMAND

First Jet Command on B757 based at Manchester

It was relatively peaceful in the quiet of the Boeing 757 flightdeck as we finished our preflight briefing. Outside all was chaos. Palma airport in Majorca on a mid-summer Saturday is mad busy anyway, but this evening was exceptional. French ATC were working to rule. Only five aircraft per hour were being accepted heading north back to the UK through the Bordeaux control sector, therefore the departure 'slot' delays were huge.

As I explained to the passengers on the PA, "Ladies and gentlemen, our *friends*; French Air Traffic Control... *Ahem!* Are playing their joker here today. They have allowed all the holiday charter flights southbound, but are now delaying the returning planes going home. We did have a slot for Manchester to depart in about four hours from now, but the reason we have got you all onboard is that we have refiled the flightplan for Santiago in Spain. Needless to say there are no delays for Santiago, so we are going to quietly slip out of the back door here..."

I knew that I sounded more confident than I felt and dearly prayed we would not actually have to GO to Santiago. My plan was to change our destination midair with Madrid ATC and then head north straight across the Bay of Biscay for the UK.

The trouble for me was that I had only had my Command as a B757 Line Captain for less than six months and if this went wrong... I had seen it done before, especially out of Palma, when some of our aircraft filed flightplans for places like Gerona in Spain and then after performing a low approach and go-around to the Gerona runway, they brought the landing gear up again and climbed on their new flightplan for their original UK destination airport. For sure, other airlines didn't like us doing it, but we were focused on trying to keep the show on the road and look after our passengers the best way we knew how in a very busy summer schedule.

After profound thanks to our helpful local handling agent (on the back of whose motorbike I had journeyed recently to the flightplanning office), we closed the doors and called for push and start. The Paramount Airways flight on the stand next door immediately protested on the ATC Tower frequency that he was ahead of the Air2000 757 and demanded to know why we were going out of sequence. ATC politely informed him that the Air2000 757 was flight-planned for Santiago...

The tug took up the strain now and we started moving backwards off the stand as I listened to the Paramount Captain arguing with the controller – he also wanted to "change flightplan for destination Santiago", to which he was told bluntly, "Captain, if you FILE for Santiago...YOU WILL LAND AT SANTIAGO!" My heart skipped a few beats and I felt very cold all of a sudden as I heard these chilling words. I thought, *well there's no going back now mate... we're committed!*

The next hour or so was one of the longest of my life as we climbed out of Majorca into the west towards Madrid. Of course it was pointless to ask too early to change our destination; we had to avoid the ATC barrier to the north of Barcelona airspace. The cabin crew came and offered food, but I was definitely not hungry, in fact my stomach seemed to have shriveled up completely and it felt like my insides were tied in knots. We were getting closer and closer to top of descent point for Santiago and I was possibly in the process of losing my first Jet Command, or that was how it felt... *Oh why did I not just accept the slot delay? Why did I have to try and be clever...? This is agony now...*

Eventually as we were handed off to the next Madrid controller, I took over the radio and asked the fateful question. "Madrid, this is Jetset 123. Please Senor; can we refile for destination Manchester now, EGCC...?" There was a long pause as the controller considered our request...

*

One of the most significant milestones in the career of a commercial airline pilot is when they swap seats from right to left. The difference in salary is usually substantial (a 50% pay rise in most cases) but more than this, there is a dichotomy between the two roles. As First Officer you can be as good a pilot as you like, but you are always second in command. Even with modern Crew Resource Management which is designed to share and improve the quality of decision making, at the end of the day, the Captain's word is law. Quite literally, the Captain of an aircraft must shoulder the responsibility for the safe outcome of every flight and their command is backed up by international aviation laws.

Being aware that the promotion to 'Commander' in an aviation career is so important, it is amazing that some of our colleagues have thrown it all away so easily in the past. Although a rare occurrence, quite often it has been as a result of inappropriate behaviour downroute in crew hotels. Back in the 1990s at an airline where I worked, there was the case of one newly promoted

Captain deciding to have a large noisy crew party in his Captain's suite at the hotel. This ended with some scantily clad crew members, whose judgement may have been impaired by alcohol, delivering a very large suitcase to the hotel lobby and leaving it there.

Unfortunately the suitcase contained one more crew member wearing only her undergarments and with her head sticking out of the zip of the bag... Five star hotels don't take kindly to their guests misbehaving in this manner, (especially in a Muslim country) and the fallout from this event lead to the suspension of several crew, including the Captain who was demoted.

At the same airline another newly promoted Captain, was found to have grossly inflated his flying hours totals to achieve an earlier (than usual) promotion ahead of fellow First Officers. When the matter was raised with the Flight Operations Manager and the new Captain was asked to bring his flying logbooks in for verification, mysteriously one of them seemed to have been mislaid.

It goes without saying that most professional pilots consider such a thing to be equivalent to a cardinal sin; however it seems that for some, the temptation is just too strong. The final sting in the tail was that this particular gentleman was given a period of time in which to produce evidence of his flying hours and having failed to do so, was summarily demoted and then did not have his contract renewed as an FO.

I think it is quite rare for a newly promoted pilot to lose their Command due to any failing in their flying performance, because these days all the airlines spend so much time ensuring that the candidate is up to standard during the upgrade process. It is a very tense time as they (the trainees) realise there is so much at stake, but by then they are usually ready for the challenge.

*

Back in the dark skies over Zaragoza, the Madrid controller called us up. "Jetset 123...?" My colleague immediately keyed the mike, "Yes go ahead Madrid..."

"Jetset 123, you are clear to turn to the North, heading towards Santander and expect a handover to Brest Control. Your flightplan has been changed... destination is now Manchester". I could have hugged him. *YES! Thank God for that, WHAT a relief!* As we replanned the Flight Management Computer with the new route, it became obvious that we would land in Manchester with loads more fuel than we needed – no bother. What's an extra few tonnes between friends?

The atmosphere in the cockpit now was close to euphoria, I knew that the FO was worrying about the situation nearly as much as I had been. To have been forced to land in Santiago would have been a catastrophe and potentially career limiting for me. As it was, I had taken a bit of a gamble and instead of the flight running more than four hours late, we would be back only 20 minutes behind schedule – a big improvement and a bonus for the airline.

As I breathed several sighs of relief, I resolved to be much more careful in future - bearing in mind that we had taken the decision to refile the flightplan with only minimal involvement of the company flight operations department. Soon we were talking to the Brest Controller. Never had the French accent sounded so lovely to hear on the R/T. "Welcome Monsieur, you are cleared on direct track to Berry 'ead". This was a straight line of some 400 nautical miles – sweet!

At which point I pressed the intercom call button for the forward galley, it was answered immediately. "Yes Captain, what would you like?" to which I replied.

"Please give my compliments to the Number One and advise her that we are now heading straight home to Manchester... good news eh? Oh and by the way, have you still got some crew meals left? I'm feeling a bit peckish now..."

(This was the summer of '94 and it is fair to say that airline Flight Ops Depts. are much more ahead of the game these days. It is unlikely that a crew now would have to refile their own flightplan for a European trip).

--0--

11 - OUR DARKEST HOUR

On 24th March 2015 when Germanwings flight 9525 crashed into a mountainside in the French Alps our profession was changed forever and not for better. With haunting similarities to the events of September 11th, 2001, we were left facing the possibility that evil intent had been the cause of yet another catastrophic loss of life. Worse still was the realisation that one of the systems which were introduced post 9/11 – the locked/armoured cockpit door – may have been used to prevent a life-saving interruption of a killer's intentions.

Airbus Cockpit Door Switch

It is highly creditable that one of the major UK Low Cost Airlines (easyJet) reacted so quickly, by announcing immediate changes to their SOPs such that never again would a solo crew-member be permitted to occupy the cockpit in flight. Similarly another major European LCA confirmed that their policy was always to ensure one pilot was never left alone at the controls. It was less praiseworthy however, when some large flag carriers were *instructed* by EASA to follow suit after they had initially expressed reluctance to do so...

*

For those of us who have had the experience of using armoured flightdeck doors on a daily basis since 9/11, we understand very well the principles involved. In the majority of companies I have worked for in the past 14 years, they have had similar Operating Procedures. The reason which we were given for having another member of crew join us in the cockpit, when the only other pilot enters the cabin in flight, was to protect against the rare possibility of pilot incapacitation. This incapacitation might be as a result of sudden illness or even hypoxia due to depressurisation.

Either way, the solo cockpit occupant might be unable to unlock the door from inside. In truth, when we initially heard about a modern European airliner leaving cruising altitude in apparently automated flight and then fly "controlled" into terrain, most of us reviewed our TUC (Time of Useful Consciousness). At 38,000 feet in the event of rapid loss of cabin pressure, the TUC would be a matter of 15 or seconds or so and beyond that, the effects of hypoxia may prevent a pilot from being able to don his or her own oxygen.

The seriousness of all of this was brought home to me some time back, when I was carrying out contract work as a Trainer/Examiner for a foreign airline in their Simulator. The recurrent Licence Proficiency Check (LPC) syllabus required that the crew experience and take appropriate actions for a rapid depressurisation at cruising altitude.

Naturally this would involve them immediately donning oxygen masks, establishing communications and commencing an emergency descent using the autopilot. Note that current best practice is to leave the autopilot engaged, to guard against the possibility of pilots becoming incapacitated in the descent. If that happened, the automatics would level the aircraft at the preset altitude (10,000 feet or MSA whichever higher) which should result in the pilots regaining consciousness.

Prior to reporting for the Simulator, the candidates had received a written brief of the syllabus outlining "the rapid depressurisation" scenario. Not only that, but I took plenty of time in the briefing to ensure that they understood exactly the vital actions which they should take in the event of sudden loss of cabin pressure. I reminded them about TUC at cruising altitude and that they should, "GET ON OXYGEN!" as fast as possible.

Sometime later as the aircraft (Simulator) was established in the cruise at Flight Level 360, I activated the "Explosive Decompression" failure. This resulted in a very loud metallic *BANG!*, the sound of rushing air; with all the alarms and the Cabin Altitude climbing out of control on the gauge... To my surprise, both pilots turned round to me and said, "REALLY? You *REALLY* want us to use the oxygen masks...?" I was astounded! The seconds ticked away as I then engaged/distracted them in a brief discussion on the subject, terminating with the words, "...GUYS! BY NOW - YOU'RE BOTH DEAD ANYWAY...!"

This galvanized them into action pronto and both of them ripped off their electric hats and donned the crew oxygen immediately. It took them plenty of fumbling and blundering with switches to actually manage to talk to each other, (remember the 'establish communications' bit?) and even then they were lost for words. I froze the simulator and asked them to take their masks off and we went through it all in slow time. Step by step; I gave them chapter and verse on how to use the flightcrew oxygen system, including all the required switch selections to facilitate proper comms.

I was mystified by their reactions (or lack of them) while they were flying the Simulator. After all, in the comfort zone of Europe, we are at pains to stress to every crew who fly the Sim, *"...treat it like the real aeroplane. If you do something during your proficiency check in the Sim, then we must assume you would do that on the line".*

Their debrief took some time and while we did so, I discovered for the first time that I was unique. Even though these gentlemen were regular line pilots and had been operating the aircraft for two years with their airline, apparently I was the only Training Captain who wanted them to use the flightdeck Oxygen system for real.

Up to then, the airline had only used internal examiners; I was one of only very few foreign trainers they had ever seen!

Operating an airliner with oxy-mask and goggles is hard work

Over the next two weeks, three out of the five crews whom I checked did exactly the same... My feedback to the airline's training management was urgent and succinct. Fortunately the department responded rapidly when they saw the flight safety implications of having 60% of their line crews operating like this.

*

It is not only pilots who sometimes exhibit incorrect responses to potentially life threatening situations regarding lack of oxygen. I recall from a previous airline that one of our London based holiday charter jets was returning home over northern France when it suffered a rapid depressurisation at cruising altitude. The 'rubber jungle' deployed without warning, halfway through the cabin service.

The cabin crew reacted immediately as their excellent training kicked in; each grabbed a mask, pulled it towards them and put it on, then sat down on the arm of the aisle seat and assisted passengers. They said afterwards at the debrief that the weirdest thing for them was that all the children reacted quickly too, but then they (the kids) had to help the grown-ups to fit their own oxygen masks – completely the opposite way to how it goes in the preflight safety demo! The pilots did a textbook job of descending to a lower altitude in a very short time and even managed to make a reassuring PA announcement to the cabin, assuring all that the aircraft was under control.

*

There is no industry which is more safety led than commercial aviation and we can hold our heads high with what has been achieved these past short decades. While it is dangerous to speculate upon the cause/s of accidents until the final report is published from the AAI team, in the case of Germanwings 9525, an unprecedented amount of factual information was released to the public almost immediately after the event.

That this was done so quickly, can be attributed to the intense commercial and media pressure which resulted from an accident where an apparently serviceable airliner flew into a hillside. The fact that European registered and regulated carriers have such an impressive safety record makes such a hull loss in Europe so rare.

Once again our industry is in the process of learning lessons the hardest way possible. As always we remain professionally committed to making our operations safer, while we acknowledge that some of our colleagues and customers have paid the highest price for us to learn more. Often, while we study such previous fatal accidents, we say to ourselves and to each other, that "we should remember to have respect" for our fellow crew who lost their lives while doing their job.

*

At the publication of the final report; the loss of flight 9525 could well prove to be our Darkest Hour, on our saddest day. If that is the case, then it may be that one of the deceased crewmembers deserves no respect at all.

*(Note 1: A depressurisation in an airliner is an **extremely** rare event and the vast majority of airline crews will never experience one in their whole career. For a passenger, it is even less likely. Note 2: Statistically, Airline flying is STILL the safest form of travel and gets safer every year. Note 3: The airline with the Simulator, was **not** a European carrier).*

--0--

12 - UNWILLING TO LEARN

Whoever said "Only fight the battles you can win" may have had some airline management experience...

*

There was a lull in activity after we had been cruising at 35,000 feet for some time and the airliner cockpit was quiet. With another eight hours ahead of us, we would have plenty of time to chat, but I was curious as to why my colleague (and co-Captain of this flight) had recently joined our company. I knew that he had been one of the 'wheels' of another operator - i.e. a senior management pilot, in fact the very top one as he had been a Director Flight Operations (DFO). He had apparently separated from that airline very suddenly and I was intrigued why that should have been. A delicate subject though and how best to tackle it? I decided that a straight question would probably do it... one way or another. I looked across at him and said, "So Jeff, why DID you leave your cushy management job as the DFO at Fly Xxx then...?"

*

I recall many years ago, a long time before I ever went flying aeroplanes for a living, that there was a time when I had a hard lesson to learn. Back in 1979 I remember standing on a pavement outside the official driving test centre with my failure slip in my hand, after I had just stuffed up my motorcycle licence test for a second time... Stupid me, I had retaken my test at the same centre as the first time, having been unreasonably cheeky to the Department of Transport Examiner. As the reasons for my second failure were debatable, I was left with the almost certain knowledge that I was the author of my own misfortune. It was a small office and for sure, the second examiner was a friend of the first guy. I was angry with myself for not thinking it through and learning from my experience, although at my third attempt, two weeks later, at a test centre some thirty miles distant, I passed without any adverse remarks whatsoever.

Wind the clock forward to a time when I was a commercial airline pilot, a First Officer on a B757. Simultaneously I was doing some part-time civilian flying instruction for ATPL trainees to prepare them for their instrument rating. At the instrument rating training school where I was working, we had a very good track record with quite a high percentage first time pass history for our candidates. You would think then that the new students would all listen carefully to our instruction, training and advice about how best to approach their Commercial Pilot Instrument Rating Test (IRT) with the UK CAA Examiners. However there were always a few trainees who believed they knew better than we did...

One such gentleman was an ex-military pilot whom we trained for his IRT and he was very, very good. Literally, he could fly the aircraft on instruments like it was on rails. His instrument scan-rate was incredible and within an hour or two of flying the light twin engined Seneca, it was obvious that he would breeze through the test. He did have a problem though and it was this. Because of his vast military flying experience and obviously above average instrument flying skills, he was rather selective about what advice he thought he needed to pass his test.

We used to specifically teach our trainees that they should be very careful about what they listened to on the second VHF radio. As is normal commercial practice, VHF 1 was used for ATC communications and the second box would be used to pick up weather broadcasts. As the candidates were being assessed for 'Single-Pilot' Instrument Ratings, they would have to "request the latest weather" from ATC. Alternatively they could inform the controller that they would be "reduced listening watch" for a minute or so while they listened to the automated transmissions on VHF 2.

When our man went for his test, he decided that because he was so proficient at multi-tasking, he would listen to VHF 2 for the latest weather without letting ATC know. He would monitor both radios. Effectively the sound from VHF 2 in his headset obscured the ATC for a minute or two. Imagine the poor old CAA examiner's shock when his candidate turned up the volume again on VHF 1 to hear the controller giving urgent Avoiding Action instructions with his official "EXAM" radio callsign on it!

They then received a lecture from the controller on maintaining a good listening watch in controlled airspace. Needless to say matey-boy partly failed his IRT and had to retake the Airways portion of the test. An expensive scenario for a private individual, an IRT retake cost thousands even then, but he could have been more willing to learn from those of us who had gone before.

*

These days I occasionally get some challenging trainees going through for their Boeing airliner type rating and the work of a Type Rating Instructor (TRI) can be frustrating if they appear to have barriers to effective learning. Sometimes this will occur with quite experienced pilots who have many thousands of hours on other aircraft types and who are sponsored by their new employer to get the rating. The trouble is, we have to play a fine balancing act as the type rating which they are training for is based upon the manufacturer's and regulator's (EASA) requirement and NOT on those of the airline.

So as a trainer I am often faced with a trainee who says, "That's not the way our airline XXX flies the airplane...!" To which I have to be very patient and explain to them again that we are training to the standards set by EASA and Boeing, which of necessity have to be 'generic' and they will learn their own airline's SOPs later.

I will usually go on to talk about the different ways I have seen airlines operate their aircraft upon a particular aspect. I can speak with authority having myself learned some twelve different sets of Standard Operating Procedures over the years, all of which were applied to Boeing Airliners. Of course being a freelance instructor/examiner for a long time exposes one to more than an average line pilot, so there I have an advantage. Quite simply I am able to assure my trainees that I have seen it done in different ways by many operators. Some better and some worse, "but on this course, we are going to have to teach it THIS WAY...!"

Well they normally get the message at this point; however some of them still display a resistance to learning which I have to deal with. One example some time back now was when I was training them to fly the single engine go-around in a heavy B767 in the simulator. One of my chaps was consistently failing to press the all important "Go-Around" paddle switch at the back of the thrust levers. This is really important in that low altitude, low speed situation when you need to get that big old bird climbing again away from mother earth. Let's face it, you have just flown a precision instrument approach down to a decision height of only 200 feet above the ground in 100% cloud, seen nothing and now you have to promptly climb away again...

In the Boeing 767, if you DON'T hit the GA paddle at that time, then you will NOT get the oh-so-important magenta Go-Around (pitch-up) Flight Director bars on the master attitude instrument. Thus you will find it VERY hard work to fly the jet, because the existing FD magenta bars are trying to fly you into the ground – not good! On several previous approaches I had reminded this gentleman to do so, but this time again he had forgotten.

As they reached their Decision Altitude and saw nothing, he commenced the single engine Go-Around. Correctly he pushed hard on the thrust lever of the live engine and called "Going-Around Flap Five" at the same time as pulling back on the control column to pitch the nose of the aircraft up. I then remained quiet in the backseat of the simulator as I saw him struggling to ignore the erroneous indications from the FD bars and then as his instrument scan broke down and he failed to put enough rudder in, the speed washed off as the nose went too high. Then the wing dropped, then came the synthetic warning voice "BANK ANGLE, BANK ANGLE!" And then the stickshaker stall-warning started...RATATATATATATAT!

"BANK ANGLE, BANK ANGLE!"

I pressed the "Flight Freeze" button in the back of the 'box and there we all were in suspended animation. His colleague was equally uncomfortable with the fact that the aircraft was effectively stalled at an extreme bank angle only a few hundred feet above the ground. I activated the CAVOK (Clear Skies) button and took all the fog away from outside the windows. The lack of height was clear for all three of us to see. I chose my words carefully and loudly..."YOU SEE GENTLEMEN – when I TELL YOU that it is vitally important to hit the GO-AROUND PADDLE for this manoeuvre you REALLY MUST LISTEN TO ME! I am not speaking just for the good of my health..."

I know it is a hard lesson for them to learn, but learn it they must and if I have to use the Simulator Flight Freeze function to drive that learning point home, then that is exactly what I use it for. Of course, you could say he MIGHT have been able to get away with it and he MIGHT have been able to recover from the 'unusual attitude', in total cloud only a few hundred feet above the airport... But we must not take the chance. At the end of the day this is public transport operations we are talking about and for the type rating proficiency check, the safe outcome of EVERY manoeuvre cannot be in any doubt.

*

So much for learning to fly; but how about learning to manage? In that quiet cockpit enroute to Mumbai in India all those years ago, my fellow Captain looked at me and smiled; "Well, I decided to experiment and see *how many times* I could say **'NO'** to the Managing Director of the airline... I found out it was only **ONE!"**

--0--

13 - LETHAL NUMBERS

There is nothing more depressing in our profession than to observe the results of gross negligence on the part of fellow aviators. Whether that is to read an official accident report, view a well constructed TV documentary or visit the site of an aircraft accident, the effect on the psyche is always the same.

It is similar to the feeling I experienced while touring in Northern France and passing the military cemeteries of the Great War. There are many. Row upon row of identical, carefully preserved gravestones. I recall shaking my head sadly and saying to them "Oh Boys...WHAT were you doing...?"

Of course they were for the most part, following orders, fighting and dying in the line of duty. Boys fighting for territory and dying for principles. Many of them will have met their end as a result of direct engagement with the enemy, but some will have been from the error of their own judgement or more likely that of their superiors... God Bless them all. "They shall not grow old, as we that are left grow old..."*

...we shall remember them

*

Naturally as trainers of professional airline pilots, it is our prime function to help our trainees make fewer errors of judgement as they progress in order that the standard of their flight operation may be enhanced. In doing so we are governed and regulated such that we apply the same standards in all of our training delivery. Part of that 'standardisation process' is to ensure that the instructors/examiners do not develop their own ideas or 'pet hates'. We are carefully groomed so that we never give criticism on a personal basis, for example "...I don't like to see you doing..." or "...I didn't approve of such..."

Personally we try to make a point of not using these forms of words in our briefing or debriefing and we specifically avoid any expression of personal preferences when it comes to how to operate the aircraft. There are times however, when the trainees question the 'standard' training guidance which they have been given and at those times I inform them that there are several different ways to operate the aircraft, some better and some not. At the end of the day it is often down to the operating company to decide on what is their method of choice – "He who pays the piper, calls the tune".

Even so and after many years doing the job, I confess that I do have a pet hate. I cannot help myself. I confess now that my personal bête noire is when pilots persist in neglecting basic safety measures which can imperil the whole operation. It is not acceptable - in my humble opinion - to erode established safety margins by a casual approach to 'the numbers'. In our game, digits are king. Seriously, they rule and limit everything we do as aviators. They keep us safe and they can kill.

A slapdash approach to some of the numbers we use in everyday airline operations can have lethal results for all concerned. A good example is the '**cleared** altitude or flight level'. The management of this vital information inside the confines of the flightdeck between two pilots is key. When received on the radio by the pilots it is customary (if the autopilot is engaged) for the flying pilot (PF) to change the altitude setting in the mode control panel. The monitoring pilot (PM) should acknowledge the new clearance correctly with ATC on the R/T and simultaneously crosscheck with PF that the new altitude/flight level limit has been set correctly.

"Gentlemen! THIS IS THE KILLER!" I can hear my own voice even now as I have frozen the Simulator to drive the learning point home. Usually as a result of a breakdown in the correct sequence of procedure, between the two pilots in the front seats when setting the altitude window on the autopilot MCP. I indicate that a wrong heading or speed insertion would probably not have such fatal consequences, but a wrong **altitude** will result in either a possible mid-air collision with another aircraft at that level, or perhaps Controlled Flight Into Terrain (CFIT).

Another part of the critical path with this sort of error/mistake is the use of unapproved, non-standard or incorrect R/T procedures. There are two numerical digits here which form the majority of the risk. They are numbers 2 and 4 – they are killers. I have lost count of the number of times I have informed quite experienced commercial aviators that they are introducing an unnecessary level of risk into their operation by saying things like, "StarWing 757, passing level two eight zero, descending to one two zero..." or even worse, **"...descending to four zero zero"**.

This was the last transmission from the Flying Tigers B747 cargo flight which crashed into the ground in early 1989 during an approach to Kuala Lumpur. Their actual altitude clearance had been **"Descend altitude two four zero zero..."** They read back and set **400** feet in the altitude window of the autopilot. Of course there were other factors involved; naturally, there always are. CRM issues on the flightdeck, poor weather, degraded ATC service and poor R/T procedures by Air Traffic Control.

Add to that the fact that the crew did not initially respond correctly nor promptly to the GPWS** Terrain "PULL-UP!" warning and the accident was inevitable. Such a sad loss - and completely avoidable too. I often use this accident as an example of the importance of getting it right on the R/T.

In addition, when the trainees in the Simulator make potentially confusing/ambiguous R/T transmissions to ATC (played by me in the back of the box) - then I make a point of misinterpreting these, usually with amusing results. Humour in teaching is always good, as it often helps to consolidate newly received information into the long-term memory. One recent example of this was when the crew called me with the transmission, "StarWing 757, in the left turn, passing two eight zero **for** two two zero..."

Naturally the low Transition Altitudes in the European operating area are a predisposing factor in many 'altitude busts' and mis-readbacks, but in reality these are simply environmental threats which we are well equipped to manage. Awareness is key of course, the environment applies to all. It is up to all of us to increase our own vigilance to maintain acceptable margins of safety.

This includes, (but is not limited to) standard and clear R/T practices, preventing numerical errors – VHF frequency mis-readbacks are common. Employing sterile cockpit procedures during critical stages of flight, such as eradicating non-essential conversation between crewmembers in the climb and descent is often mandated as SOP in the airlines.

The insistence of the senior members of our profession (Training Captains) on the maintenance and promotion of healthy, safe cockpit procedures is so important, it cannot be overstated.

I recall an incident many years ago, as we taxied out from London Heathrow on a wet and windy night. We were bound for the Indian Sub-Continent with a newly joined First Officer in the right-hand seat and were just about to launch off into one of the busiest ATC terminal areas on the planet.

He would not stop talking. For some reason he had the urge to comment on anything and everything which came to mind or into his vision – known as verbal diarrhoea. Of course his vocalisations were mostly irrelevant and simply distracting to the operation, to the point where we missed an important R/T call from the overworked ground controller.

I brought the aircraft to a halt on the taxiway and applied the parking brake. I looked directly at him and said very slowly, "Listen to me Mister _____ either you cut out the verbal diarrhoea and pay attention to your duties in a quiet and professional manner or we are going back to the gate and I will offload you! Your Training will be suspended and you can explain to the airline the reason for the delay of Flight XXX tonight. IT IS YOUR CHOICE SIR! WHAT IS IT TO BE...?!" Needless to say I had his full attention at this point; in fact he had the good grace to look a bit shocked; maybe he was shocked. After all I had just announced formally and categorically that his career was like a train about to hit the buffers...

He shut up and did his job well for the rest of the night. He was not in essence a bad pilot, but he did have some personal tendencies which required active management to ensure that he did not adversely affect the cockpit communications environment. Sometime later while working for the same company, he came to me privately and thanked me for being so honest with him that night. It gave him clear guidance with regard to the expected standards of behaviour and acceptable code of conduct that the airline required.

*

In the recent past while researching an airliner CFIT accident I ended up on a hillside on a sunny afternoon, overlooking the Mediterranean Sea. The view was "breathtakingly beautiful" as the novelists would describe, yet I felt so very, very sad. I was deeply affected by the evidence of human frailty in front of my eyes and the huge memorial white cross which had been erected. *"Oh Boys...what were you doing...?"*

If there is ONE THING we can ALL do as professional aviators to help make the future safer... it is to remove the words "TO" and "FOR" from our R/T transmissions- these are NUMBERS. Believe me it is easy when you try. "Hello London. SmartFlight 757, passing **Flight Level** One Four Zero CLIMBING **Flight Level** Two Four Zero..."

*

* *"They shall not grow old, as we that are left grow old... At the going down of the sun and in the morning...We will remember them".* 'For the Fallen' by poet Robert Laurence Binyon – September 1914.

**GPWS – Ground Proximity Warning System - It does what it says on the tin.

Note: All references to male gender in this chapter apply equally to the female and vice versa.

--0--

14 - AIRBORNE INTERCEPTION

Maintaining listening watch will avoid this outside your window

A couple of years back there was the much publicised interception of a Latvian operated cargo aircraft by RAF Typhoons over southern England. The incident was resolved when the cargo aircraft obeyed the orders from the RAF interceptors to land at Stansted airport. It was interesting for professional aviators from a variety angles, not least of which is the fact that clearly the crew were not maintaining a listening watch on the emergency frequency 121.50 MHz.

A frequent occurrence these days is to hear calls on 121.5 from aircraft calling on behalf of ATC agencies when a flight has gone too far away from their ground transmitter and can only be reached from an airborne station. Usually this is after the ground agency has tried several times unsuccessfully to make contact themselves. The phenomenon is called PLOC – Prolonged Loss Of Communication.

In the vast majority of cases the crew respond and there is no need for an interception from the military. There are those who question whether intercepting civilian aircraft travelling on recognised airways is the right thing to do as a response to lack of communication. Maybe they have not thought it through properly. You don't have to look back very far to think of some flights which have gone awry and we're not even considering September 11th, 2001.

Think of Malaysian flight 370, think of Helios and there are others too, flights lost after communication also ceased. In the case of the Antonov 26 Cargo aircraft allegedly crewed by Estonian flightdeck crew, it is likely that simple negligence or finger trouble was to blame, nothing more sinister than that. However after all that has gone before, including the September 11th attacks, then you can certainly understand the British Government's policy regarding aircraft arriving into UK airspace being uncontactable by normal air traffic control methods.

Civilian airliners being intercepted by military fighters are not as rare as one might think. Going back many years now when I was working for a charter airline flying B757s to and from holiday destinations all over Europe, one of our flights (early '90s) was intercepted in Austrian upper airspace by an Austrian Air Force fighter. The reason given at that time was that the airliner flight number had been incorrectly filed – I think it had something to do with inexperience in the Ops Dept who filed an HM Government trooping flight as a holiday charter by ineptitude.

The Austrians were probably making a point... Whatever the reason, I recall the B757 Captain relating the story of how in the middle of the night, their TCAS system went crazy as the fighter came rushing up from down below in line astern position. I think nowadays the fighters turn off the TCAS or switch to Standby mode prior to formating on the target aircraft.

*

When I was working for the Low-Cost Operator in the late 1990s we went through a period when we had more than a few interceptions of our flights coming back to the UK. Funnily enough these were over central Europe, not arriving into the UK. On investigation we found that the most common flight being intercepted for being uncontactable on the R/T, was the inbound flight from Athens in Greece.

Further enquiries revealed that the flight was scheduled to arrive in Athens during the early hours of the morning, (local time) and then had to remain on the ground until 6am local time before departure. Therefore the crew were reporting for duty late evening in the UK, flying the three and a half hours to Athens, being forced to sit around onboard the aircraft for three hours or so, prior to flying back home to Luton.

Needless to say this sort of duty is likely to have the most debilitating effect on the flightcrew's awareness and arousal levels. It was decided that it was possible that some of the pilots MAY have actually fallen asleep while operating the flight back home again... Therefore the scheduling policy was changed - the flight to Athens became a day flight only and in fact it was at that point I believe that we effected a change to SOPs.

There was introduced a very strict ruling whereby ALL flights were instructed to maintain a listening watch on the emergency (guard) frequency, 121.50 MHz on the second VHF box at all times while airborne. No surprises then that the interceptions stopped and I would be surprised if there have been any since for that airline. In reality most of our crews had already been listening out on Guard on VHF2 for many years as a policy of good airmanship, but once it was enforced, then it became 100% across the fleet.

Maybe if the A380 flight from one of the Gulf States had been listening out on 121.5 on VHF2 recently over Europe then it too might not have been intercepted by fighters. This particular incident - although not widely reported, lead to a disciplinary hearing and the Captain's resignation from the airline. In addition the First Officer was censured and his career prospects took a nosedive. There were many pilots within the airline who stated that the disciplinary went against the modern trend of no-blame culture which exists as part of modern Safety Management System practice. It should also be borne in mind that the Captain involved was very senior in the company, an influential figure and highly popular among his work colleagues.

That being said, the 'no-blame culture' should not be used to shield individuals whose acts or omissions produce consequences which effectively may be construed as Gross Negligence. For example a charge of Gross Negligence could be levelled at any employee whose action or inaction brought the company's reputation into disrepute. In this case, having your aircraft intercepted by fighters unnecessarily through not maintaining a listening watch on the radio, contrary to SOPs could qualify and in fact could have resulted in summary dismissal.

The outcome of the hearing was a Final Written Warning for the Commander, which meant that any further transgression within the following 12 months would result in dismissal. Apparently, this would have meant that the Captain's savings in the company provident fund would have been at risk, which he could not accept, so his choice was to resign. In essence his was a business decision and you can understand it from his point of view.

*

So there is no doubt about it. It is a serious business and we should all be aware of the potential consequences when we operate commercial flights. That being said, airborne interceptions are surprisingly common. In fact over the past few months there has been a rise in the number of intercept missions flown by NATO forces, (including the RAF) as Russia flexes her muscles on the diplomatic front over Ukraine. The funny thing about the reported interceptions for me and probably other not so young aviators is that the Russian aircraft being intercepted by the RAF are the same types that were the targets from the 1960s and '70s.

Seriously, have a look on the internet under TU-95 interception images and you will see old photographs of Phantom F4s and Lightnings in formation with the 'Bears'. These days the interceptors are Typhoons and F16s, but the TU-95s are the same! How OLD are those airframes? It makes you think eh?

Not all airborne interceptions are hostile however and I have had the good fortune in the past to be on the flightdeck of airliners when we have been intercepted by fighters as an escort, while carrying troops and government supplies into bandit country.

From experience the main thing is to get in contact with the interceptors early (via ATC) and keep it simple – they need to know height, speed and heading. Also it helps if you fly entirely predictably of course. The autopilot stays in and quite often they have asked us to keep our speed up; 300 kts is good for middle airspace if memory serves me right.

While on the subject of memory, it reminds me of the old, old joke on this particular subject. Forgive me if you've heard it before.

A couple of Fighters are escorting an airliner trooping flight, and their pilots are chatting with the Captain of the airliner to pass the time. Talk comes round to the relative merits of their respective aircraft. Of course the fighter pilots contend that their airplanes were better because of their superior speed, maneuverability, weaponry, and so forth, while putting down the airliner's deficiencies in these areas.

After listening to this for a while, the airline pilot says, "Oh yeah? Well, I can do a few things in this old girl that you can only dream about..." Naturally, the fighter jocks challenge him to demonstrate.

"Just watch," came the quick retort. And so they watch... But all they see is the airliner continuing to fly straight and level. After a few minutes the airline pilot comes back on the air, saying "There! How was that?"

Not having seen anything different, the fighter pilots reply, "What are you talking about? What did you do?" And the airline pilot replies, "Well, I got up, stretched my legs, got a cup of coffee, then went back to the forward Lav and took a leak!"

Tornado F3 on fighter escort duty saying "Bye-Bye"

--0—

15 - WEATHER AVOIDANCE

Cumulonimbus (Cbs) on the ITCZ can reach 45,000 feet.

"What does this do?" was the question over the intercom from my brother Mike in the passenger seat as I was carrying out the preflight checks in the Piper Chieftain Mail plane.

"Oh! That's the weather radar... I haven't used it much" I replied airily. I was new to the aircraft and new to the job - 'Air Taxi Operations, Single Pilot'. To make him happy, I said, "...you can play with it if you like once we're airborne, I have never seen much on it to be honest..."

It is paradoxical in commercial aviation that the least experienced pilots (usually with the ink still wet on their frozen ATPLs) are put in the unenviable position of carrying out some of the most challenging flying jobs. Single Crew IFR Operations in northern

Europe during the winter has just about got it all. Normally the aircraft are piston twins or turboprops with limited performance, often carrying 'Acceptable' Deferred Defects because the small operating company has limited cash flow. Not only that, but there are also the overloaded cargo flights, the dubiously extended flying duty times and the vagaries of the weather to contend with.

Of course the pilots do not complain or demur because they really need the flying hours and after paying out so much to get qualified are just happy to be paid anything at all for the use of their newly found skills. I recall when I went for my commercial Instrument Rating Test with the UK CAA in Stansted back in the mid '80s; my instructor told me that if the examiner asked what job I was going to do afterwards, to tell him I had an offer of a safe job as First Officer with a UK airline. The inference being that if I was to inform the examiner I was destined for Single Pilot IFR Ops, he would judge me more critically. In those days it was legal to dispatch for commercial flights, single pilot without a working autopilot.... imagine!

Well I passed my test with the CAA examiner and never looked back, but at that time, little did I know, how little I knew. My real learning phase was just about to begin, as I entered the world of the air taxi pilot. One of the benefits then was that we could take a passenger on flights with us and often friends and family would come along for the ride. They would be included on the crew list and we (the pilots) were responsible for their safety and security.

On this particular night I was very glad to have my brother along who had a keen interest in aviation although not himself a pilot. It was while we were heading southwest in solid clag at around Flight Level 70 down the airways that Mike managed to get the weather radar screen lit up. It was one of those old ones which only swept about 45 degrees either side of the nose, but it was enough. I said to him on the intercom, "Yes it's supposed to show green areas on the screen where the radar returns are from the heaviest precipitation, which also means thunderstorms of course..."

"What? You mean like THAT one?" he said in a curious sort of way, to which I replied,

"YIKES BRO! You've found A MONSTER!" and it was true. There was a huge mass of solid green about 20 miles ahead of us exactly on our track and smack over the beacon at Daventry. I immediately called the London controller for a turn away from the build-up, our request was swiftly granted. Needless to say I always flew with the weather radar on when operating in IMC after that, during day or night. In fact the forecast had indicated 'embedded Cumulonimbus' and it was not wrong. Later on when I mentioned the incident to my Chief Pilot, he laughed it off, referring to "the Duty Cb over Daventry".

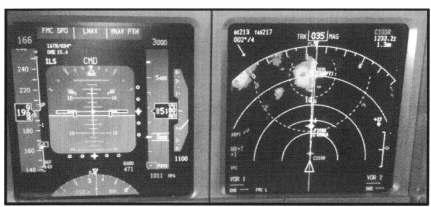

Some WX is difficult to avoid, here the CB is close to the airport

Embedded Cumulonimbus (thunderstorms) are one of the greatest dangers which we face flying airliners even now. It is the unique factor in our operating environment which cannot be controlled by designers, technicians, engineers, pilots or regulators. The dangers to aviation include severe air turbulence and airframe-icing both of which may potentially result in loss of control of the aircraft. No pilot would opt to fly through a thunderstorm.

Of course our weather forecasting has improved markedly since the days when I was flying air taxis. Often for example when I note the time, fuel and Met Data passing a waypoint on the route, the wind vector is close enough to be within only a knot or two of the forecast and the direction within 5 degrees, astounding accuracy. The Static Air Temperature is also usually within a couple of degrees Celsius and often it is exactly spot on. I look at the operational flightplan and then compare it with the instruments in the flightdeck and there it is, bang on at -53C. How do they do it?

It is worth considering here that when talking about 'avoidance' of potentially hazardous weather conditions, there are some flights when it is impossible to avoid everything. Isolated Cbs are usually easy to avoid, especially during daylight hours when simple deviation from heading will suffice. In northern Europe it is often possible to cruise over the tops of many build ups as it is not uncommon for the upper limits of Cumulo-Nimbus to be limited, reflected by the usually lower level of the tropopause.

Closer to the equator it is a different story where build-ups and storms generated by, or close to, the Inter Tropical Convergence Zone (ITCZ) can reach 45,000 feet. Airliners generally cruise in the regime of 33 to 39,000 feet depending largely upon their weight. The heavier they are; the lower is the maximum cruising altitude for any given aircraft. The reason for this is that the buffet boundaries become closer together, the higher you climb as a result of the thinner atmosphere. This is so called 'Coffin Corner'. The gap between high speed buffet, where the high-speed (Mach) stall occurs and slow speed buffet, where low-speed stall happens gets narrower and narrower.

Compounding the issue is the fact that this critical gap is dramatically reduced by adding bank angle as in a turn, which is why the automatic systems will limit the autopilot bank angle for aircraft flying at high altitudes. Bear in mind we are talking about being close to 'maximum cruise altitude' here, i.e. higher than our normal operating cruise levels. For normal flight operations airliners endeavour to fly at Optimum Cruise altitude which is the most fuel efficient and safe cruising level, while maintaining adequate buffet margins. As fuel is burned off and the airframe becomes lighter, this Optimum Cruise altitude increases of course.

There is speculation that a recent airliner loss, (Air Asia) in the Far East was due to the pilots trying to out-climb and then turn away from a Cumulonimbus. Although this may have some truth in it, that cannot be the whole story and we should wait until the official investigation is completed. The instances of *adverse weather conditions alone* being responsible for the loss of an airliner are extremely rare, especially in modern times.

Statistically it is the least likely complete explanation, although it may well have been a significant causal factor. One thing is for sure, once the accident cause is established, there will be more lessons for our poor industry to learn. Although we often learn from our own mistakes, it should be remembered that it is a privilege to learn from the mistakes of those who lost their lives for our benefit.

So what conclusions can we draw from our musings on the presence of and avoidance of weather on the routes we fly as commercial airline pilots? Well, in some ways not a lot really, but then in others we should be deeply respectful of the omnipotent power of nature.

I liken it to the very wholesome attitude of seasoned mariners when they consider their relationship with that incredible element, the ocean... The home of King Neptune and Davy Jones's locker; that source of a thousand scary stories about its unstoppable force and the catastrophic damage which it is capable of producing.

When making comparisons with the ocean, I am reminded of a

great philosophical quotation. Maybe you have already seen it, or perhaps it is new to you - either way, it is a profound statement and one that I have personally had on my study wall at home on a plaque for many years as a warning to myself, lest I forget...

"To an even greater degree than the sea, aviation is terribly unforgiving of any carelessness, incapacity or neglect".

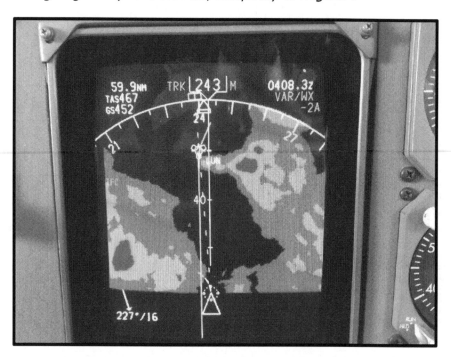

The HSI photo shows us tracking out of Delhi in the Monsoon season with storms (painting darker returns) all around. B767 WX Radar – threading our way carefully between the cells. Note we would not try to out-climb a Cb in these latitudes as has been suggested in the press recently. In fact if we could not avoid possible areas of known or expected turbulence, then 'lower is better' because of the greater protection against stalling – i.e. further away from "Coffin Corner".

--0--

16 - THE ANGRY PALM TREE*

With Army Air Corps pilot Danny McBride (brother)

The fatal Eurocopter accident which occurred in July 2012, brought to mind one of my pet hates. *'Reading about rotary wing accidents which might have been avoided'*. I don't mean to be trite here and with due respect to the casualties of helicopter accidents (and their loved ones), but many of these accidents could have been avoided. In fact taken to logical extreme, **all** rotary wing accidents could have been avoided if the helicopter had not been invented in the first place.

I have heard people talk about helicopters as "all those moving parts all wearing out together at the same time..." and there is some truth in that. Everything in a Helicopter is "life'd" and in simple terms this means that the designers and technical engineers have calculated how long each part will take to wear out. They then apply a factor to this and specify how many flight hours (or calendar point) earlier the part should be changed. This point then becomes the "life" of the part and it is changed for a new one at or before this time. It is interesting to note that when the British royal family go flying (i.e. in the Military for example when Prince Andrew served in the Falklands conflict) everything is half-life'd as an extra insurance policy for their protection.

Without going into the politics of royalty and the relevance of the monarchy to modern Britain, it is clear that some extra precautions should be taken when helicopters are used by extraordinary individuals. Consider the maintenance back-up and attention to detail and planning of "Marine One" the United States armed forces helicopter which carries the US President for example. This is as it should be of course, because there are special individuals who are VIP or VVIP and need protection in the interests of the good order of society. There is no doubt about it, rotary wing operations can be complex and there is even more potential for catastrophe than fixed wing flying. Even the aerodynamics of helicopter flying is complicated; with 'flapback' and 'inflow roll', joining 'translational lift' and 'vortex ring' as weirdly named phenomena of the spinning disc which sits above the 'cab'. Then there's 'retreating blade stall', 'fenestron stall' and... Well it just doesn't stop; there is SO much to learn when you start to fly helicopters. If an example was needed of the possible dangers regarding operating a powered flying machine with rotating wings, consider that traditionally the piece of hardware which holds the main rotor assembly in place is called the "Jesus Nut"...

The positive side of rotary-wing is easy to identify. Just think Air Sea Rescue or Air Ambulance. You can instantly visualise the life-saving potential of a vertical takeoff and landing machine which can hover in mid-air and recover people from dangerous situations. Those of us old enough to remember watching 'Thunderbirds' on TV as kids the first time round, appreciate the philosophy of International Rescue – such a wonderful philanthropic concept.

There is a dark side to helicopter flying though and it is this. It is far too attractive and glamorous to the extent that people are drawn to fly these machines that really should leave well alone. Let me explain. If you Google three words "businessman, helicopter, accident" the list of search results exceeds 2 million – this is not good. Furthermore you will see that the helicopter accidents involving successful businessmen cover the globe. From Mexico to Moscow and from the Caribbean to Calcutta "businessmen" have been killing themselves in these infernal devices for years.

Not only that, but there is another appalling aspect to the continuous stream of helicopter disasters involving rich and successful people – they usually take one or more of their family members with them. This just adds to the tragedy and can be evidenced by accident reports such as the one involving Colin McRae (ex World Rally Champion) who killed not only himself in 2007, but his six year old son and two family friends at the same time. Steve Hislop (former World Superbike Champion) suffered a fatal accident in 2003 which was devastating news not only for his family and friends, but for thousands of fans around the world. These two accidents are significant and indicative of where the problem lies. Both men had clearly demonstrated that their reaction times and locomotor skills were at above average level compared to the general population. Both of them were relatively young and fit and in neither accident was it suggested that mechanical failure had been a cause.

With the incredible sporting record of both these men, and their renowned achievements you can hardly say that the helicopter "attracts the wrong sort", but still the accidents continue to happen. Usually the occupants (and often the pilots) of helicopters are not only rich and famous, but they are also talented, gifted people who have so much to lose. They are the movers and shakers of society, they are often key individuals to their businesses and their loss to society is felt all the more keenly.

*

Many years ago when I was instructing at a flying school, I remember that the owner of the school was learning to fly helicopters and often he would arrive and or depart from the airport in a lightweight machine accompanied by his QHI. The funny thing was that even though the owner was an accomplished and experienced pilot himself with many thousands of hours in airliners, he was an incredibly slow learner in his new environment. You could see it from his point of view. The facility to be able to fly directly from his farmhouse home to the flying club and back again was potentially wonderful and would save him hours of driving, if only he could master the beast! Those of us who had trained on military helicopters in a previous life, watched with amusement as he grappled with hovering outside the flying club. On the quiet I asked his QHI one day what the score was and received the inside story. "He just has too much else on his mind to concentrate on learning new skills" was the professional assessment. He was right too, because after some weeks, the lessons stopped, we saw less of the owner and eventually the little red budgie device disappeared also. He never did get his PPL(H).

Before the machine was withdrawn, I did manage to blag a quick go in it myself when the QHI was taking it over to the other side of the airport for refuelling. Amazingly sensitive and not a little bit twitchy, I was surprised at how manoeuvrable it was. The other quality which hit me was how damn flimsy everything seemed. Bear in mind that I had trained on Aerospatiale Gazelle with the Royal Navy and thereafter the mighty Sea King, so I was used to substantial machinery with lots of superstructure around the pilot seats – this thing was like a Go-kart! Increasing the throttle while pulling up the collective lever was another revelation – the gas turbine powered aircraft I had been used to in the past were marvellously well equipped by comparison.

Especially the beautifully racy and powerful Gazelle with its Stability Augmentation System (S.A.S.) which I even now recall with fondness. You could sit in a steady hover in the Gazelle, then simply pull up on the collective to increase the pitch on the disc and without consciously pushing on the yaw pedal; the thing would hold its heading – VERY clever! The 'studes' were never normally informed of this by the instructors, so there we were, all pushing our yaw pedals this way and that while going up and down in the hover. My QHI was different however and decided to show me the trick – I was amazed and thought to myself, next time out, I will try that myself. This was a mistake.

The next day dawned bright and clear at RNAS Culdrose where one Sub-Lieutenant McBride thought he would impress his instructor with his in-depth knowledge of the machine. Once the engine was running and the rotor engaged, with all checks completed, I (as handling pilot) was ready to lift into the hover. What I did not know, was that the clever system ONLY worked once the machine was actually airborne in the hover, in all other cases (like getting airborne) yaw pedal was most definitely required... The ground crew out front of the bubble canopy gave the signal "clear to lift" and I simply pulled the collective lever with my left hand! Doh! As the skids broke loose from the friction of the concrete, the machine started to yaw dramatically and I have never seen a marshaller react so quickly or run so fast either before or since – *"I HAVE CONTROL!"* shouted the QHI in my headphones and immediately brought the machine into a stable hover. Needless to say I never did THAT again.

*

Much later came my conversion onto the Sea King with twin engines and five bladed main rotor. It was at this point that I came to appreciate the incredible capabilities of a machine which can lift ten tonnes vertically and fly at 120 knots across the earth's surface – phenomenal.

The helicopter has given so much to the human race which cannot be denied, however Leonardo da Vinci's creation is genius yet flawed. I just wish there was some way to stop rich businessmen putting themselves at risk in them.

*

The nickname of the military helicopter by some of the 'customers' - The Marines call it "The Angry Palm Tree".

--0--

17 - THINGS PEOPLE SAY

Do you know it's funny, but apparently according to modern myth, all airline pilots sound like Chuck Yeager on the PA. That steady, calm reassuring voice coming through all the speakers in the cabin "This is your Captain speaking, welcome onboard..." You would have thought that we all went to the same charm school together. In fact these days due to potential customer litigation most companies are quite prescriptive about what the pilots should and should not say on the Public Address system. In the old days it used to be different...

*

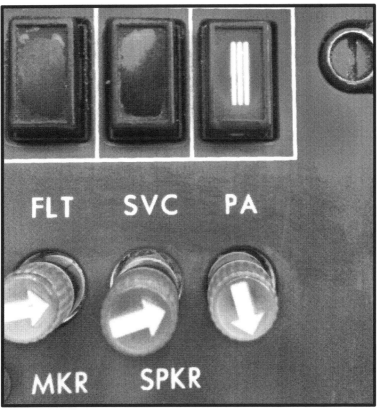

Press the switch and they will hear everything you say!

When you first commence your line training as a junior Co-Pilot in the flightdeck of a jet airliner, it is the most amazing experience. Everything is new to you and not just the scenery passing the window, but absolutely EVERYTHING. Your uniform, the functions of the seat, the paperwork and of course even the type rating on your pilot's licence. Of course you are keen to learn all the new skills which come with the territory, so although you do not feel it, you are soaking up information like the proverbial sponge.

Even really basic things, such as to know which VHF radio to use for which purpose. In the past if you had experience flying light aeroplanes, it was often up to you which 'comms box' you used for which purpose, but once you are in the airline system, there is no latitude for creative thinking about such matters. For example, it is normally standard practice for the left (number one) VHF to be used for all Air Traffic Control communications.

The first time I found this out was on my B757 type conversion course when I tried to select this radio to listen to the weather broadcast – I found out very quickly that this is "not the done thing old chap!" I dare say the Training Captains of today might be rather more direct... There is one element of flightdeck communications however which nobody looks forward to learning about, me included and this is using the PA system. There are hand mikes in most flightdecks and it is also possible to make PA announcements using the headset boom microphone.

If you then adjust the settings on the headset earphones, you will be able to hear your own voice just like it sounds in the cabin – scary eh? Normally in most companies it is a shared duty and the Pilot Flying (PF) on their sector will make the announcements after the initial "Welcome Aboard" - usually done by the Captain. Apologies for delayed departure and explanations of technical issues/defects are commonly performed from the LHS also, as the passengers seem to expect to hear this sort of bad news from the top.

I recall with horror the first few times when the Line Training Captain on the B757 said to me, "and of course as you are the PF this sector, all the PAs are yours..." Yikes, what do you say? Well everybody has to start somewhere and usually you begin with writing out a little script of what to say. The old pro's just pick up the mike and start talking and when you watch them it leaves you dry mouthed and speechless when you are in the other seat, thinking to yourself, *I've got to do that myself on the next sector – GULP!'*

The really daunting bit is the thought of *ALL THOSE PEOPLE* sat back there listening intently to what YOU are going to tell them. In reality, many will not listen and the ambient noise level in the cabin may reduce the audible effects of your voice anyway – but this does little to allay the fear of *PUBLIC SPEAKING.*

The Line Training Captain can help or hinder during this phase and I distinctly recall being distracted by the Skipper during one of my early attempts at an informative PA announcement to the passengers, by him holding up a piece of A4 paper with the helpful advice ***"TRY NOT TO SAY FUCK!"***

It's hard not to laugh out loud at times like these and in the natural progression of things, eventually my turn came to 'help' my trainee Boeing pilots in their early announcements. In addition to the foregoing, distraction technique, I would also encourage them to prepare well for their PA by muting all other headset inputs on their side.

If they forgot (inevitable in the early days) then I would wait until they were well into their prepared speech and then key the intercom on my side making farm animal noises which came flooding into their ears from they knew not where! The look on their faces was hilarious as they fought to continue with the PA, with me "Mooing and Quacking" in their ears. They did learn a valuable lesson – ALWAYS take care to ensure you cannot be distracted by other audible inputs to your headset before you start speaking.

Once when I did this to a new First Officer, she laughed afterwards and said that the previous day on another flight while she was making the PA close to the top of descent point, the Line Training Captain shouted **"RETARD!"** verbalising the change in autothrottle mode as the power was retarded. She was sure this had been broadcast to everybody in the cabin also. The funny thing is that the SOP for the airline was that ALL autoflight mode changes should be called out by the first pilot to notice if they were unexpected, so in a way the Captain was just following SOPs... (Thank you Capt Paul Barnes wherever you are).

FO Anze Slivnik makes inflight PA with distractions going on...

When you are nervous, it is often the case that a situation which might otherwise be serious, could make you amused, like the time when I have flown with one pilot who used to make the most ridiculous faces at me while I was trying to be serious on the microphone to the cabin. I was so affected by the sight that I had to stop talking and take my finger off the button mid sentence. After a long pause I was able to compose myself enough to resume my speech with apologies.

Of course once I became a Captain it became my 'pleasure' to help my junior colleagues to carry out their PA announcements while trying to ignore the distractions from the left-hand seat...

*

In those bad old days there were also plenty of jokes on the PA too, often between the pilots and the Flight Attendants. Even though I never saw it at the expense of flight safety - in our modern litigious industry, things are much less light-hearted. Occasionally you will hear pilots making mistakes with their comms switchery ('finger-trouble' they call it) and one of the funniest of these is when a pilot transmits their PA to the passengers all over the ATC frequency. Although you could say it is an easy mistake to make, most pilots are very careful when they set-up to speak to the passengers and are careful about which transmit switch they select on the audio/comms box.

Needless to say if they have done it once, they usually have previous form – it's a case here of the usual suspects. The trouble with this particular 'switch pigz' is that it blocks the ATC frequency and if you are at a busy airport this can be not only frustrating, but dangerous too. The good news is that this erroneous transmission is unlikely to occur on the approach or tower frequency, but I have heard several quite nice "Welcome Aboard" PAs transmitted on the ground or delivery frequency. This is usually followed by a chaotic scramble of aircraft calling for pushback, mixed with the ATC ground controller trying to redirect taxiing airliners and one or two clowns who think it's SO funny to add to the mess by transmitting "Thank you Captain, we ALL enjoyed that! Have a nice flight yourself!"

When this sort of mistake happens on the airways frequency, it is not usually such a big issue as everyone instantly recognises what has happened. The subsequent ribald comments which follow a truly boring announcement sometimes provide comic relief to an otherwise featureless cruise segment. When pilots get together on the ground talking about these sorts of mistakes with PA announcements and RT transmissions, there is always one story which gets told and is a cautionary tale for any pilot who does not wish the *private conversation* in the flightdeck to be aired to all the passengers.

I have heard it several times, so there is likely to be truth in the original version. It allegedly happened with an American airline when the Captain's voice came over the cabin loudspeaker system talking to his Co-Pilot while the aircraft was in the climb to cruising altitude. He drawled, "Yeah well, did you see that pretty new Flight Attendant we got working in the rear galley called Angie? She's a REEEL honey and when ah've finished havin' ma cawfee, ah'll jess be takin' a stroll down there to see if ah can git ma hands on her pretty little ass! That oughta make her wake-up an' take notice, eh?"

Well of course Angie heard this and blushing bright red she made a dash up the aisle to alert the flightcrew that they were being heard over the PA, she was worried what he might say next! Halfway up the cabin, a little old lady grabbed her arm to stop her and said with a twinkle in her eye;

"Whoa! Not so fast l'il lady... he ain't finished his coffee yet!"

--0--

18 - DON'T LOOK DOWN...

...if this isn't the first rule of mountain climbing, then I think it ought to be. I mean it makes such eminent sense from all angles – especially from above! You see we all need basic rules of thumb to go by when we are carrying out complex tasks as human beings. In fact when you think about it, mountaineering and flying have much in common. There are various comparisons which can be made regarding ascending and descending; the overcoming of obstacles; continuous improvement in the technical kit and always there are the common denominators, gravity and altitude.

The mighty 747 passing head-on 1000ft above us on the airway

Now surprisingly enough, the latter of these two can be a problem for some pilots. You would think that being 'unafraid of heights' would be a primary quality for becoming an aviator, not so. I know many pilots who cannot go up a ladder outside their house, or get terrific anxiety when standing at the edge of a big drop, whether it is a tall building or a natural precipice. Non-aviators are often taken aback when they hear this and immediately look sceptical when told that we are scared of heights. They say things like, "It cannot be true, what happens when you look out of the cockpit window?" But I explain that this is completely different although I am not sure why.

In my own case I freely admit that I am not good with big drops, sheer cliff faces or being near the top of tall buildings. When we visited Paris a few years back and went up the Eiffel Tower, the kids were running up the stairs ahead of me and then rushing towards the railing, "Come BACK! Don't go near the EDGE!" I recall shouting, much to the consternation of other tourists as the children fell about laughing and I wanted to drop onto all fours to stay low and keep safe. We had only reached the first level... In reality of course it was me who was close to the edge, the edge of reason!

Logically the steel structure has been standing perfectly safely and sturdily since the 1800s in all weathers with nobody falling off it, so why on earth should it suddenly become unsafe just because an Englishman brings his kids to see it on a sunny day? But that's the funny thing about phobias; they are irrational and very hard to overcome. I was trying to think if there had been any times in my flying career when I have experienced my fear of heights actually while in an aeroplane. I could only count twice.

The first was in a helicopter while on the rotary wing course with the Royal Navy when one of the details was to climb to 10,000 feet over Cornwall. The normal operating environment of the helicopter is at low-level of course, but this exercise was part of the syllabus to explore the envelope of the machine. It took ages to get up there and the thinner atmosphere had a quantifiable adverse effect on the power and effectiveness of the controls. In the glass bubble of the Gazelle, I looked down past my military flying boots and there was the earth, a very, very, long way away – now that felt scary!

The second time was some years later in an open cockpit biplane over Florida while practising aerobatics. The aircraft was a Pitts Special and the lesson was 'inverted spinning'... I must admit even though we had briefed extensively prior to take-off, I had not really given it much thought, but then when we turned upside down at about 8,000 feet and flew inverted for a while I looked 'above' me to find that the ground was down there, over a mile away!

..soon learned all there was to know about tightening harnesses

Now I thought I had done a pretty good job of tightening my safety harness preflight, especially the wide aerobatic negative 'G' lap belt – but after this incident I soon learned all there was to know about **REALLY** tightening harnesses.

I recall that once we were actually spinning it did not feel as bad as there were plenty of other things to think about. It was just the inverted flying leading up to the spin, hanging from the seatbelts with nothing visible preventing a very long drop which got to me. Once again, this was an irrational fear because the aircraft had been doing this many times before without accident and the aerobatic instructor/display pilot in the back was highly qualified and experienced. So what could possibly go wrong?

In fact there was much more likelihood of not recovering from the spin, than falling out of the airframe. Talking of which, I remember many years before while I was doing my initial flying training in a Chipmunk with a military instructor that I got temporarily confused between the recovery actions for a Spin and a Stall. We had already made three turns in the spin and I was the handling pilot in the front cockpit when I heard the words "Recover now..." in the earphones of my helmet. There was a laconic tone to his voice and a bored quality which I found fascinating.

After all, how could anybody become bored when this whole flying thing was SO EXCITING!? Literally everything about it was brilliant and I was enjoying learning all these new skills in my new element (the sky) very much indeed. It sounded like my instructor (a retired ex WW2 veteran) was half asleep in the back as the nose of the Chipmunk circulated around the horizon as we entered the fully developed spin. I was quite tense in the front and being eager to please, when I heard the command I immediately recovered from the *STALL*...?? Doh? WRONG...!

Applying full power in a 'Spin' has the effect of raising the nose to the horizon, flattening the spin attitude, dramatically increasing the speed of rotation and makes it much harder to exit! Well, I had his full attention now. He shouted, "WAYHAAAY! I HAVE CONTROL!" and horrified, I let go completely with both hands and feet. Very soon the rotation stopped and we exited from the flat spin with a huge swooping dive, pulling up into a steep climb and trading speed for altitude.

I could not stop apologising – in those days we called our instructors Sir. Well as they say, I learned about spinning from that, but there was much more. It was a salutary lesson in paying attention to the preflight briefing and making sure not to lose focus when you fly. You've got to get your head straight and keep it that way if you want to be a good pilot. And you have got to get over the fear of falling or failing, in other words Don't Look Down.

One of the most intriguing aspects of the whole flying game for me has been making the transition to another aircraft type. Every time you feel that you have mastered one cockpit and all of the controls seem to have a familiar, homely feel to them, then you pass on to another stage. The next aircraft type always seems so much more complicated than the last one and it appears to require superhuman powers of concentration to fly the damn thing!

This is normally most evident in the early phases of training, but can come as a surprise to some of the more senior members of our community too. I recall an ex Cathay Pacific B747 Captain regaling us all with his story of making the transition "from steam to glass". (From the old analogue instrument display to glass cockpit EFIS setup on the B747-400 in Hong Kong).

As they climbed away on the first take-off in the simulator, with everything happening too fast for the trainees, the instructor pointed out several of the new automatic functions which occurred to the instrument displays as the aircraft climbed through the first few hundred feet. The trainee Captain turned in his seat with wide eyes and asked *"How did you know we were airborne!?"*

*

Back in 1989 the glass cockpits of the new (in those days) generation Boeings, made us feel very special – they seemed to be far ahead of their time and we were the envy of colleagues operating much older 'round-dial' equipment. Now of course, these same flightdecks look quite dated and old fashioned, but 20 years ago, they were "the business". Of course some of us older chaps have missed out on the revolutionary technology which now equips all GA aeroplanes. We hear Garmin this and GPS that, but we are still not quite sure what it all means.

In the days when visitors were allowed to visit the flightdeck, they were often genuinely overawed by the instrument displays of the B757 for example and many times we would hear the question, "How do you know which switch to use?" They perceived that we were at the sharp end of information overload and were worried that we would not be able to cope if we needed to use all of the information coming in at the same time.

I used to try and reassure them with phrases like "We only ever seem to use one bit at a time" and "When you sit in here for 5 or 10 years it does become familiar to you". Eventually I crystallised all of the above into the maxim, "Learning to fly, is all about learning **when** to look **where!**"

...beautiful snow capped peaks *far below*

This was driven home to me a few years ago when I managed to blag myself a flight in one of the new VLJs – a Phenom 100. With a range of only 1000 nautical miles and a limited payload capability, we could be forgiven for thinking that this business jet is more of a toy than a workhorse. I have to say that I was pleasantly surprised by the experience and can confirm that the aeroplane is a delight to fly.

My only problem (well I have lots of problems, but the one I am thinking of...), was the instrument displays in the Phenom. To a chap who is more used to seeing an old fashioned EFIS and EICAS setup designed in the 1970s, the cockpit in the Embraer machine is like something out of Star Wars. Experienced jet pilot I may be, but Luke Skywalker I ain't, so I spent lots of time asking questions trying to discover the secret of when to look where...

Embraer Phenom 100 – a delight to fly

Fortunately the old faithfuls did not desert me and Attitude, Power and Airspeed kept me on the right track even though the huge multicolour TV screens appeared to have more information than 3 pilots could cope with at the same time. What kept running through my mind was that this aeroplane is supposedly certified to be flown single crew by a competent PPL holder.

On the face of it I would say it is a 'big ask' and prior to flying it, I was very sceptical. Now I feel that it is justified and without doubt some of the very experienced PPLs whom I know, would have no issues with learning to operate these VLJs safely. The aircraft is very capable from the performance aspect and climbing out of Geneva we were soon cruising at 36,000 feet and tanking along at 380kts or so – wonderful.

The view out of the cockpit window is dramatic crossing the Alps, but I did feel that I was very close to the glass at the side of me, my gaze naturally was drawn to the beautiful snow capped peaks *far below* and my breathing rate increased.

I straightened up and looked dead ahead and exhaled deeply... *'BREATHE!'* – phew! I said to myself, *Whoa! Steady mate, don't look down!* You see mountaineering and flying have lots in common.

--0--

19 - DECISIONS, DECISIONS...

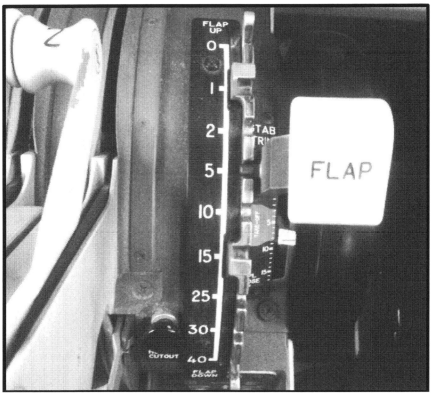

...I repeated back and moved the lever to the Flaps 5 position

For once the controllers had been kind to us. They had given us a very gentlemanly arrival to the ILS Localiser for Runway 25 at Barcelona and now we had around 18 or 19 nautical miles to run to landing... luxury! I say "We", because of course there were two of us in the cockpit of the B737 and we had enjoyed a very leisurely flight down from London. The weather was gorgeous, one of those lovely blue sky, sultry southern Spanish days with a light sea breeze and to top it off I was doing a final Command Check for a very competent pilot who was sat in the Left-Hand Seat.

Not only that, but this pilot was an old acquaintance and a good friend – it would be a real pleasure to "sign-him-off" as was we say in the trade. Nigel's Command Upgrade course had gone very well, he was always ahead of the game; well prepared and I had no doubt that today's flight would be a simple formality. It was to be his last flight with a Training Captain in the right-hand seat before flying with "real" First Officers. I should not have been so confident.

Now we were established on the localiser beam with the autopilot engaged; visual with the airport 16 miles ahead at 4000 feet and the controller had cleared us to descend with the glideslope. We still had another few miles to run, so my colleague called "Flaps 5", which I repeated back and moved the flap lever to the Flaps 5 position. Nigel reduced the speed to Flaps 5 speed on the autopilot mode control panel and then in a very relaxed manner stated, "I'll fly it manually as it's such a nice day..." After which he disengaged the autopilot and autothrottle modes. I noted that he was making very smooth corrections with both the control column and thrust levers. I thought to myself, *'yes he's really got it, excellent'* and admired the fact that he anticipated the glideslope so well such that the cabin angle changed so very gently – *'back there they will hardly have felt a thing'* I mused. There were at least two more Flap selections and the landing gear to extend before landing... We had so much time, it was great.

It was very satisfying to be working alongside a professional aviator, who was also a good mate too. I would almost be sorry not to play Nigel's FO in the future... "Cabin Secure for Landing" I called as the intercom had come through from behind the flightdeck door, to which he responded "Check". I noted we were now down towards 7 miles from the runway, nearly 2000 feet above the sea/airport and we were handed over to the Tower Controller. We were exactly on the centreline and glidepath – this was going like a dream for him.

"Surface wind two three zero at ten knots, Cleared to Land

runway two five" came the call on the radio, to which I responded correctly. I looked across at Nigel and could see from his face that he was enjoying this. Even though he still only had three gold stripes on his shoulders, you could tell he was thinking, *'I can eat this job...'* But there was something missing... All of a sudden, I felt very afraid, seriously I got such a tingle down my spine that it was like a small electric shock...!

My sixth sense had kicked in and I KNEW it was not right. Everything SEEMED so perfect, SO easy, this was his last flight of the series, and surely he couldn't cock-it-up here? The day was beautiful, the approach was smooth and established, (we had been nicely established from SO FAR OUT...) this was Barcelona, one of the easiest airports to operate into for heavens' sake.

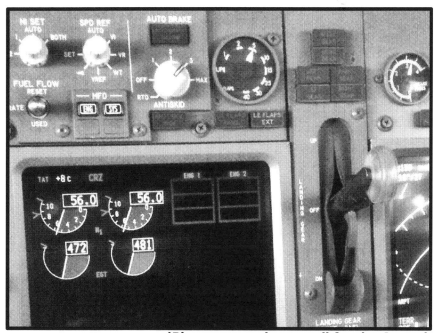

'Please remember to call for the Gear...'

'ARGGHH! He's forgotten the GEAR...!' OH NO! Big problem... my inner senses now screamed at me SO LOUDLY! I could NOT ignore them. But how in God's name do I tell him and when? *How on earth?*

I looked across the cockpit again, the sharp crease down the white shirt, left-hand on the control yoke, right-hand laconically on the thrust levers, a picture of serenity, sunglasses, ID card and three gold bars on his shoulders - proper Captains have four of course. Only three... and at this rate it may be three for quite a while. *'Please remember to call for the Gear Nige'... PLEASE FOR HEAVENS' SAKE!'* I thought to myself, *'but I can't tell you YET mate, I cannot TELL you...'* If I tell him NOW, then the learning experience from this error will be diluted and he might do it again.

That is unthinkable; I must wait and of course *I* must not forget... because if we get to 500 feet on the radio altimeter, then the Ground Proximity Warning System will give us "TOO LOW GEAR!" and then we will be forced into a Go-around, no question. Damn, what's it going to be...? I sit there terrified as I see fifteen hundred feet coming up on the altimeters. Only five miles left to run and we are doing nearly three miles per minute... *seriously* there is not long to go...

*

You see training professional pilots to fly commercial aeroplanes can be quite tricky really. The foregoing is just one example of a situation when the LTC (Line Training Captain) has to decide how far to let a situation develop, before intervening to prevent a serious incident occurring or worse. Not uncommonly it can be during the approach and landing phase of flight, sometimes it can be during takeoff/departure as these are the critical parts of the operation. Quite frequently the issue is one of good old fashioned Situational Awareness, or lack of it, on behalf of the trainee.

Lack of SA was the case on the approach into Barcelona when the Captain under Training had forgotten to call for the landing gear and pre-landing checklist. Remember that airlines do not promote duffers to command their airliners for them, so if a pilot is in the position of actually Line Flying in the LHS, then he or she must be pretty close to getting signed off as "Commander". Already they will have been through an extensive assessment, training and checking process to determine their suitability for the role. Even then, it is down to the LTC to decide how far things can go when errors and mistakes are made. It is all very well for the LTC to "trap the errors" as soon as they appear, but that has to be balanced against the training value for the student (Pilot U/T).

Gaining knowledge from the errors of others is a privilege of course, but to learn from your own mistakes is the most vivid learning experience that we can have. Of course LTCs don't always make the right decision early enough themselves, but it should be borne in mind that it is not an easy mission. The task of being the legal Commander and therefore 'signing for the jet', combined with playing an often subservient or passive role is a huge responsibility. There is no getting away from it though, when you are training 'new Captains', there is only so much Simulator time you can use – after that it is has to be done in-vivo; you have to get real.

Whereas in the Sim you have the choice to freeze the motion, in Line flying, that is not an option. Everything happens in real time with a real aircraft and live flights. Sometimes there is not even enough time for the LTC to explain what is happening to the student so they may correct their error or the flightpath; they just have to take control of the aircraft themselves.

Like the incident which occurred in a previous company to a colleague of mine. The RHS pilot, a mature First Officer still under line training failed/forgot to engage the autopilot on a night departure from Hamilton, Toronto and took his hands and feet off the controls. The LTC in the LHS didn't notice as he was distracted with a radio frequency change as the B767's nose continued to pitch up and up until the stickshaker alerted them both to the imminent stall... "I HAVE CONTROL!" he shouted as he grabbed the control column on his side and pushed forward to lower the nose while pushing the engines to full power...

Perhaps if the airline had heeded the warnings from previous LTCs about this particular trainee, then this event might not have happened. The student had demonstrated his lack of spare mental capacity on many line training flights prior to this. Fortunately, the stall was prevented and the LTC retained control as Pilot Flying (PF) for the rest of the flight back to the UK. The airline training department carried out a review of the trainee's progress and suspended his training subsequently. He left flying for aeroplanes a living and returned to his previous profession, which was a wise move.

*

The Barcelona Tower controller had cleared us for landing, we were passing 4 miles and still no gear... Arrrggghhhh! Inside my guts were in knots as I sat there playing the passive FO – *just as somebody might do next week if Nigel passed his Command Course. Come-on fella, notice it...* The Radalt was now coming down towards 1000 feet as I looked across to him and said "It's ALL going RATHER WELL isn't it...?" A completely non-standard thing to say and therefore as big a hint as I can give him, to which he replied airily, "Oh yes, I think so TOO!" with a big cheerful grin. DOH! So I nonchalantly asked, "Are you PLANNING to land with the wheels up then....?"

Immediately his face changed, total shock and deadly serious, eyes wide open as he looked from me to the landing gear lever and back again, "FUCK!... GEAR DOWN! GEAR DOWN! FLAPS FIFTEEN! LANDING CHECKLIST DOWN TO FLAPS! FUCK! FUCK! FUCK!" He commanded urgently. Naturally I obliged swiftly and we rapidly completed the final landing checklist with the flaps running to 30 degrees (the landing flap position) just before the GPWS alert was about to go off...

"Three Greens" – a reassuring sight on short Finals!

Of course he was appalled that he could have made such a huge mistake at this stage of his training. The training debrief took a long time as we analysed what went wrong and when. However the main thing in my mind was that he had come so close to committing the cardinal sin of a professional aviator (trying to land with the wheels up) that I was confident he would NEVER do it again. The biggest learning point which both of us took away from this flight was that it is a danger flying with our friends; especially people whom you trust to do the job right. It is a real 'threat' (to operational integrity) which should be considered as we report for duty.

--0--

20 - WHY THE LONG FACE?

The outside air temperature was nearly 40°C as we shutdown the engines on the Boeing 767 at Ahmedabad in India. We had just arrived direct from Heathrow on behalf of the national carrier Air India and it was time to carry out a crew change. As we waited on the concrete by the side of the airliner in the stifling heat, the turnround crew was hard at work unloading baggage and cargo, refilling fresh water and draining the lavatory waste tanks. What we did not know was that we were about witness to one poor man's worst nightmare coming true.

One of the Honey Truck* workers was standing directly underneath the large bore drain hose for the lavatory waste tank when all of a sudden it split in two completely. There was no warning, he had no time to escape and most of a tank of filthy brown sewage emptied itself all over him – there was nobody close enough to shut the "dump valve". It even filled the pockets of his overalls and his oversize wellington boots. Appalling though the sight was; it was nothing compared to the smell... In that heat and with a faint breeze we were all subjected to the most horrible stench imaginable. Seriously, even years later, if I close my eyes and visualise the scene; I swear I can still smell it.

Time literally stood still as everybody, horrified, held their breath – (there was a good reason for that). The poor man was standing there in a spreading puddle of brown, not knowing what to do. His colleague on the Honey Truck* was quick thinking however and jumped onto the top of the wagon, where he grabbed the huge fresh water hosepipe. The delivery was almost too much to withstand, but the man under the fuselage of the aircraft was stronger than he looked as the powerful jet of water sluiced all over him. Right there and then under the gaze of everyone on the ramp, he took off his overalls and boots, down to his underwear and had the shower of his life. Unbelievably he started to laugh and as he did so, everybody else joined in. All of his co-workers, the fuel bowser driver, the ramp agents, dispatchers, baggage loaders and even our crew, we all laughed with him. Fortunately our crew bus arrived and we were not slow getting aboard for the short journey to the terminal, the smell on the ramp was enough to choke a goat!

For me, this incident was a perfect example of the indomitable human spirit which exists in large measure throughout the Indian subcontinent.

*

They say that bad news travels fast and this is certainly true in aviation. As evidence, you only have to look at the plethora of aviation related internet sites, including those spreading "the news" or gossip. Unfortunately there has been a spate of really depressing stories recently which have involved major loss of life. Without going into detail, Malaysian 370 and 17, Air Asia, Germanwings and Shoreham all have tragedy in common, which if viewed alone would lead an observer to think that aviation is in decline and becoming more dangerous.

This is far from the truth. In reality we have much to be grateful for and must continue to view it all in the round. To focus on hull losses and human failings without consideration of the positive side of the aviation sector would be wrong. It would be doing a disservice to the millions of hard working professionals who deliver global excellence in their jobs every day of the year. Like the poor man in India who got the shock of his life when the lavatory waste pipe burst, he still found a way to see the positive side and we should follow his example.

I am pleased to observe and report that having been involved in commercial aviation for three decades, it is evident to me that there are key areas of the industry which have never been so healthy. Recently I have had the pleasure to be closely involved with crew training for two of the major low-cost airlines in Europe. What has impressed me the most about the training by these companies is the diligence and thoroughness of the training standards. The quality is simply world-class and I have every reason to believe it has had a beneficial effect upon the standards of training delivered by some legacy carriers.

Not only this, but the same operators have not been slow to take advantage of recent breakthroughs in technology. Just one example is that of EFB (Electronic Flight Bag). This particular development has contributed enormously to the safety and efficiency of airline operations and those companies which have adopted it have also integrated it with their training programmes. In fact it has happened so quickly in the past couple of years that in some parts of the world the regulators (national Civil Aviation Authorities) have been running behind the airlines trying to catch up.

Commercially too, the industry has been enjoying unrivalled success in recent years. Regardless of the falling oil price which has provided an unexpected bonus for some, commercial aviation is growing globally in excess of five percent annually. Traffic volumes continue to swell as the market expands not least in China and the Far East. The reassuring part about all of this for anyone in Europe considering a career in aviation is that countries like China are offering huge incentives to draw experienced personnel from the west.

The rapidly expanding companies there are acutely conscious of the fact that they do not have enough home-grown talent to support the growth of airline operations within the world's largest economy. Additionally, foreign companies encouraged by their governments have been sending unprecedented numbers of young people to the west for professional aviation training. In EASA-land this is all to the good of course as there is now a new structure in place which regulates the quality of training delivery by ATOs (Approved Training Organisations). Quite simply, when it comes down to the delivery of quality training, nobody does it better than Europe.

Looking more widely at the effect of aviation upon the world we should remember that no other invention in history has had a more positive effect upon communications, transportation and prosperity for mankind. From the rapid deployment of vital aid to disaster areas in remote regions, to empowering millions of people to travel freely, movement by air is the key. When it comes to ensuring peaceful skies and no-fly zones, military air power provides the answer. Even the exploration of our solar system could not have begun to take place without the development of powered flight by manned vehicles which were able to defy Earth's gravity.

*

There has never been another transportation system which is so safety conscious. Unlike older modes of transport, because aviation came so late, the established governments of the world ensured that regulations could be applied to the phenomenon which protected both workers and customers alike. There is a safety led culture within every company, operator and airline engaged in the transportation of the travelling public.

We are prepared to learn by our mistakes without blame and those of others to make future operations safer. Information gained from accident investigations and analysis of incidents is actively used to improve the quality of the training for personnel. This combined with modern CRM (Crew Resource Management) – uniquely developed within our industry – is what makes aviation special.

This pursuit of excellence does not stop or even begin with the airlines of course. The UK CAA has recently launched a programme to improve the safety of light aircraft operations with their PROUD initiative - the word being an acronym for Pilot Recognition for Operational Up-skilling and Development. The message here is "Be Proud and keep learning". It is aimed at improving the knowledge and skills of GA pilots. Also it will be beneficial at reducing the high dropout rates of newly qualified pilots. We should consider that emphasis and focus on the grass roots of our profession is good for us all.

In summary, although there have an unfortunate spate of tragic accidents recently, we have much to be grateful for. Even though sometimes it is hard to see the positive aspects, perhaps we should ask ourselves the same question as the barman to the horse in the old joke?

A horse walks into a bar and the barman asks; *"Why the long face?"*

*

*Honey Truck is the industry slang name given to the toilet servicing vehicle which goes from aircraft to aircraft "like a Bee collecting honey" – although it is not honey of course...

--0--

'Ebony' – with a not-so-long face.

21 - FLYING THE SOUTH ATLANTIC

The South Atlantic Ocean is one of the largest areas of uninhabited space on the planet. Whereas the North Atlantic has an organised track system for commercial traffic to fly across, arranged in parallel lines 60nm apart, the Southern half of the ocean has so little crossing traffic that there is no need for the same provision. Most of the flying is done in straight lines across the chart with points of Latitude and Longitude used to plot the route. Some of these positions are 350 nm apart and perhaps more. All of the radio transmissions are on the long range HF system which is notoriously difficult to use and some of the radio stations seem to have little input into our flights. We are very much left to our own devices out there, which is why our procedures are so stringently adhered to.

In June/July 2009 I was engaged in flying in this remote region of the world on the B767-300ER. Doing this gives you a different perspective on life in many ways. Naturally the first thing that you notice is the vast distance between airports and the complete remoteness of some of the destinations. Of course it is winter in the southern hemisphere at this time, so the weather combined to make life more than a little challenging at times.

Add to this the fact that communication is difficult at every level and you get some idea of the problems faced by the crews down here. When discussing airline flying in this region, thoughts automatically turn to the loss of Air France 447 which was en-route from Rio to Paris. It was such a terrible tragedy of course, but even more of a shock to those of us working in the industry that an airliner might break up in mid flight because of weather as seemed possible initially.

It certainly concentrated the minds of me and my First Officer (F/O) on one of our flights in the middle of the night when we had a very large band of huge embedded storms which lay across our intended route. The tops of these large Cumulonimbus (CB) clouds were around 45,000 feet and due to the aircraft's gross weight our optimum cruising altitude was FL350 (around 35,000 feet) so we couldn't climb over them. At one stage we were something like 80nm off our track and working hard with the weather radar to find an easy route through the storms in moderate turbulence.

Squall Line on the ITCZ

The seatbelt signs remained on for a very long time and no doubt there were some of our passengers who were having trouble sleeping. Meanwhile there was no problem for us in staying awake, as we carefully snaked our way round the heavier (Red) returns on the radar screen. As I was Pilot Flying (PF) I asked my colleague to put the engine ignition systems to "Continuous" setting and I set the autopilot speed to M0.78 which was our recommended speed for turbulent air penetration. Our normal cruise speed in the B767 is M0.80 or thereabouts, decided by the

Flight Management Computer (FMC) when all the winds, weights and temperatures are fed in to it. The FMC then computes the most economical cruising speed (ECON CRZ).

Even though the autopilot is engaged in these conditions, I am always in the habit of following through on the flying controls and therefore we were both sat forward in the flightdeck with full harness applied. Additionally the cockpit and instrument lighting was dimmed to enable us to observe areas of the sky outside for lightning activity. I was anticipating that we would get St Elmo's fire on the windscreens, but this didn't happen. I have seen it many times before and the visual effects are most dramatic, although it is a harmless by-product of atmospheric conditions in some weather systems that we fly through.

It appears as spidery electric blue miniature patterns of lightning on the inside of the flightdeck windows and according to my colleagues, if you point your finger at the glass and move towards the screen, a small flash of electricity will jump the gap on to your finger! Quite honestly I have found it far too spooky to try this myself and usually I am pretty busy concentrating on flying the aeroplane.

Talking of which, I recall that as we approached the band of CBs across our path, we warned the cabin crew to expect turbulence on the intercom, but even we were surprised at how bumpy the ride was. We monitored the outside air temperature closely, because at these latitudes (close to the equator) even at cruising altitude it can warm up to higher than -40 degrees Celsius. At temperatures below -40, all the cloud particles are assumed to be ice crystals and therefore not a danger to us, but once it gets higher than -40, we require to use the engine Anti-Ice systems which direct hot air to flow from the engine 'bleeds' to the front intake cowling to keep it free of ice.

In common with other aircraft, ice and engines do not mix well! A regular check of the windscreen wiper arm just outside the window is also carried out as this is our first indicator of airframe icing. The detrimental effects of airframe icing on aircraft are well proven and these checks are very important to us – at night we use a torch to shine out from the flightdeck to see the wiper. Fortunately on this trip, we managed to avoid getting ice on the wipers. On the flight before however we were forced to fly through a heavy snow shower during the initial approach phase to reach our destination airfield and noted that we picked up a lot of ice on the wipers very quickly.

When it comes to airframe icing, the Boeing is well equipped to deal with such unwelcome accruals. Along the leading edges of the wings there are fitted large air ducts through which can be ducted very hot air from the engine bleeds which will melt the ice which is formed here. On other airliners which I have flown it is actually possible to see something of the leading edges of the wings from the cockpit and there is nothing better than watching a whole load of ice being shed in chunks as the Wing Anti-Ice (WA-I) system is switched on.

It is much preferred to leave the use of the WA-I until there is definitely plenty of ice on the leading edges. If you hit the switch too early, the ice just melts and the water then runs back on to the wing surface to *refreeze* at a point on the aerofoil section behind that which is capable of being de-iced... The potential consequences of this are obvious.

Even outside the Cbs, we found ourselves bouncing around in the tops of the large Cumulus clouds and this we could tell by checking every once in a while with the landing lights. As 500mph fog coming at you can be a distraction, these were only used momentarily to check whether we were in cloud or out of it.

From time to time we began to see more and more of the star constellations above us and this gave us much cause to celebrate.

The weather radar was showing fewer clusters of red on it and we were finally able to regain our track having added possibly as much as 200 nm to our route. In the overall scheme of things however this is small beer, as on this occasion our flightplan was over 3000 nm long!

We monitor the emergency frequency 121.5 on one of our VHF radios and also the information (chat) frequency 123.45 on another while flying at cruise altitude. On top of this we regularly try to maintain radio contact with the ATSU agencies which allegedly cover large sections of the South Atlantic. However the only station which is really of any use to us is aptly named "Atlantico" which I think is based at Recife on the Brazilian coast. To give an idea of how big the sky is down here, you only have to consider that in an eight hour flight; we maybe only ever hear one other aircraft on the radio and never see any contacts on our TCAS system. Even though we are on a 'random track', our standard operating procedures recommend that we fly an offset of 1 or 2 nm to the right of track as one more precaution against meeting somebody coming the other way at the same cruise flight level.

B767-300ER on the ramp at Ascension Island

After passing through the weather and with dawn slowly breaking in the East we passed close to the area where flight AF447 went down. We were very quiet for quite some time in the flightdeck after we had noted our location and ruminated on their fate. The size of the task of looking for the wreckage also came to mind as we looked down at the Atlantic and realised that the vital flight data recorders might never be found. If the sea is 12,000 feet deep here as they say and the area to be searched is as large as reported, then the search team is going to have to be spectacularly fortunate to recover the FDRs. A couple of years later the Flight Data Recorders WERE found in an amazing operation – see 'Never to be Found' in The Flightdeck Survival Manual.

On short finals to Wideawake Airfield - RAF Ascension Island

A couple of hours later and we were on final approach to land at Ascension Island after a long and tiring night. This was to be a crew change stop and refuelling before another equally long journey for our passengers. In the meantime my crew and I would be able to take life easy for a couple of days of well earned rest. After landing, the F/O and myself happened to bump into the ATC tower controller who had popped down to the airport operations room while the aircraft was being turned round. The tower controller was a lovely old American guy called Bill and we loved to tease him on the radio sometimes, I think he liked our "British sense of humour".

It was good to see him and he asked about the brightness of the PAPIs* which we had asked to be increased to full on our final approach, "Oh, hey! The brightness was fine Bill", we said, but could you have the *ANGLE* adjusted for us please?" He paused for a moment and then said.

"Whatd'ya mean guys? Ain't they set right for ya? They should be at 3 degrees right?" to which we replied with, "No Bill, they are supposed to show us 2 reds and 2 whites, but they kept changing while we were flying the approach... you need to get that sorted out!" He chuckled as the penny dropped that he was having his leg pulled again and responded.

"NO BOYS! THAT'S YOUR JOB! You gotta keep 'em two reds and two whites yourself!" We feigned mock amazement and shook our heads as if we had learned a valuable lesson, *"Gosh! Is THAT how they work?! Well now that explains EVERYTHING!"*

*

*(PAPIs - Precision Approach Path Indicators at the side of the runway, normally sited at the 1000 foot point where the airliner should touchdown. On an ideal 3 degree slope approach they should show 2 reds and 2 whites, going low on the slope brings more reds and going high on approach makes more whites).

--0--

22 - ABNORMAL OPERATIONS

An early clue to the security status of our flight was when we were given an instruction by the American Military controller, "XXX you are cleared *direct to destination airport"*. This was received as we crossed the National FIR boundary at cruise altitude. No mention of airways, navigational beacons or waypoints; just that, "...cleared direct to destination airport". Certainly nobody listening to *that* transmission was going to be able to work out where we were headed...

Sometime later, the flightdeck of the VIP Boeing 757 was very quiet as we descended through 30,000 feet in the darkness. I carefully crosschecked our electronic map display (HSI) position again with raw data from a VOR beacon. Now was definitely NOT the time for an unexpected 'map-shift' to occur – as aircraft Commander, pilot flying and sat in the left-hand seat, the safety of the flight was my ultimate responsibility. When people say "it didn't happen on My Watch..." well this *WAS* my "My Watch" and for sure I knew it.

Not only were we descending into a remote airport in a Middle Eastern country recovering from a very recent civil war, but we had the country's President onboard. It should not matter who is in the cabin of course, as pilots we do our job with the same level of professionalism at all times, but it is a very human thing to feel the pressure of carrying VIPs... in this case a VVIP. Heads of State are always considered VVIP. The silence was broken by the co-pilot as he turned to me in the dim night-light of the cockpit.

"He's actually not very popular you know..." and then immediately from the jumpseat behind us, "...Yes. There have been a few assassination attempts this past year..." The speaker behind was a former senior airline captain and a local national, he had been born and raised here. Certainly his opinion would carry a lot of weight on many subjects and I listened carefully as he explained in brief our VVIP's lack of support among the population.

I did occur to me that it was a bit late in the day to be having this sort of discussion on this particular VIP flight, but their main point to me was made when they both said, "So, ARE you going to put the lights on then...?" In common with many airlines' SOPs we always put the landing lights on in the descent passing 10,000 feet, plus the tail-fin logo lights for better visibility by other aircraft.

It was a clear night with open desert and some mountainous terrain beneath us. With the 757 lit up like a Christmas tree, we would be visible for a hundred miles. Their last comment sealed it for me, "and we would be a big target..." Target for what; was not in doubt of course. A 50 calibre machine gun, shoulder launched SAM; even a well aimed AK47 at low altitude could cause a lot of damage. The altimeters were now showing 15,000 feet with a high rate of descent and I had to make a decision...

... in the dim night-light of the cockpit.

In contrast with the opinion of many people I do not think that

154

flying airliners is boring. As I am quoted as saying before, "the perfect flight does not exist". Regardless of how well the crew are trained and how slavishly they follow Standard Operating Procedures, something; no matter how small, will go wrong on every flight, guaranteed. If enough 'things' go wrong in the wrong sequence without intervention, a tragic accident may occur. Without being too saintly about it, I think this is what keeps airline pilots focused and engaged in the profession for years at a time... we are all striving for perfection.

It cannot be denied that repetitive routes on the line with similar destinations, weather, navaids and briefings can get a bit 'samey' when carried out day after day. No longer is there quite the challenge of adapting and reacting to different circumstances at potentially difficult airports which have not previously been visited. Now the major threat becomes one of trying to maintain high levels of vigilance and attention to detail when all the details are so familiar. This is probably one of the reasons why older, more senior pilots tend to really enjoy their work when the operation becomes rather 'less normal'. Into the category of abnormal operations would fall things like, empty Ferry Flights, Test Flights, Base Training Flights, Demonstration Flights, Air Display Flights and adhoc VIP Flights. All these types of aerial movements have potential additional risks involved and therefore for an experienced pilot can be quite alluring. Something out of the ordinary always focuses the mind.

Not only are pilots of VIP flights required to fly the aircraft, but they are often drawn into the operational planning of the mission. The company will usually consult them, making use of their experience and knowledge when considering how best to fulfill the task. Pilots who have been flying commercially for decades tend to accumulate more knowledge through experience than any other operational personnel. It comes down to the things you've seen and the places you've been. No matter how studious, diligent or experienced a Dispatcher, he or she can only ever have a limited perspective. Remember that old maxim? *"The Pilots are always first on the scene of the accident...",* which tells you all you need to know about which profession faces the most operational risk when things go wrong.

The crew of a VIP aircraft will often find themselves multi-tasking and performing jobs which are alien to normal airline flying personnel. Planning and ordering special catering for the passengers, dealing with special baggage requirements or planning to operate to completely remote airfields with limited Navigational aids for example. Or possibly having to make arrangements to accommodate a VIP coffin onboard, not just in the aircraft hold, but actually in the cabin with the mourners. Not only that, but it must be absolutely secure for takeoff and landing... It can be a fascinating occupation to be sure. On one occasion we were tasked to fly 20 VIPs plus another 30 valuable hunting birds - Falcons. The Falcons were tethered in the rear cabin, but there was really no proper space for them apart from sitting on the tops of the cream leather seats. You can only imagine the mess after the customers disembarked having been onboard for over six hours. The cabin crew were protesting loudly that their job description did not include cleaning bird crap off leather upholstery!

*

Meanwhile as we approached 10,000 feet in our descent I had made a decision. "All lights OFF" I ordered and we switched off even the Navlights. Also in the cabin they followed my instructions to "darken ship" and now we were confident that we could not be seen visually by anybody on the ground. Due to lack of approach radar, we had to carry out the whole instrument procedure from flying over the top of the airfield, tracking outbound on the VOR radial to turn inbound and establish on the ILS for final approach.

With some VERY high terrain nearby it was a challenging process to ensure we stayed above the minimum safe altitudes, yet descended towards the ground in the right place. I was pleased to see that we were all three of us working well as a team in the cockpit and it was clear that our extensive approach briefing had worked well to provide us with heightened Situational Awareness.

"XXX cleared to land runway __" came the instruction from the tower as we were about 6 miles out on final approach, still with no lights. The runway lighting was good however and the PAPIs were doing their job well holding us at two red and two whites, confirming that we were on glide path. At around one thousand feet I disconnect the autopilot and we completed the landing checklist, "...gear down, flaps thirty, cleared to Land". As we crossed the perimeter of the airfield at around 150 feet on the Radalt I could see in my peripheral vision the co-pilot's hand up on the overhead panel ready with the landing light switches, "Lights all on NOW please..." I said in my most measured tone of voice and there was a series of audible rapid clicks as the switches went home. Outside where I was looking the runway was flooded with light as the 757's landing, taxy and nosegear lights lit up the night.

After landing as we vacated the runway, we reduced the lighting again to minimum, just one nosegear taxy light to see where we were going all the way to the apron. Within 10 minutes after the doors were opened, our valuable guest and his entourage had disembarked, the baggage had been offloaded and we were getting ready to depart for our empty ferry flight back to Europe. Later still while waiting in the darkness at the holding point of the runway ready for departure, we were amused to see three other aircraft come onto finals and land with no lights. They had military callsigns and American accent voices on the R/T, but that was all we knew. In our darkened flightdeck, we looked at each other and said almost simultaneously, "We made the right decision then!"

--O--

23 - PRESS-ON-ITIS?

Cessna 172 – always better to be wishing you were up there...

As a professional in the industry, I know how important it is not to jump to conclusions when an aviation accident is reported. That being said however, from the early TV coverage of the helicopter accident in central London early 2013, it seemed that bad weather conditions, which included poor visibility combined with a high obstacle were likely causal factors. No doubt partly due to the location, the focus of media interest was intense - much was written and said about the pilot, his mission, the weather, the unplanned diversion to Battersea Heliport etc. The question in my mind then and now is; *"Could this one have been avoided?"*

*

Helen Krasner is a columnist in the aviation publication Flight Training News and only a month before the accident in central London, she wrote about a similar situation. At that time she was attempting to fly from Blackpool to Welshpool (VFR) through the

Low-Level Corridor which separates the Liverpool and Manchester air traffic control zones. When the weather closed the route, she proved that it is always better to be "down here wishing you were up there", as she diverted with her colleague back to the airport of departure for an unscheduled nightstop. No doubt she learned a valuable lesson at that time, which she articulately conveyed to the reader.

By coincidence, I had a similar event in almost the same location while attempting to ferry a Cessna 172 from Barton GA airfield in Manchester down to Tilstock airfield in Shropshire. I think the year was around 1990 and at that time I was employed as a co-pilot on the B757 for a charter airline based at Manchester international airport.

As a part-time instructor with a flying club at the weekend and ferrying a type which I knew well over familiar countryside, it is true to say I was in my 'comfort-zone'. Not only that, but I had been looking forward to the ferry flight for a week or more after being asked to do it by the owner of the club. Once you are employed as an airline pilot, it is not often you get the chance to fly solo in your jeans, so it is quite a buzz really.

The day came and the weather was disappointing to say the least, with rain, extensive layered low cloud and reduced visibility beneath it. The forecast indicated that it would be brighter in the afternoon and better the further south towards my destination. I checked the aircraft over carefully on the ground at Barton and went to chat to the guys in the tower. They did not seem very positive about much flying at the airfield, but I do recall saying to them, "Well the cloudbase must be around a thousand feet or so and at the speed of a Cessna you don't need to see very far ahead..." I was thinking of the VFR definition 'COCISS' (Clear of Cloud in Sight of the Surface) and its applicability to the ferry flight.

Being conscious that the owner wanted the aeroplane back to work as soon as possible (there were customers booked at Tilstock for the afternoon) I felt obliged to give it my best shot, *after all*, I thought, *the weather is better the further south I get...*

By now, the visibility had increased such that you could see beyond the edge of the airfield; *yes there was definitely an improvement in the local conditions.* I booked out VFR with ATC and ran through my preflight preparations which included strapping the map to my kneeboard and checking the route carefully to orientate my departure once I was airborne. I would be heading straight for the low-level corridor and must be careful not to infringe Manchester TMA above and/or the Control Zone on either side. Remember this was in the days before GPS became widely available.

The aircraft had just been returned to service after maintenance, so everything was working as it should have been. Even the minor snags had been fixed and I murmured to myself "You boys have done a good job", as I taxied out to the threshold of the grass runway 27 for departure. There were a few people around the hangars as I trundled past and no doubt some of them were wondering "Where's he off to?", but of course they didn't know that *"...the further south you get... the better the weather..."*

It felt good to be flying on my own again and I knew it was not far through the low-level corridor to open airspace to the south. In the corridor, the maximum altitude is only 1250 feet so the vertical gap is quite narrow, but looking at the weather I might not get above 800...

The engine felt strong as we launched over the grass and with only me onboard, the ground run was very short. As soon as I was airborne, I realised that there was no visual horizon and the visibility was even worse than I expected. In anticipation of this I elected leave the first stage of flaps extended and adopted the bad weather slow flying technique which I learned at instructor school – this would give me more thinking time. I was still working with Barton airfield on the radio and they were keen to know what the conditions were like – I informed them that it certainly wasn't good enough for teaching circuits as the lack of horizon was critical.

It was while I was trying to judge how far I could actually see, "is that two kilometres?" that I first ran into cloud, so I dropped the altitude a little lower, now we were at 900 feet, just at the base of it. Suddenly, ahead of me there seemed to be sharp reduction in vis and I knew that I couldn't fly through that – it was like an impenetrable white curtain and even at my slow cruising speed, I did not have long to think about it. I started a turn to the left at 30 degrees angle of bank, but because of the lack of external horizon references, I was more than partly concentrating on the attitude indicator. While I sat there in the turn at a steady angle of bank at slow speed, I was checking the map to ensure I knew the location. One orbit followed another as I realised there was no way through the corridor, *"Harrumph! I will have to go back!"* I felt cheated.

It was while carrying out my low-level orbits and weighing up the options that Barton tower received a call from Manchester International asking why the recently departed light aircraft was going round in tight little circles on their radar screen. I rolled out of the turn onto the reciprocal heading and made my way the few miles back to the airfield while talking to them on the radio again. *"How embarrassing?!"* I thought to myself as I came into land after only 15 minutes airborne, but mostly I have to say I was really relieved.

Taxiing over the grass towards the parking area outside the hangars I knew then I had just had a lucky escape. Because there was what had seemed to be a wall of cloud in the corridor, there was no way through, therefore the decision to turn back was made for me. Where I really made the mistake was actually getting airborne in the first place! *"Always better to be down here..."* I muttered as I shut everything down and climbed out, *Hmmm, time for a cup of tea.* I put a brave face on it and strolled to the nice warm clubhouse. Everything happens for a reason...

*

There is a phenomenon which we used to talk about in the military which was commonly referred to as "Press-on-itis". The clue is in the name. In fact these days with modern CRM, it has been identified as a significant causal factor in many accidents where the crew becomes goal-oriented to the point of disregarding some of the basic elements which keep us safe. There is no doubt in my own mind that I had been suffering Press-on-itis to try and get my ferry flight done.

Perhaps the fact that I had graduated to flying all weather airliners for a living had made me drop my guard - but I should have remembered it is horses for courses. What can be achieved with triple ILS and full Autoland systems at the airport just up the road, is a world away from flying from a grass strip, VFR with no autopilot trying to keep the shiny side up and read a map at the same time.

Whilst reading one of the more informed newspaper reports about the 2013 London helicopter accident at the time, it mentioned that the pilot was 'aware of the poor weather conditions prior to getting airborne', but stated that he decided to '...*press-on regardless...*'. There it was in black and white. Possibly the major cause of the accident, but we would have to wait and see what the AAIB report stated to be sure.

Everything happens for a reason? Well, yes I sincerely believe in this concept, but as I sat down to my pot of tea and some cake in the clubhouse that day waiting for the weather to improve, I was scratching my head as to what reason there could be for my being there...

"Hello Jim, fancy seeing you here?!" a familiar voice came to me from across the cafe as a chap in engineering overalls entered. I recognised him with a smile and replied, "Hello Dave, I could ask you the same mate. What brings you to Barton?" Dave Budden was an old pal of mine from Hawarden Flying Club and although we had lost touch, it was always a pleasure to see him. In addition to being an experienced PPL holder and keen private flyer, he was also a licensed aircraft engineer.

"Let me show you round the beautiful old aeroplane I am working on in the hangar Jim. The owner's going to start doing air displays in her soon and is looking for a commercial pilot preferably with ex-military experience to help him..." As we entered the darkness of the hangar and my eyes adjusted to the dim light, I could see a large shiny aluminium airframe with two massive radial piston engines.

There on the left side of the nose was the nose art declaring she was called *Southern Comfort.* 'Wow! She's a beauty mate! What is it...? An Anson?" to which he replied;

"No, she's not an Anson Jim, she's a Beech 18 – or rather she's a Beech C45, which was the military variant. Come and have a look in the cockpit..."

*

Note: *This chance encounter led to some of the happiest days of my flying life, as I flew the Beech C45 Southern Comfort with the owner for the next seven years.*

--0--

24 - FLYING SOUTHERN COMFORT

Southern Comfort Crew (Photo Seimon Pugh-Jones)

Our First Air Display Season 1992

This article was originally published in Flypast Magazine Airshow Special 1995. Southern Comfort, a 1941 Beech C45 ex USAF Expeditor was based at Bryngwyn Bach on the North Wales coast from the early '90s.

When I think back to the summer of 1992, when we first started displaying the Beech C45 Southern Comfort, the term 'much to learn' comes to mind. That's not to say we were inexperienced – as pilots we had a few thousand hours between us – but as far as the airshow scene was concerned we were certainly uninitiated.

As the Americans say, we were about to enter a whole new ballgame. During the first season we only had five airshows booked, but when we looked back at the end of the year and people asked us how many shows we had done, up went the cry "Six, including Caernarfon!" The reason we included sleepy old Caernarfon airfield was that it had been the chosen venue for our pre-season practice, although the weather had different ideas. In fact we flew the display three times in pouring rain under a ridiculously low cloudbase.

This was the first time that we had flown Southern Comfort in a downpour and to our great dismay, we found that the windscreens leaked... badly! Due to the time element involved, "We've GOT to practice today, our first airshow is at the end of the week!" we had to carry on regardless (there's a title for a film in there somewhere). As rainwater cascaded down the instrument panels, we switched off all the radio/navigation aids apart from one Comms radio tuned to the tower frequency, which was used to monitor any other aircraft movements.

Cockpit of the Beech C45 – Southern Comfort (on a dry day)

We need not have bothered – even the birds were walking. We recorded the practice session on video, but the sound of the engines was drowned out by rainwater pouring off the roof of the Air Traffic Control tower, mingled with the frequent roll of thunder. I vividly recall sitting in the right-hand seat, simultaneously demisting windscreens, stuffing rags round the tops of the instrument panel, while operating the wipers on command and keeping up a running commentary on height and speed, while reading out the next manoeuvre in the sequence from the disintegrating piece of sodden paper draped across my left knee. The thought passed through my mind, *how did I get talked into THIS?*

From such an inauspicious beginning, it amazed me that we achieved so much. In seven full display seasons with the Beech we enjoyed a near 100% reliability record. We made it to virtually every venue, which considering the aircraft was over 50 years old and the British climate not the kindest, was no mean feat. During the seven seasons which Anthony displayed the Beech, it was my privilege to accompany him on virtually every occasion.

We were not helped by the fact that our home base airfield was a coastal grass strip only 2,296ft (700m) long and with an elevation of 700ft (213m) above sea level. There were times when low cloud caused us one or two problems...

It always amused me when we discussed operating the Beech with anyone interested in flying (usually PPL holders) that their side of the conversation often went something like..."Oh Yes, it must be a nice day out for you really. Go flying, arrive at an airshow, watch all the other acts for free, do your own display, scoff the free food and drink, then shove off home – it must be a piece of cake!" Days like that were very rare indeed. What people forgot of course is that it is not LIKE private flying at all.

When flying for pleasure – you decide which day you want to fly –

we did not; the airshow dates are fixed and we were required to operate around them. If the weather was a little bit unkind, then the prudent private pilot could say "Ah well, perhaps another day" We had to view the weather differently – we looked at the TAF and METAR very closely and we asked ourselves, "Is it feasible?" We then considered, "If the worst forecast weather happens, have we got a safe contingency plan?" If the answer to both questions was "Yes", then and only then would we launch. In many ways our flying had a great deal in common with both commercial and military aviation. When we finally shut down back at base at the end of a difficult day, someone was often heard to say, "Another mission accomplished". Indeed as the airshow calendar on the hangar wall charted our progress through the summer we began to think in terms of "seven down, only twelve to go!"

The learning curve

Our first display was an eye-opener in many ways. We arrived at the RAF base the day before the show and as the bosses there were happy for us to practice our routine, we took advantage of this to become familiar with all the landmarks etc.

After we had landed and taxied in, the RAF groundcrew who had been very friendly and helpful asked us to fuel up that day rather than after our display when they would have less time. We took on 100 gallons of Avgas at 7lbs per gallon, put the aeroplane to bed and went to the airshow party. The following morning dawned bright and clear, with the temperature climbing to over 30°C by lunchtime – our display slot was at 2pm.

We took off some 700lbs heavier than our practice session, at the hottest part of the hottest day of the year and commenced the display routine exactly as we had done the day before... As Anthony (aircraft Captain and flying pilot) was pulling the nose of the Beech round the top of the first tight wingover (90° angle of bank), I was cheerfully reading aloud the airspeed.

As we slowed to 110mph on a wingtip above the RAF married quarters, the buffeting from the elevator gave us the first warning of an impending stall. At the same instant we looked at each other, simultaneously answering the question of our degraded performance, a small voice in the background could be heard saying, *"Gentlemen... welcome to the learning curve...!"*

The rest of the display was flown in a much more circumspect manner and as we taxied back in we knew we had learned a valuable lesson. Never again would we get caught out by that one. In future, our ideal display fuel load would be three tenths in the main wing tanks and the other four tanks empty. Well for our second display we went from the sublime to the ridiculous. From a 10,000 feet concrete runway at a large RAF base, our next display was at a charity garden party at a small grass strip.

Beech in the centre with THAT HANGAR behind

The runway itself measured 1,968 feet which would not have been so bad if the owner had not built a large hangar across the eastern end of it. Our arrival was something akin to an aircraft carrier landing. With that hangar across the upwind threshold, there was no chance of 'going round again' here. As we shut down Southern Comfort's Pratt and Whitney radials, we were acutely aware that this was the largest aeroplane ever to have visited this particular airstrip. We eyed the hangar suspiciously as we taxied out for our display. We had joked with the owner that the first thing they would know about us having an EFATO towards the hangar, would be a hurried radio transmission... "GET THOSE DOORS OPEN...!"

There was an Extra 300 aerobatic aircraft which was also supposed to be displaying here on this day, but the pilot was waiting for the cloudbase to lift. Very wise I thought as I chatted to him by the side of the grass strip. "How much height do you need for your aeros?" I asked to which he replied casually, "...oh only a few hundred feet really". Not long afterwards I heard him start his engine and watched him taxi out for the runway. As the base of the cloud seemed to be just about as bad as before, I assumed he had decided to go home, but no.

The Extra roared along the runway, got airborne very quickly and with speed building rapidly - my God those things can accelerate – he cleared the hangar roof by about three feet then pulled straight up into the clag. We lost sight of him and I thought, well he's surely gone home now then, but wrong again! He's back! Roaring out of the cloud, rolling out level he shot straight down the runway again trimming the grass – or so it seemed. "WOW! HE'S DISPLAYING!" I shouted to the crew from Southern Comfort close to where I was standing... "WHAT THE F_____!?" Fortunately my last word was drowned out by the snarl from the Extra's powerful Lycoming 540 engine as he whizzed past us all again – this time inverted...

At the end of his pass he rolled upright and immediately pulled up again – we lost sight of him for half a minute or so, then the distinctive shape of Walter Extra's design appeared again this time coming straight for crowd centre. The aircraft rolled once then pulled hard into a turn to parallel the crowd line, before rolling again and pulling up out of sight. The noise of the engine and propeller roaring away was still there even though he was invisible to us on the ground. A few more passes, some inverted and he was done, bringing the Extra onto a very tight right-hand baseleg to land on the grass runway in front of us.

As far as aerobatic displays went it was a complete masterclass by a seasoned professional at the top of his game, however if you looked at it in the cold light of the display 'Regs', it was very iffy to say the least... As the propeller came to a stop and he flipped the glass canopy open I went up to the side of the cockpit to congratulate him – he was covered in sweat. I said, "Hey Paul! There's a psychiatrist over there looking for you mate! YOU'RE A NUTTER!" He laughed, "HAH...! just doing my job mate!" but he was grinning more from relief that the ordeal was over I think.

There must have been quite a few times when he lost sight of the ground during his display – for sure there was hardly any visible horizon due to low cloud and reduced visibility in the continuous light drizzle. However, looking at the Extra's cockpit instrumentation, it was easy to see that an aerobatic display would have been possible with flight instruments alone. There was a massive Attitude Indicator in the centre of the panel which would no doubt have been completely "topple-free" in all axes and the other instruments were large and clear.

*

I recalled then that in 'a former life' we actually used to practice our Aeros display routine in the BAe Hawk Flight Simulators at RAF Valley and RAF Chivenor back in the mid 1980s. In fact there was one time when I was training on the Hawk at Tac Weapons Unit from Chivenor when the QFI in the back decided to give me some sort of special test. There was an airborne evolution which we used to practice called an 'emergency low-level escape manoeuvre'. The reason was that sometimes when we were flying tactically at low-level, (we're talking a steady 420 knots indicated at 250 feet MSD) we might turn into a valley where the cloud was too low to continue visually. Of course you have to assume the valley is too narrow for a 180 degree turn at that sort of speed so the only way is UP!

If you suddenly run into cloud at low-level in a military jet, there is no possibility of carrying on without Terrain Following Radar (TFR), which we did not have. In those early days of low-level flying we were equipped with a quarter-mil map and compass, a stopwatch and the "Mark One Eyeball!" I forget what the exact call was on the intercom (or R/T to your mate if flying in formation), something like "EMERGENCY PULL-UP!" and before you had uttered the word up you had already slammed the throttle fully open for maximum power, rolled wings level and pulled hard back on the control column.

Flying the Hawk was hard work at low-level

We were taught to apply 4G until we got to a pitch attitude of 45 degrees nose-up then a quick push forward on the stick to hold the nose there. Naturally being keen young chaps, 'bright eyed and bushy tailed' etc. we practiced this manoeuvre in the simulator solely on instruments as if we actually had run into cloud at low-level. Additionally of course we practiced our aerobatic routines, which is where the problem really started I think. After a while we did get quite good at flying aerobatics on instruments alone – of course the Air Staff Instructions (ASIs) prohibited any aerobatics in IMC conditions for real.

Hawk T1A instrument panel with large Attitude Indicator – note the speed in this one... 550 Knots at Max-Chat! ☺

So... fast-forward to our low-level sortie over the Bristol Channel. I think we might have been on our way to the range to practice Strafe and in the back seat as my TWI was Ian Gore. He was on an exchange from the RNZAF I think and his nickname was IGOR among the other instructors. As part of his brief for the mission he told me that I could expect to have to perform an emergency escape manoeuvre at any time and that I should react as if it were for real. So far so good. However it was not long after takeoff and we were over the sea at about 1000 feet, blatting along at 420 knots just underneath a solid overcast at 2000. I knew from the Met briefing that this cloud was solid all the way to something like 15,000 feet. I was planning my arrival into the range in South Wales and had the map out in the front, when he shouted "LOW-LEVEL WEATHER ABORT!" Immediately I called back "EMERGENCY PULL-UP!" I checked we were wings level, looked up simultaneously to make sure the area was clear, then slammed the throttle open and pulled back hard... "UNNGGGFFHH!!!"

We both made similar grunting noises as the G piled on during the pitch-up, then we were at 45 degrees. A slight bunt forward and the AI was showing us exactly where I wanted it, the pipper was 45 degrees above the horizon and we were climbing like a homesick angel. We were climbing fast in thick Nimbostratus with a steep pitch attitude – 45 degrees nose-up and with something like 6000 feet per minute rate of climb... Suddenly he shouted on the intercom from the backseat "AIRWAY ABOVE!!... THE BASE IS FLIGHT LEVEL NINER ZERO!" I was pretty sure there wasn't because I had checked the map only a minute or two previously. But NOW was not the time to argue as I looked at the altimeter. This was showing us rocketing up through 8,200... YIKES!

"ROG!" I panted in the oxygen mask. While we were still 45 degrees pitched up in solid clag, I whacked the stick hard over to the left, the Hawk rolled inverted in what felt like half a second - almost full aileron applied. My vision was glued to the Attitude - as we reached wings level upside down, I blipped the ailerons the opposite way to stop the roll fast, then immediately pulled back hard. Inverted, but with lots of positive 'G', the nose came down to the horizon really quickly, I stopped it there and rolled out level... The altimeter read exactly 9,000 and the whole thing was over in about three seconds...

From the rear I heard him mouth-breathing heavily on the intercom in my ears, he had been grunting during the manoeuvre; now there was quite a pause... Then he said "*STREWTH MCBRIDE...WHAT THE HELL...?!*" still breathing hard... I replied quickly, "SORRY SIR! I had to act FAST, you said there was AN AIRWAY ABOVE US and it was the only way to stop the climb!" We were over the Bristol Channel at the time. Now barreling along at Flight Level Nine Zero at 300 knots, I was bringing the throttle back before we started to accelerate away. To be honest, in my mind at that time I didn't think it was a big deal – I suppose it had been all the simulator sessions practising Aeros on instruments, from Igor's perspective though I bet it was quite a ride!

In reality of course that is exactly how we would have flown it anyway. Hardly much thought involved apart from the briefest of checks to make sure that there wasn't an aircraft above us before we pulled up hard into the murk. He actually gave me a very good write-up for that particular sortie and I overheard him relating the tale to one of his mates on the squadron later in the day. Needless to say I bet he was a little more circumspect about shouting "There's an airway above..!" after this. I still smile about it when I think about it these days. It was literally three seconds, from climbing fast and steep, shiny side up to; rolling inverted-pulling to horizon-rolling out again... WHACK, PULL, ROLL, BANG – WINGS LEVEL!

*

With this experience in my own background, I knew where Paul the Extra 300 display pilot was coming from when he said "just doing my job mate". His real job these days is actually flying as a senior Captain for a major UK airline. It is nice to know that there are people flying airliners who have done plenty of other sorts of flying before – you never know when that experience might come in handy. Recovering an airliner with minimal height-loss, from an unusual attitude at night or in IMC for example...

Happy days – Tactical Weapons Unit 1986 with Hawk T1A

Now the display organiser came to us and asked when were WE going to fly...? After what we had just witnessed, it was going to be rather difficult to refuse. We had another look at the weather and a good study of the large scale map to assess topography and potential obstacles, a quick brief and we were ready to launch.

As the cloudbase was somewhat unhelpful, we gave our special 'flat display' which included fast passes in the clean configuration and slow passes with all the flaps extended and the gear down. The Beech could fly at amazingly slow speeds with full flap and we took advantage of this for positioning in the grotty cloudbase at very low altitude. There was just enough space below cloud for us to get the display done, but we had to work hard to keep ourselves oriented safely – there was no way we wanted to be doing any aerobatic manoeuvres in cloud thanks. Basically Anthony flew mostly on the instruments, while I called the visuals for him with my neck stretched right forward in the windscreen of the aircraft.

"Keep it coming mate, hold that bank angle, another 30 degrees of turn or so... NOW start your roll out... wings level NOW! The runway is in your right one o'clock..."

When we finally came into land from a very tight curving baseleg turn (so we didn't lose sight of the field), we touched down with a very slow three pointer landing. We tended to land the Beech in the three point attitude on grass and used the wheeler landing technique for hard runways. So far this strategy had worked okay, with the advantage on grass of a very slow touchdown speed, thereby reducing the ground run. With that hangar at the end of the strip we needed to be sure we would stop before the end... Sorry... did I mention THAT HANGAR before?!

It goes without saying that we refuelled at another airfield on the way home – you see we WERE learning.

Early August 1992, saw us preparing for our third airshow with an early morning departure to Jurby on the Isle of Man. Bryngwyn Bach was clamped in and so was the island. Everything was ready to go, but the weather prevented our take-off for several hours. Telephone calls to Jurby revealed that other aircraft had cancelled from southern England – we all wondered if this was going to be the one airshow we couldn't make? The latest Metfax (who remembers those?) indicated a frontal clearance at 1500hrs local time through Bryngwyn Bach and coincidentally the latest time we could get airborne for Jurby and perform was 1515hrs local...

After kicking our heels all day, predictably the weather cleared just enough to give credence to the Metman's forecast and we knew we could get back in again on our return. We launched almost straight into cloud – a little instrument flying later had us in the cloud over the Irish Sea heading for the northwest corner of the Isle of Man. On arrival at Jurby, we were met by one of the display committee with a very worried look on his face and a big ask. "Can you display in ten minutes time, after the Wessex Helicopter?" Of course the answer had to be yes. After what we had been through to get there, it would have been churlish to refuse. On completion of our display routine, a quick refuelling stop at Ronaldsway (main airport on the IoM) and then we were homeward bound once more.

Our fourth air show of 1992 was at a huge USAF base about a week later and as we taxied out for our display slot, the crosswind was reaching our maximum limit, with occasional excursions above it. Mindful of the fact that that it could result in our landing elsewhere we left a VHF radio with the family and groundcrew so we could tell them where to meet us by taxi. Fortunately Plan B was not required and some very relieved faces greeted us after we landed back at the USAF base.

There was then some negotiation with ATC about our 'going home time' at the end of the day. The crowds had thinned out, it was late afternoon and there were huge gaps in the 'flypro', but ATC was reluctant to let us go for no apparent reason. Although not wishing to offend our hosts, it became obvious from the illogical transmissions from 'the tower' that no-one up there was making any sensible decisions. Aircraft departing for Duxford were cleared to taxi out, but then told to hold at the entrance of the empty runway without any reason – engines were overheating and so were tempers!

Eventually "Duxford formation clear take-off" came through just before the Spitfire boiled over.

Prior to the Beech C45 – I had to check out on the Harvard

Harvard G-JUDI (FX301) – 'G' meter reading +4.5G and -1.0G

By then we had been waiting patiently for 45 minutes, all closed up and ready to start our engines. It was time for us to push for a departure slot. Another transmission to the tower reminding them that we were still ready for start-up, resulted in a curt "Southern Comfort STANDBY!" Then suddenly the handheld radio burst into life with, "Southern Comfort, you are cleared to taxi AND cleared for IMMEDIATE TAKE-OFF!" Pandemonium ensued as Anthony and I did our version of 'one-legged paper-hangers with St Vitus' dance' much to the amusement of our passengers just behind us in the back – they loved it! Clearly this departure slot could disappear just as quickly as it had arrived and therefore our hands were a blur as we fired up the Pratt and Whitneys.

As soon as one of the big radials was running we waved the chocks away and started taxying even before we were developing any power from the second one. It was a great feeling to have the wheels retracting into the undercarriage bays after airborne and as we set climb power, it felt like all our worries were over - we set course for North Wales. The tower controller's clipped transmission "Contact departure g'day" conveyed no hint of apology for the debacle we were leaving behind. We were disappointed, I turned to Anthony and said, "*...and this is the nation that put a man on the MOON?!*" We were still chuckling an hour or so later as slipped onto finals at homebase – after overflying to check that the sheep had been cleared...

Our fifth and final air show of 1992 also turned out to be quite an adventure. We had been very much looking forward to 'Great Warbirds' Air Display at RAF Wroughton Airfield in Wiltshire for many months. It was a highlight moment in the calendar for anyone interested in antique/veteran aircraft and military types in particular – the clue is in the name. Of course we were only just starting out on the airshow circuit and as newcomers we should be grateful for any display that we could get – it is quite an exclusive club and we were not yet really welcomed as members.

Author, Anthony Hodgson (owner) & Dave Budden (Engineer)

In consequence there was some doubt as to whether we would actually be invited to *attend* Great Warbirds, let alone be permitted to fly in the show. Eventually we received word that the organisers would pay fuel costs for our appearance, but we were under no illusion that we would be simply required as a static display – no flying for us.

Well that was better than nothing and in our view as enthusiastic amateurs, it would be an amazing experience just to be there and be able to mingle with the best in the business. As usual for summer 1992, the forecast was not very promising with the probability of high winds and heavy showers appearing on the menu. When we examined the weather in detail, it was agreed that although difficult it was feasible especially as the occasional gust to 40 knots at Wroughton was straight down the runway – well almost.

The transit flight that early morning was very bumpy and we needed to carry out a radar letdown at the nearby RAF Base just to get under the cloudbase. We duly arrived into the visual circuit at Wroughton and landed in what could be described 'sporting' conditions. It was clear that we were one of the very few aeroplanes to have flown in that morning – the majority having been invited to arrive in much clearer weather the day before.

"Great Warbirds" Airshow - 1992

After making such a determined effort to get there, despite the conditions, it was disappointing to think that we would not be allowed to fly in the airshow. A quick glance at the flying programme for the day confirmed that we were not included – static display only for us. C'est la vie. During the Aircrew Briefing however, it became apparent that the programme was falling apart... The forecast of near gale force winds and thundery showers for the day put paid to the hopes of Tiger Moths and most other lightweight aircraft. In fact some of the heavier metal was dropping out also and leaving huge gaps in the display schedule. That being said, there was still no invitation forthcoming for us to fill a vacancy – it rather felt as if our presence had not been registered. We were very much the 'Cinderella Crew' as we waited outside the briefing room to buttonhole the main display coordinator and offer our services.

While we were waiting the wife of one of the other display participants while commiserating with our "shoddy treatment" (her words not mine) suggested that perhaps we should "just take the free fuel and go..." It must be said that the thought had crossed our minds, however as we agreed at the time, "...if we do that we will always be known as the crew who pitched up, took the fuel and pissed off!" Eventually the briefing room door opened and we got our chance to plead our case with 'the head-waiter' himself. He listened for a couple of minutes and then gave us the 9 minute slot we were looking for - We had to be airborne in 15!

We literally raced back to the aircraft to get it ready for display, just as a particularly malevolent shower made its presence felt – all and sundry got a good soaking. The rain was horizontal as we reached Southern Comfort – carrying out the external preflight checks was definitely not the usual pleasant experience. As we taxied out in the howling wind, Anthony had to employ all the tricks of the trade to prevent the tail lifting and I privately questioned the wisdom of getting airborne in such atrocious weather, but there was a feeling that, "We haven't come all this way for nothing" and the wind was inside our crosswind limits most of the time. It would mean a 'wing-down' takeoff and 'Gawd knows' what sort of landing...

"Southern Comfort. You are clear takeoff - straight into display, the surface wind is 25 gusting 40 knots..." came the business like tones of the tower controller on the R/T.

Never *quite* upside down during display... but we did get close!

Our takeoff roll was, I think, the shortest we have ever done before or since and the wheels were up in the undercarriage-bays well before crowd centre. We had to 'beat' a long way into wind before the first turn for the downwind pass and our groundspeed then was quite startling. Indeed the commentator was moved to say, *"Southern Comfort... and here she comes, showing all the speed of a little fighter!"* Of course it was just an illusion really with our airspeed at around 190mph, but with the benefit of 60mph up our chuff we were certainly motoring on the fast passes.

All too soon it was time to finish and we turned finals for, what would prove to be our toughest crosswind landing yet. Apparently some of the other display participants drifted out from the bar in the pilots' tent to watch the event, which had all the makings of a big 'moment'. Fortunately Anthony was able to disappoint the ghouls among them as he struggled to put the aeroplane down on the runway in one piece. The fact that he did so by touching down cross-controlled, abeam the pilots' tent was pure coincidence and icing on the cake!

As we sauntered nonchalantly back into the tent, a ripple of applause from the cognoscenti indicated that the achievement had been recognised. Although not taking this to be a sign that we had been welcomed as members of an exclusive club, at least we were not invisible anymore!

Beech History

One of only four Beech 18/C45s on the UK register, G-BSZC, Southern Comfort joined the UK airshow circuit in 1992. Built in 1941, it was first used as a navigation trainer (AT-7 42-2490). Between 1952 and 1961, almost 2,300 Beech 18s were re-manufactured for military service and Southern Comfort was one of these, becoming C45H Expeditor 51-11701. During the early years of the Cold War between East and West, the aircraft carried out communications work for the USAF's Strategic Air Command.

The twin-Beech was civilianised in 1963 and allocated registration N9541Z. With one owner over some 20 years and having recorded only 2,000 flying hours the aircraft eventually fell into disrepair through lack of use. It was saved from almost certain death in the scrap yard by a serving USAF F-16 pilot Col Blake Thomas who supervised the restoration work between 1986-89. Blake flew the aircraft across the Atlantic in November 1990, along with another ferry pilot. It was fairly obvious that more restoration work was required, because the ocean crossing took 30 flying hours and the aeroplane consumed 50 gallons of engine oil!

1991 saw the aircraft pass to the new owner Anthony Hodgson, who had his sleeves rolled up for much of that year, preparing the Beech for Airshow work. Anthony was ably assisted by a band of volunteer 'polishers' whose reward for their hard labour was to accompany the aircraft to airshows throughout the summer.

Real Flying? – 1994 Southern Comfort formation (Seimon Pugh-Jones)

--0--

Signing for the fuel at an airshow

--0--

25 - PUSHBACKS, PULLBACKS AND POWERBACKS

Shannon Airport May 1989...

...nose in to stand 30 at Shannon – tugs attached ready to pull?

I recall distinctly the first time I ever encountered the term 'Powerback'. It was on that day in May 1989 when we went to Shannon airport in Southern Ireland for our Base Training with Air 2000. Not that Powerbacks are a normal part of Base Training of course. No, the Base Training is simply to ensure that the newly trained pilots can actually land and takeoff safely in the real aircraft, before the CAA puts the type on their licence. It is 'circuits and bumps' again basically.

These days it is a less common practice as many airlines have "Zero Flight Time" (Level D) simulators which means that the CAA will grant the type rating without the pilots actually having flown the real machine. Back in the 80s and 90s however there were no fancy simulators capable of this, so all companies had to put the pilots through the mill on the jet.

Ours was the first in-house Boeing 757 Type Rating course and there were three "flightcrews" composed of one Captain and one First Officer in each crew. Once our Groundschool exams were passed, it was up, up and away... to Singapore where we experienced the complete Simulator package for the Boeing 757. From memory this was three weeks long and after our final Sim exam check (LST) we returned to the UK to await our Base Training Circuits.

In fact here we are below in our official course photo in February 1989 – at the Westin Stamford Hotel in Singapore, just over the road from Raffles.

L-R Peter Headley, Sandy Cameron, Sheldon Osborne, Tony Storey, Self, Mark Kleynhans

Why Singapore? Well in those days there were very few B757 Simulators available in the world and time was at a premium, so our top Flight Operations people decided to do the course in the Far East. Singapore Airlines were extraordinarily helpful with business class air tickets and Hotac etc. For sure, we had no complaints...

Although I do recall we sent a nice postcard back to Neil Burrows our Director Flight Operations in Manchester – something along the lines of *"Dear Neil, Having a lovely time, hotel nice, weather sunny and girls very pretty, but BEER EXPENSIVE – please send more money! Yours sincerely, The Boys!"*

*

B757 Base Training

The Training Captain in charge of the Base Training mission met with all of us in the Manchester Operations centre where we boarded the aircraft. He had reviewed the options and although the weather was not perfect, they decided upon Shannon in Eire. There are many factors to be taken into consideration while doing circuits with a big jet, not least of which are noise and weather.

Most airports are unsuitable for one reason or another and many prefer not to have "training" going on while they are trying to operate commercial flights in and out. Bear in mind that each trainee usually requires 6 landings and you can see the problem.

Chief Pilot in a good mood BEFORE we landed at Shannon!

In our case there were 6 of us, so that would be a minimum of 36 takeoffs and landings – it was going to be literally hours bashing the circuit. In addition they were upgrading a new Training Captain to become a Base Trainer, so that would be even more circuit time.

The message came back from Shannon Airport however that we were good to go. They had accepted the aircraft for circuits. Back in the late 1980s / early 90's, Shannon was pretty much a backwater. Although it had a large main runway and could handle big aircraft, there was not much traffic, so in many ways it was perfect.

We arrived into the visual circuit from a radar vectored ILS approach and started doing the "Touch and Go" (roller) landings. It was not intended for us to stop flying the circuit throughout the entire detail as we were able to swap pilots in the large flightdeck midair. I think it was approximately 90 minutes after we had started the training when ATC on the tower frequency made their announcement that the runway would be closed in another 30 minutes for several hours! Needless to say this came as a surprise to our Training Captains onboard and they decided that we would, "land and sort this out with them..."

Personally as a newbie trainee F/O I was not too concerned about us having a break for a while because the continuous takeoffs and landings were making me feel nauseous. I was very conscious of the experienced, professional pilots I was with, so I kept my concerns for my stomach to myself.

We landed and taxied in towards the terminal and were guided by the marshaller nose-in onto Stand 30. Where they could put a set of steps up to the aircraft door. Up to this point I must admit I was so new to the industry, that it hadn't really occurred to me that airliners are such ungainly beasts on the ground. They need all sorts of special equipment designed for the job...

'Bright-eyed and bushy-tailed', 4 of the trainee pilots

So, after the engines were all shutdown and the steps were attached, we disarmed and opened the L1 door. A representative from the handling agent came onboard. He addressed our senior Trainer and the conversation went something like this;

"Well that's the runway closed for four hours now for maintenance..."

"Why was the closure not on the NOTAMs?" A fair question.

"Well... to be sure. You would NOT have come here for your base training circuits if we'd done that now would you...?"

He did have a point and the logic was inescapable, unfortunately so was our parking position! When the Senior Trainer asked them for a pushback tractor and towbar to push us back from the stand, there was a very awkward silence. Then:

"Ach! Well. D'ya'see, we will not be havin' one of those now..." His voice trailed away as he could see the effect his words were having on an already pissed off Airline Training Captain who has just been told that he cannot continue with his planned training mission. All because Shannon didn't want to put it on the Notices To Airmen that they were closing the runway for four hours in the middle of the day.

I looked at our Chief Pilot and thought he was about to explode as he said to the hapless dispatcher,

"What do you mean you haven't got one...? We NEED a towbar to push the aircraft back from the gate here and if you didn't have a 757 towbar... WHY THE HELL DID YOU MARSHALL US INTO THE STAND...?"

"But could you not be REVERSING BACKWARDS off the stand now Captain – you have the reverse thrust now isn't it...?"

"OH RIGHT!? And blow all your bloody windows in...? I DON'T FLIPPING THINK SO!"

The dispatcher then realised the stupidity of the situation and wisely kept his mouth shut. I noted also that my feelings of nausea had subsided now and I was looking forward to the next

chapter in this drama. A couple of walkie-talkie calls from the Dispatcher confirmed that Shannon airport was not in possession of a towbar which would fit our beautiful 757.

We looked outside and it was clear we were VERY close to the terminal building - the large yellow number 30 indicating our parking stand was huge in the flightdeck windows. In fact Oscar Charlie was perfectly parked on the gate ready for pushback... IF the airport had owned a towbar which fitted the linkage on the nosegear. What to do?

An executive decision had to be made and fortunately we had some of the very senior pilots from Air2000 here with us. Capt Bob Screen was Chief Pilot and I think it was he that said, *"Right chaps! It's Durty Nelly's then!"* I could barely believe my ears. We were going to stack (finish work) and go for an unscheduled nightstop – how exciting!

Not only that, but it was clear by the conversation among our seniors and betters, they also knew a watering hole with a fascinating name... "DURTY NELLY'S......" I couldn't tell you the name of the hotel we stayed in, but the pub....? Brilliant!

Durty Nelly's, complete with cèilidh band and absolutely packed with customers all enjoying the craic. The history of the pub is very interesting and I was curious to know more about the original landlady... It turns out she was described thus;

"...a buxom lady, tall in stature, but shapely and appealing to all". She was keeper of the toll-bridge over the river Owengarney and although times were hard, she always found ways to make ends meet. A woman of considerable charm, she was known to the virile men of the day from Galway to Cork, Dublin to Limerick. Her hospitality to the travelers coming across the bridge gained her a place in many a man's fond memories..."

So – quite a woman then eh? With a bit more research I found out that there was also such a thing as Nelly's blessing. It crossed my mind that she was going above and beyond the call of duty here in looking after her weary travelers – literally she couldn't do enough for her boys...

"May the road rise up to meet you. May the wind be always at your back. May the sun shine warm upon your face, the rains fall soft upon your fields and until we meet again, may God hold you in the palm of his hand".

*

So, God was holding them all "in the palm of his hand" and I am sure that He alone knows how we ever got out of that bar before closing time! However, I think it was probably another Command decision – the next morning we had a job to do!

Pullbacks

Which is how we came to be attaching ropes to the maingear bogies of our ship of dreams on a wet ramp in Shannon. In fact it wasn't us that attached the ropes, but some very nice chaps from the Aer Lingus pushback teams. Needless to say everybody was a little embarrassed about the situation – it was certainly a new experience for our training captains as they had never been towed backwards off a stand either!

As with all non-normal situations, the senior training captains took time to establish the methods of communication with the Groundcrew to ensure that everyone was on the same page. While the steps were still attached I took a moment to go and have a look at the towropes – they were huge! Of course the B757 weighed around 80,000kgs so the ropes would need to be quite strong... Additionally the pull of both tugs needed to be coordinated equally.

Tugs ready to take up the strain...

Eventually all was ready and we were "cleared to pull and start..." usually in the airline industry this is clearance to PUSH and start of course. Once the aircraft had been pulled back into a position on the taxiway where it could manoeuvre under its own power.

The parking brake was applied, the tugs and ropes disconnected and we were cleared to start engines. This all took some time, however there was enough light in the day to complete the Base Training Circuits and then fly home to Manchester without any further embarrassing incidents.

All of the foregoing was actually quite an eye opener for a newbie First Officer. My appreciation of the ramp handling required for a large airliner was improved considerably and from this episode my Situational Awareness (SA) of Ground Operations was heightened.

At the time I thought of it as an added bonus to the invaluable training which we received in flying the jet round the circuit for takeoffs and landings. The other bonus was a free trip to Durty Nelly's of course – but I think my appreciation of that was apparent in the previous paragraphs.

In those days yellow Hi-Vis jackets on the ramp were optional

*

Powerbacks

Although our problem was fairly easily solved by the use of two large aircraft tugs, there have been occasional times during the operation of airliners in faraway places that Powerbacks have been required. By 'Powerback' of course we refer to the aircraft using its own reverse thrust to manoeuvre on the ground, backwards away from obstacles such as terminal buildings.

In some cases, there are airliners which do this routinely, I am thinking of MD80s and the like with high mounted engines, situated at the rear of the fuselage and therefore unlikely to suffer from FOD damage with re-ingested exhaust gases. So although inappropriate in the case of G-OOOC at Shannon on Stand 30 where a Powerback would have caused a lot of damage to the terminal windows, the suggestion was not completely out of whack with all of the options available.

In those days (up to the early '90s) there was an actual documented procedure in the Boeing 757 Flight Crew Training Manual, (FCTM) although there were several cautionary notes regarding its use. I believe it was also in the FCOM (Flight Crew Ops Manual) from Boeing.

The threats mainly centred on three areas. Firstly the potentially damaging effect of the re-ingestion of exhaust gases which would have mixed with dirt, dust and FOD (Foreign Object Debris) from the ramp. Secondly, the effect of the high energy exhaust gases being directed forwards towards buildings, vehicles and personnel. Finally the possibility that the aircraft might tip backwards onto its tail if the brakes were applied while it was still moving in reverse.

As my interest had been aroused by the 'Pullback' fiasco in Shannon I was eager to learn more about the possible Powerback abilities of the B757. I studied the chapter on Powerback very carefully, but then had no need to use the information while I was flying for Air 2000 during the next seven years.

It was only after I had moved on to another airline that I was required to carry out a Powerback myself as Captain and it was an unnerving experience to say the least. Suffice to say when I was looking for the information to refresh my memory on the subject I found that Boeing had actually removed the procedure from the FCTM and FCOM. If I had not been aware of the original instructions, then we might still be trapped on the tiny ramp in Agra in India – but that, as they say, is another story.

It never fails to surprise me while working with airlines that there are some people who rise to positions of very senior operational responsibility, who lack some of the basic knowledge which the rest of us take for granted. In short, they should take time to get out there and see how the operation actually functions so that they can speak with authority on the matter.

*

There was one particular Chief Operating Officer who made himself look very foolish in a meeting at a low-cost airline long ago. Clearly the COO had never really understood how aircraft were handled/serviced on the ramp. We were in a closed meeting room, there were approximately 10 senior managers present, some from Flight Ops Department (my speciality) and some from the Ground Ops team.

The meeting had been called in order to discuss cost saving measures for the turnarounds which would not have a negative impact on the planned 25 minutes turnround time. We had been discussing some ideas quite openly and the meeting had relaxed into a brain-storming exercise, when all of a sudden the COO interjected with – "WAIT...! I'VE GOT IT...!"

All of us in the small meeting room went quiet out of respect and I thought to myself, *this will be interesting...* Frankly, up to that time I had not noticed 'our glorious leader' to be capable of much in the way of innovative brainwaves, but there was always a first time... He had decided that he had struck on a brilliant idea to save ground handling costs on the turn-rounds. "...don't you see? We can *remove the need for pushback tractors*, saving money and time on every turnround – *the pilots can reverse the aircraft onto stand...!"*

There was a very awkward silence... The majority of the aviation professionals looked down at the table, their notes, a pen; anything but up at face level and possibly catch his eye... Bear in mind these people were good solid airline industry personnel.

They had worked their way up from the ramp and the hangar to positions of middle and senior management in the head office and had many, many years working in the industry. They KNEW the operation inside out and they also KNEW that airliners cannot reverse themselves unless under VERY specially controlled circumstances and then only in extremis. Frankly the COO was talking nonsense and they KNEW it...

I thought quietly to myself, "Whoah! What on earth is he talking about? Maybe it is some sort of joke...?!" But looking round, no such luck, just a very awkward silence. Somebody MUST say something surely...? Was there a hidden camera? April fool? No he wasn't smiling, just looking earnestly for everybody's reaction – ANYBODY...?

Okay here goes I thought. I opened my mouth to speak with an effort. Somebody had to relieve the tension here and I had a sudden realisation that he REALLY was serious. This one was easy, he was clearly speaking without proper knowledge of the operation, but how to let him know that and at the same time allow him to save face and not look like a complete idiot?

"Well... that's a good idea in principle yes boss... But, that would put the door for the airbridge on the wrong side of the aircraft do you see? All of the airports would have to change the build of their terminals first."

"Oh Yes!" he said relieved, "You're right James. Well let's break for coffee everybody shall we? Back here in say... fifteen minutes?"

We all breathed a sigh of relief as we left the room.

--O--

26 - KISS AND FLY

In our ultra-modern, overheated, multi-media, global-village, you could be forgiven for thinking that Romance and Aviation parted company several decades ago... you would be wrong. If you have not seen a movie called 'One Six Right' (2005) and you are at all interested in aviation, then you should make time to do so – the clue is in the name... Focussing on Van Nuys GA airport in Southern California, the movie reveals the history of an airport where Amelia Earhart broke a world speed record; Marilyn Monroe was discovered working in the hangars; and the closing scenes of Casablanca were filmed. Seriously, it has something for everyone.

*

One of the 'airplanes' in the film reminded me of a nostalgic flight from years ago – the Boeing Stearman. I had the good fortune to be offered a flight in one by the engineer who was maintaining her and didn't need to be asked twice. Bearing in mind that I had long been acquainted with the flying qualities of Boeing products, (earning a living with them since 1989), the chance to fly one from the 1930s was not to be missed. It should be remembered that during the same period, the British equivalent was the very sweet handling and beautiful Tiger Moth. The Tiger, although light and simple to operate, required a firm hand to fly well as it is slow to respond to control inputs – not undesirable qualities for a trainer. By contrast the Stearman was a better rough/short field aircraft having large wheels, brakes and generally being a heavier machine.

The Stearman cockpit is large and roomy

Getting into the Stearman was not difficult as the cockpit is quite large and roomy. It reminded me of the Second World War P47 Thunderbolt Pilot's description of that aircraft when he stated that his cockpit was large enough to run around inside to dodge the bullets... All the controls seemed massive compared to a Tiger and taxiing the aircraft was easy, with feet comfortably planted on huge rudder pedals, large wheels, stick held back to ensure no nose-over – it felt like a child's toy!

Almost like an overinflated version of something a kid would run round the garden with, most odd. Plenty of positive rudder control was required for takeoff, but in reality it seemed fairly innocuous. Once airborne, the 7 cylinder Continental radial engine gave a good rate of climb and the ailerons and rudder were very effective with good harmony in yaw and roll. I noted that the rudder needed attention to stay in trim and it kept me on my toes for sure. Of course us jet-airliner pilots have very dull feet these days, a result of only ever using the rudder pedals for steering on the ground, or very rarely in the case of engine failure.

- it felt like a child's toy!

Aerobatics were a delight however, once you got used to the visual perspective. Again, the feeling of flying a model aeroplane on steroids came to me as I pushed and pulled on the huge joystick in the cockpit. Nicely balanced in all axes though, rolls and loops were a doddle. Unlike the Tiger, the glide ratio of a Stearman is more similar to that of a drain cover. All that weight and drag have to act somewhere and she required plenty of throttle on final approach to control the rate of descent for landing. A three point landing was not difficult; I just followed the numbers given to me by Dave the engineer. In many ways THIS was the biggest similarity with the modern Boeing, just go by numbers.

Certainly when you are first learning on the beast, simply fly her at the recommended pitch attitude and power settings (in-trim of course) and listen for the audible cues of the radalt. "50, 30, 20..." In the Boeing 737 for example, at "50" you are over the threshold, at "30" you are getting ready for the flare and at "20" you flare (just double the pitch attitude, no more than that) and simultaneously/smoothly close the thrust levers - **while holding the attitude.**

This last bit is most important as there is a distinct tendency for the nose to drop in the airliner as the thrust is reduced from those under-wing pod mounted CFM56s. As the main gear touches down - remember you are STILL flying the aeroplane – positively fly the nosegear onto the runway. Again control of back-pressure on the control column is important here.

As the main landing gear touches down, that is the time to move your hand forward onto the thrust reversers and raise them to the interlock position. If you develop the bad habit of reaching for the reversers earlier, prior to maingear touchdown, then it is only a matter of time before you inadvertently (absent mindedly perhaps) raise them while the aircraft is still airborne. The danger then is that the groundspoilers may deploy which destroys the lift very suddenly with predictable results... a hard landing would be guaranteed.

Turning the clock back to the 1930s, the Stearman was rather simpler to land, although in common with the Tiger there is a limited crosswind capability – they both prefer to land into wind for sure. But as the ground roll is short, this is less of a problem for most airfields. Allegedly the Stearman has a penchant for ground-looping at a low speed "around 35 mph", but I didn't see it. Mind you with taildraggers I am ultra-conscious of the possibility of a sudden swing during and/or after the landing. As far as I am concerned the landing ain't over till she's back in the hangar...

The main thing I recall being in common with the Tiger was... THE COLD! Brrrr... Even though I was wearing plenty of stuff and had borrowed a HUGE sheepskin flying jacket for this flight and the subsequent ferry flight, it was very, very cold. I suppose this is something you get used to after a while; we modern pilots have gone soft. Our ferry flight was to a maintenance hangar for engineering work. My most striking memory was the reception. As we shutdown outside the busy little flying club, everybody came out to have a look!

If you half closed your eyes for a moment you could roll back the decades to an earlier, more innocent time when airplanes/airmen (and women - sorry Amelia) were rare and respected sights. A golden age when the truly rich and famous travelled by Pan-Am Clipper across the oceans. Where airport security consisted of a piece of rope across the entrance to the apron, or perhaps just a polite sign reminding that the area was off-limits to unauthorised persons.

There is still romance in the airline industry today, although it is more subtle than it used to be. There is humour, friendship and much happiness too, in the airlines this tends to exist more in the smaller crewbases which have a family atmosphere. In our crewroom you will hear the happy hubbub of conversation intermixed with formal briefing procedures among the crew. There will be lots of witty jokes too from time to time, passed confidently among people who enjoy an easy working relationship together; "___ are you ready...?" and the response we heard was

"I was BORN ready!" which brought a smile from all nearby.

At our base, when whole crews meet either on the ramp, the airport bus or on handover of an aircraft, there are handshakes, hugs and kisses all round. In fact this is sometimes a distraction especially when we are trying to get the next flight away ontime. Although it is really heart-warming to see the comradeship and friendly ambience... to "...feel the lurve!" Wait, did I really say that? Yes, well I have never been afraid of the truth and that's just what it is, L-O-V-E... There are times when ours really is the most romantic industry in the world and in the modern times this togetherness is actively promoted and fostered by CRM.

A very simple example is a line from the script of 'Yorkshire Airlines', the Hale and Pace short comedy sketch (see on YouTube). A voiceover in heavy Yorkshire accent describes the stewardesses lovingly as *"Ow-er AIR-DORISES welcome you all onboard..."* etc. This bizarrely provides evidence of the loving respect with which the Pilots treat the Cabin Crew - true. There are many more examples, but let's not wallow too much in nostalgia. Suffice to say that when international airports like Nice, JFK, Chicago O'Hare (to name but a few) signage their short-stay drop-off points "Kiss and Fly", they knew what they were doing!

--0--

27 - THE FACE OF GOD

Speaking generally, I think it is fair to say that 'Religion' has a lot to answer for. That said, I wasn't specifically thinking about religion as we pushed back from the stand at Gatwick for a nightflight to Taba airport in Egypt in our B757. The weather forecast had indicated Nil Significant Cloud, but there were two other factors which made life more complicated instead. Firstly the wind was entirely in the wrong direction so we would be required to make an approach to land on Runway 22R instead of 04L. The consequences of this were that we would have to fly a very tight visual circuit onto finals for Runway 22R to avoid crossing the border with Israel only 5 miles away to the East – not easy at the best of times. The second worry was the recent desert dust storm which had passed through the area and left some very poor visibility behind it, down to 1500m in dust haze... Yes it was going to be quite a night, I could see it coming. Oh, and it was a Line Training flight for my colleague in the right-hand seat who was converting onto the Boeing 757...

*

There have been many occasions when 'religion' in all its various guises has impacted commercial airline operations over the years; sometimes with only mild effects, but at other times with rather more serious consequences. You don't have to think very deeply to link religious extremism for example with some of the worst terrorist atrocities which have yet been enacted. However, some long lasting and less dramatic after-effects of religious conflict can be more subtle. For example consider Taba Airport in Egypt (ICAO - HETB). Built by the Israelis in 1972 during their occupation of the Sinai Peninsula following the Six Day War, the airport was handed over to Egypt as the Israeli forces withdrew. Demilitarised in 1982, a new terminal building and night-lighting were added in the 1990s and it was then used for holiday charter flights to and from Europe, in addition to domestic shuttles to Cairo. The main runway used for landing and takeoff was 04L - the approach lighting system for this runway was quite effective and much money was spent – the same could not be said for the opposite end (22R).

You can see why. The prevailing wind was north-easterly and therefore only rarely would the airport have to use runway 22, plus it was SO close to the Israeli border. In fact close enough that it was undesirable to vector air traffic anywhere to the east of the airport just in case of an international incident. Because of the "history" between these two nations, they are rather sensitive when it comes to border and airspace infringements. The root cause of all this angst...? Religion.

More recently I have noted a few airlines which have not been shy to exhibit their beliefs with religious symbols on their aircraft. One of these was the recently collapsed SkyGreece which had a one aircraft fleet based in Athens. The aircraft a Boeing 767 was named "Taxiarchis" and bore this name proudly on the nose of the fuselage in large letters. Taxiarchis is the Greek name for the Archangel Michael whose home island is reputedly Lesbos (Mitilini). Early in 2014, the airline engaged me to carry out some training of their pilots and to fly a commercial demonstration flight for the local Civil Aviation Authority. Simultaneously, the company required that we fly the aircraft "as close as possible" to the Monastery on Lesbos so the aircraft could receive a blessing from the most senior Holy Man there. Finally when we looked at the charts very closely, it appeared that the monastery was extremely close to Turkish airspace! You can imagine my thoughts as all the foregoing was explained to me during the briefing for the flight, however I do love a challenge and this one was going to hold my full attention.

It started off in the company offices when one of the Airline Directors, a Greek Orthodox Priest, known to all as "Father Nick" gave us (the crew) a blessing prior to setting off for the airport. He also pinned some SkyGreece Wings on my uniform which was when I asked, "Have these Wings been blessed Father?" He replied very casually, "Oh, EVERYTHING'S been blessed James, don't worry about that!" Anyway, to cut a long story short, the Chief Abbot gave his blessing as we did our low flypast of the Monastery balcony, the CAA were happy with the operation and best of all the Turks didn't shoot us down!

*

Returning to our nightflight to Taba in the B757 back in 2006, we had made a point of dimming every light in the flightdeck as we commenced the descent into the desert blackness. The latest Met report gave us 1500m visibility and nil cloud cover. The wind was still 240/15. Taba itself sits on a high plateau which is 2,500 feet above sea level just to make things more interesting. Therefore when descending towards the overhead of the airport, coming in from the North, it was necessary to add this 2,500 feet to the calculations to prevent us getting too low to the terrain. I had made a careful brief of my plan for the approach and emphasised that we should be careful to ensure that at all times we remained well clear of the high ground nearby. Additionally I had drawn a planned visual manoeuvring circuit so that my First Officer would be recognising what I was trying to do.

Because the border was close to the East, it was going to be required to manoeuvre to the West, away from the Israel. That would mean a right-hand descending turn to get us onto finals, which from my point of view (sat in the left-hand seat) was not ideal. Also, the approach lighting for 22R was simply a cross of white lights on short finals for the runway. I briefed that we would descend to be 1,500 feet above the ground as we closed the overhead, which meant that the Barometric altimeters would be reading 4,000 feet, very disconcerting... The other point I briefed was the planned configuration for the aircraft. At the overhead, we would be 'Gear Down, Flap 20' which would give us the slowest speed possible for manoeuvring.

We used the HSI moving map display with a range arc plotted on the border to ensure that we stayed clear of Israel and within Egyptian airspace. Even then it was a bit of shock as we flew slowly over the top of the airport and looked down, it was only just possible to see the lights of the runways, taxiways and apron. I left the autopilot engaged and turned the heading bug on the mode control panel to the right all the way through onto North. The 757 dutifully followed the turn command and I noted 25 degrees of right bank on the EADI. The airspeed was a pleasing 150 knots or so in this configuration which gave a relatively tight radius of turn – we would need it.

We got all the landing checks out of the way early before I turned the heading bug again onto 040, the reciprocal heading and when I judged we were abeam the threshold both visually and on the moving map, I dialled in a very slow rate of descent. Now we could see nothing ahead of us, even though the sky was clear – there are very few lights in the desert. I said in a clear voice, "Technically, we are still visual..." just to assure my FO that I knew it didn't feel good to be descending into what looked like a black hole. To which he replied, "I can still see some lights of the airport out here on the right, just going behind the wing... now".

Well I was glad he could still see something, because from my seat looking out of the front windows, I could see diddly-squat! I checked again the position on the HSI – yes we would be turning onto finals in another five seconds, the clock ticked ever so slowly by... *'Do you know any good prayers...?'* Went through my mind at this point and I was surprised, it was not like me to be either superstitious or religious. *'Give us a sign Lord, GIVE US A SIGN...'* I noted we were coming onto finals at just around 4 miles out and the altimeters showed 3,700 it was time to increase the rate of descent, but not until I could actually see the runway or approach lights... The feeling was tense as he said, "I can't *SEE* anything!" This was not looking good, much more of this and we would be going around...

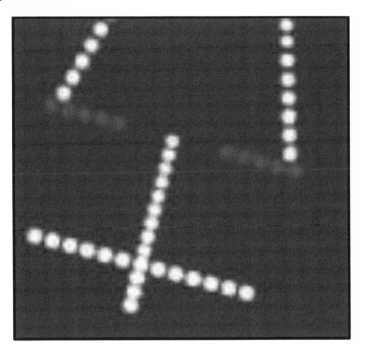

'Give us a sign Lord, GIVE US A SIGN...'

I leaned right forward now and looked upwards through the banked windows of the airliner. All of a sudden I got religion. Or to put it another way, I saw a sign! The sign of a big white lit-up cross pointing towards runway 22R. "Visual! Flap 30, complete the landing checklist!" I nearly shouted with relief. Then I called, "Disconnecting Automatics!" And with a double click I had manual control of the aeroplane, THAT felt good, to have your hands and feet firmly on the controls, to really FLY THE JET – YES!

*

After landing and as we vacated the runway, the words of 'High Flight'*, the poem written by a young WW2 Spitfire Pilot came to mind. I was especially touched by the last three lines of the poem which celebrates the celestial majesty of flight...

"...And while with silent lifting mind I've trod,

The high untrespassed sanctity of space,

Put out my hand, and touched the face of God"

'High Flight' by John Gillespie Magee Jr.

RCAF Spitfire Pilot, died 1941, aged 19.

--0—

28 - CAT'S EYES AND WINKLE

In 2016 our industry lost another hero. Capt Eric "Winkle" Brown (pictured above at Duxford) died at the age of 97 after a short illness. He was the Royal Navy's most highly decorated and distinguished pilot (CBE, DSC, AFC and more) and world record holder in the number of aircraft carrier landings and different types flown by one pilot - 2407 carrier landings and 487 different types.

It was revealed in 2015 that a US Navy pilot had been tasked with beating the record of carrier deck landings, but gave up after 1600 when he suffered some sort of "nervous breakdown". So Capt Brown was pretty special then... Not only was he specially gifted and dedicated to the cause of aviation in general and test flying in particular, he was also self-effacing and modest. Whenever he was asked to talk about his exploits he always focused on the technical aspects and had a tendency to play down the human (heroic) side of things.

*

Notably Eric Brown also had a number of creditable achievements on his extensive CV. He was the first person to land a Jet aircraft on an aircraft carrier on 3rd December 1945 with a De Havilland Sea Vampire. He was also responsible for the post-war test flying of all of the German WW2 aircraft, both fighters and bombers. He even flew the Messerschmitt ME163 Komet – the world's only rocket-powered aircraft to enter active service. This particular mission must have been fraught with danger as the machine had killed many of the pilots who had flown it – some of them being almost completely dissolved in landing accidents by the chemicals used to make the rocket fuel.

Eric "Winkle" Brown – WW2 with Carrier Landing Aircraft

He flew all three of the Nazi's jet powered fighters too and reported on their flying qualities and safety. Finally as if all that was not enough, as a fluent German speaker, he was tasked with interrogating some of the very high ranking German officers still alive at the end of the war. These included Herman Goering, Heinrich Himmler and Josef Kramer, the former commandant of the Belsen concentration camp. He said afterwards that "Herman Goering was quite charismatic", but his opinion of Kramer and his assistant Irma Grese was, "two more loathsome creatures it is hard to imagine".

A charismatic speaker himself, Capt Brown gave a very interesting account of his career to Kirsty Young on the Desert Island Discs programme two years ago. While talking about his flying life he let slip that at times he had occasionally acted irresponsibly mainly it seemed as a result of high spirits. He stated that after he had completed the successful series of carrier deck landings of the Royal Navy Seafire (maritime version of the Spitfire) and was ferrying the aircraft back to base, he saw the Forth Bridge. It was clearly too tempting an opportunity for him, so he proceeded to fly an aerobatic 'loop' through each span of the bridge!

Fortunately for him nobody managed to record the registration of the aircraft (side-number in Fleet Air Arm parlance) and because the Navy did not have any Spitfires at that time, the RAF was blamed for the event. No doubt the senior officers of the light-blue service carried out a fine witch-hunt for the non-existing miscreant!

It appears that Capt Brown kept this particular aviation 'first' to himself for a very long time, only revealing it publicly on national radio for the BBC, whereupon Kirsty Young commented "...they might be still looking for you" to which Capt Brown was most amused. Mind you at the age of 95, at that time he could afford to be relaxed about any potential consequences for his low-level aerobatics from 70 years previously.

That was one of the most remarkable facets of his aviation career; it just seemed to go on and on. Only a few years ago the European Giant, Airbus Industries was consulting with him regarding some finer points of aerodynamics while completing the design of the mighty A380. Down through the past decades, Capt Brown's extensive testflying work could be said to have had a major positive influence on the design of many aircraft including airliners and even passengers today owe him a debt of gratitude.

He had great respect from the other side of the Atlantic and it is understood that he might have even been one of the first astronauts if he had been prepared to change his nationality... To his eternal credit he had 'taken the King's shilling' and therefore decided to keep his British passport.

*

In many ways he had much in common with John "Cat's Eyes" Cunningham, another great British aviator who was from the Great British de Havilland 'school of airmen'. He joined the company as an apprentice aged 18 and then became a test pilot also, but was called up to active service in August 1939. Cunningham was highly decorated throughout an exciting and illustrious career and in much the same way as Eric Brown; he made a huge contribution to the war effort.

His main claim to fame was his skill and ability as a nightfighter ace, which was where he earned his nickname. The term "Cat's Eyes" was a ruse to explain his extraordinary success at shooting down enemy bombers at night – allegedly he had exceptional eyesight. Indeed his eyesight was quite good, but the main reason for his long string of kills was the fact that he was using a top secret invention which vectored his aircraft into the killing zone in complete darkness.

John Cat's Eyes Cunningham - WW2 with Mosquito Nightfighter

That invention was called Radar. At the time the UK government was very keen to prevent news of this being leaked out, so the RAF invented all sorts of stories, such as the nightfighter pilots were all eating lots of carrots which are rich in Vitamin A. Flying Blenheims, Beaufighters and Mosquitoes, Cunningham and his navigator/air gunner had a virtually unbroken record of success against the Luftwaffe bombers at night.

After the Second World War was over, he went back to de Havilland and as their Chief Test Pilot was probably Eric Brown's boss. Cunningham went on to perform the first flights of the new DH Comet in 1949, flying a 'round the world' trip in one during 1955. The Comet was the world's first ever passenger jet. In 1962 he flew the first Trident airliner which in itself was a major advance in airliner design being the first of its breed to be able to conduct automatic landings in fog.

He retired in 1980 and lived quietly in Harpenden, I recall seeing him at the bar of The Fox (his local haunt) sometime in the early '90s when he was pointed out to me with great reverence by my instructor while I was flying Boeing 757s.

He was described as a quiet unassuming man; quite the reverse of whom you might imagine would be an Ace Nightfighter pilot with over 20 confirmed kills during the dark days of a war which at the time looked very bleak for England. So another national aviation hero, he died in 2002 at the age of 84, having enjoyed a remarkable and noteworthy career similar to Eric Brown.

Funnily enough they actually have more in common. Not just their respective employers, (The MOD and de Havilland's), nor even their string of medals. Cunningham was decorated in the service with the DSO (Distinguished Service Order) and two bars and also with the DFC (Distinguished Flying Cross) and bar. The "bar" of course means that the recipient won it a second time – quite extraordinary!

In a similar way to Eric Brown, Cunningham never received a Knighthood. You may wonder why that is important. Well I was reliably informed that some years ago (while Cunningham was still alive) there was a concerted effort by the Guild of Air Pilots to suggest to HM Government that a Knighthood would be an appropriate award for the man's services to aviation. Apparently they made a very good case for the honour to be bestowed, however at the end of the day the members of the Guild were disappointed to be informed that it was "all too long ago now..." Presumably this will have been from a Senior Civil Servant and not the Royal Family.

*

There are parallels with Capt Brown here because even though he, "Winkle" was awarded a CBE and had been Her Majesty's ADC for a period, it was still not *quite* a Knighthood. Knighthood starts at KBE - Knight Commander of the British Empire.

In the opinion of many of us in aviation, Capt Brown should have been able to call himself "Sir Eric" long before he passed away. Certainly it wouldn't have been Sir Winkle! He never really liked that nickname, given to him in the early days of his naval service due to his short stature. Of course it is too late now, both of these heroes who achieved so much on behalf of a great nation are flying in a higher plane, but let us hope that the future work of the honours committee is rather more generous to the aviators.

*

In closing, it was interesting to note that the BBC Radio 4 presenter Kirsty Young, who featured Capt Eric "Winkle" Brown on the 3,000[th] episode of Desert Island Discs, said of him,

"When you read through his life story, it makes James Bond seem like a bit of a slacker..."

Ironically, the actor who played the original James Bond is able to look in the bathroom mirror each morning and call himself, "Sir Sean".

--0--

29 - MAGENTA CHILDREN

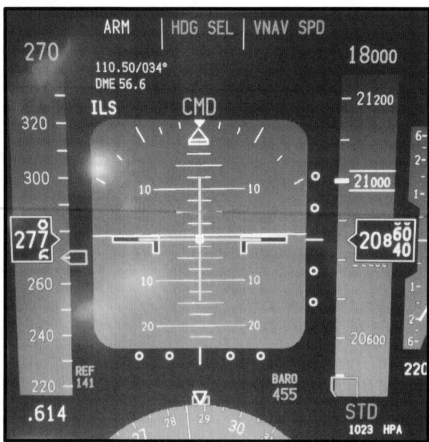

Modern PFD brings with it issues regarding dependency

Back in the mid '90s, American Airlines identified a problem. In 68% of aircraft accidents which they analysed, it was determined that a phenomenon called "Automation Dependency" had played a significant role in leading the professional airline crew "to a critical flight attitude or forcing them to extract maximum performance from their airplanes". It would be true to say that until this discovery was made, it had been assumed that increasing levels of automation in aircraft cockpits over successive decades had lead to enhanced flight safety. This was based on the premise that more automated flight systems reduced pilot workload which resulted in fewer human errors being made.

*

The first real autopilots were fitted as early as 1912 by the Sperry company, although they were little more than devices which could hold an aircraft straight and level in heading and altitude. Lawrence Sperry the inventor, also helped develop the gyro stabilised Artificial Horizon which was the grandfather of the modern Electronic Attitude Director Indicator (EADI***). There were significant advances in the 1950s especially after the great airline PanAm determined that autopilots operated their flights 7% more efficiently than when manually flown by their pilots.

By the time of the 1970s automation had truly come of age with integrated flightdecks whereby advanced automatic pilot systems had been incorporated with Flight Management Computers and Auto Flight Director Systems, which in turn were fed by Inertial Navigation Systems. These INS systems themselves were pretty advanced for their time, benefiting from the laser ring gyro technology of the NASA space missions. As Charles Draper* (Father of inertial navigation) referred to them at the time, they were examples of "astronomy in a closet", which very neatly describes Astronav in a box.

Now we entered the '80s and the introduction of even more automation – this time from the centre of Europe. In the words of the Engineering Vice President for Airbus Bernard Ziegler, "I am building an aeroplane that even my concierge would be able to fly!" We should assume that Mr Ziegler was resident in serviced apartments at the time and hope that his concierge was not offended by the remark.

The major development he was referring to of course was 'Fly-By-Wire'; a computer system so advanced that it actually senses and anticipates what a pilot wants to do with the aircraft, then smoothly and safely executes the manoeuvre. One of the major claims for this design breakthrough was that it would not be possible for a pilot to stall the airliner. So called 'Alpha Floor protection'** would prevent a pilot from exceeding 'critical angle of attack' for any phase of flight. See below the relevant part of Normal Law for Airbus;

"Alpha Max will not be exceeded even if the pilot applies full aft deflection" (of the sidestick).

That was not all though. There were many protection features built into the Airbus computer system which covered attitude, speed, low energy etc. and all were designed to keep the aircraft safely inside the flight envelope at all times. Significantly the FBW system was designed such that unlike an autopilot it cannot be turned on and off by the pilots, but it can turn itself off...

...and when THAT happens, what? Well the Airbus people are pretty smart and in their design criteria they tried to cover every contingency. They actually created a set of Flight Control 'Laws' which govern what parts of the flight envelope is being protected and controlled. Let's simplify here because the entire package is rather more than can be adequately covered in one article. Basically 'Normal Law' is the usual computer mode that is used to operate flights, but this degrades to 'Alternate Law' when "multiple failures of redundant systems occur".

Then there is 'Abnormal Alternate Law' which is only activated when the "aircraft enters an unusual attitude allowing recovery from the unusual attitude"... Note these are not my descriptions; these are direct from the manufacturer. Finally there is 'Direct Law' (pilots have direct control over the aeroplane) and one last level called rather bluntly 'Mechanical Backup' - to cover the complete loss of all electrics. Bear in mind that I have summarised very briefly an incredibly complex set of protocols and integrated functions of the Airbus FBW system. Despite all the complexity remember it was designed with the laudable aim of making flying safer.

So much for technological progress, but there was always going to be one big factor to consider. The system operators, the pilots; members of the Homo sapiens species. Bear in mind that human anatomy and physiology has hardly changed at all in the last few millennia! True we have invented plenty of stuff and the way in which we live on the planet has evolved to such a degree that we consider ourselves very sophisticated, but we are still just 'Primates with shoes'.

Now we come to the Automation Paradox, which states that "...the more efficient the automated system, the more crucial the human contribution of the operators. Humans are less involved, but their involvement becomes more critical". It is a well defined phenomenon and the consequences are not limited to aviation.

*

Sadly aviation history is littered with examples of Automation Paradox, one of which could be considered to be the loss of Air France flight 447 in May 2009 over the South Atlantic. As in all aviation accidents, there was not one single cause, but a chain of events which lead to the final result. However one of the significant links in the error chain was the fact that "the pilots never recognised that they were in a stalled aeroplane".

It took 4 minutes and 20 seconds for the airliner to hit the ocean from cruise altitude – regardless of the initial failure (icing of the pitot tubes) there was 'mode confusion' on the part of the Pilot Flying which was held to be mainly responsible. The really weird thing is that this accident happened nine years AFTER Capt Warren VanderBurgh; a senior Training Captain with American Airlines gave his series of lectures entitled "Children of the Magenta".

In these very graphic presentations Capt VanderBurgh described in great detail some of the challenges which confront pilots when dealing with levels of automation while operating their airplanes. Basically he states that there are three levels of Automation flying airplanes. The fully automatic state where LNAV (lateral path) and VNAV (vertical path) computer modes are engaged with the autopilot to operate all systems; then the direct Autopilot MCP (Mode Control Panel) level where the pilots make selected changes via a direct interface to operate the aircraft and finally the old fashioned "Click, Click" (sound of autopilot and autothrottle being disconnected) where the PF takes direct control of the flightpath through the flying controls and manual throttles.

Capt VanderBurgh's contention is that there are too many times when pilots allow the aircraft flight path to deteriorate in automatic flight before they take direct control. Indeed he states that in many cases choosing the wrong level of automation actually *Increases workload* – sometimes to the point of loss of control. He observed that our industry had trained pilots this way (to increasingly rely upon automation) and he has an endearing way of explaining this to his audience of professional pilots. "We MADE you!" he says pausing for effect, "You are CHILDREN OF THE MAGENTA!"

*

What is significant about the colour Magenta? Well it was chosen by the instrument designers in the early days of glass cockpit development as a good colour for AFDS (Auto Flight Director System) Command (CMD) information to be displayed on the TV screens (EADI and EHSI) for the pilots to follow. Red was used traditionally for warning information; Amber was caution, Blue for ancillary/location, Green for radio beacons etc. So they chose Magenta. Think of Magenta as being "Mildly Attention Grabbing" and then you can see the logic.

The phenomenon is not limited to Airbus either; there have been many instances where over-reliance upon automation has trapped Boeing pilots too. Think of the Turkish Airlines B737-800 which crashed short of the runway going into Schiphol when the autothrottle system failed and the speed came all the way back... 80 knots at 400 feet was too slow to recover.

Then there was the Asiana Boeing 777 into San Francisco in early 2013 on a Visual approach. It landed short, onto the seawall in the undershoot of the runway. In the accident report, it stated that in the final 2 minutes and 30 seconds of the flight "there were multiple autopilot modes and autothrottle mode selections made..." If only those pilots had attended Warren VanderBurgh's lecture? There is no excuse for crashing a perfectly serviceable airliner into the ground visually on a clear day with calm winds. Click, Click, take control!

*

I am reminded of the old story of the RAF Canberra taking off at very heavyweight from Gibraltar back in the 1970's.

The Canberra bomber was never famous for its single engine performance when one of the engines failed. On this day, the crew experienced an engine failure on takeoff and to the Air Traffic Controller's horror, disappeared from sight off the cliff-end of the runway – he hit the crash alarm in the Tower.

A couple of minutes later, the aircraft was visible again struggling to gain altitude away from the sea and a rather breathless pilot made the radio transmission, *"Okay God.... I have control now!"*

*

Charles (Doc) Draper; Founder and Director of Massachusetts Institute of Technology's Instrumentation Laboratory.

** Alpha, or Angle of Attack (AOA) is the angle between the oncoming air or relative wind and a reference line on the airplane or wing. AOA is sometimes confused with pitch angle or flight path angle. Pitch Angle (attitude) is the angle between the longitudinal axis (where the airplane is pointed and the horizon. This angle is displayed on the attitude indicator or artificial horizon. (Courtesy of the Boeing Airplane Co.)

*** EADI itself transformed into the more modern Primary Flight Display as shown in the leading photograph

--O--

30 - GREEKS PROGRESS

Connie at Athens Airport - 1948

It was only recently while flying in Greek airspace, that it really came home to me how much progress has been made in aviation terms here these past three decades. Is it really that long? Well, yes; unfortunately it is. The beauty of a pilot's flying logbook is that everything gets recorded. I can see that it was 27 years ago almost to the day when I landed in 'Rhodos Paradisi' airport as a very green First Officer on a Boeing 757 with a visual approach from Manchester. (G-OOOC with Captain Bob Garlick) Of course that was in the day when the island of Rhodes' airport was actually called "Paradisi" - a lovely name for an airport.

It all changed in the early 90's when overnight it seemed that all airports in Greece were "Renamed after dead Greek Generals" – according to one of the more cynical 757 Captains I flew with. In reality the government had enacted a policy of renaming all the country's airfields after historical national heroes.

*

This is not a new phenomenon of course, just think of 'JFK' in the USA and you get the idea, but I recall flying the next day when there was a certain amount of chaos on the radio. It appeared that the UK Charter 767 descending into Corfu on the first morning after the renaming had not fully understood the Notams (Notices to Airmen). In our B757 flightdeck behind them, we heard the pilot calling several times "KERKYRA Approach, this is Britannia 123, we are 30 DME inbound to KRK VOR" – no answer. Finally a very irate Greek controller transmitted with "Britannia 123, this is IOANNIS KAPODISTRIAS APPROACH, our airport has a new name now and the callsign has changed".

Well there was a fair amount of farce for a few days until we all got used to it and it provided not a little entertainment at the start of an otherwise busy charter holiday summer season. Not all of the new names were well received by the crews however. For example poor old 'Heraklion' airport on the Island of Crete, was now to be known as "Nikos Kazantzakis" – which is almost as much of a mouthful for our Northern European radio voices as Kapodistrias. It was such a shame for us Manchester based crews, who used to talk in terms of having a "Harry Kline" on the roster, or in response to the question in the crewroom, "Where to tonight?" we could reply with *"Eric the Lion!"* and a big grin.

*

The serious stuff was interesting though. We would wonder about operating our brand new Boeing 757s with three autopilots, triple ILS and state of the art Autoland systems all the way to the eastern end of the Mediterranean to carry out an NDB descent to a VISUAL approach at night! In those days of course there was hardly any radar coverage throughout Greece and all of the airways were 'procedural'. The night-skies were full of R/T transmissions with DME readings inbound and outbound from significant beacons. It is incredible to imagine now, but in those months of busy rosters with many flights to Greece and Turkey, we were not blessed with GPWS and TCAS systems. Often we would use the Weather Radar at cruise altitude on the airways to establish distances behind other airliners – an unapproved method of course, but it helped with situational awareness. Additionally it was very much accepted practice to flash the landing lights at night between aircraft on the airways when coming head to head.

Instrument approach aids were few and far between. There was no chance of using our triple IRS (Inertial Reference System) for IMC approaches – it might have been accurate enough to cross the Atlantic, but LNAV precision approaches came much later. Raw data was the order of the day and the flightdeck stopwatch was used in conjunction with DME information to time "Base Turn Procedures" etc.

Who has done one of those recently? Non-Directional Beacons (NDBs) combined with the onboard ADF equipment, meant that we were "pushing the head and pulling the tail" round the skies to manoeuvre our ships onto finals for landing, often with minimal runway approach lighting. The "Mark One Eyeball" was an essential element of all of this naturally. It is worth remembering that there were only 2 ILSs in Greece at that time and they were both at Athens!

Of course that was Ellinikon Airport at Athens (LGAT) which had first opened for operations back in 1938. When I look now at the surrounding area of Glyfada (downtown suburbs of Athens) I find it hard to believe that we made all that noise flying airliners in and out of there for so long. We were still operating in and out of Ellinikon up to the Athens Olympics of 2004. I have vivid memories of turning and descending over Aegina Island (and NDB) on a clear night, before guiding the Boeing onto finals for runway 33.

The lights of the hotels and apartment blocks in Voula/Glyfada seemed to float past the cockpit windows as we arrived with screaming jet engines onto short finals. Operations at the original Athens International Airport were always a challenge. The Jeppesen charts were quite specific about the early left turn (300 feet) over the sea after takeoff from runway 33, *even in the event of engine failure on takeoff!* This was not only to protect the residents from noise pollution, but more importantly perhaps to prevent damage to the ancient monuments of the City of the Gods. The Parthenon on top of Acropolis hill had an exclusion zone round it from ground level up to I think it was 8,000 feet from memory, but it may have been more.

*

Refuelling with passengers onboard was also problematic at LGAT. I recall that when we decided to refuel the B737 in 1998 at night with passengers already on the aircraft, the ATC controller made a big song and dance about having to call out "The big fire extinguisher..." Similarly at the outlying island stations, there were problems with facilities. For example when they first opened Kefallinia to large airliner ops (B757), in the early nineties, there were no large airliner steps available. The week before we arrived with the 757 some poor airport employees were tasked to drive a set of mobile aircraft steps from Athens airport all the way down through Greece at a steady 40 kph – the mission took three days!

And just down the road on the island of Zante (Zakinthos Airport) things were not going swimmingly either. For a start, they only had a 30 metre wide runway with pretty minimal (inadequate?) lighting which would most likely not be acceptable these days. This was designated a 'Cat C' airport, and was restricted to "Captains Only" landings and takeoffs. At one point their limited resources were exposed by the lack of a serviceable Ground

Power Unit (GPU) to provide electrics.

When we arrived with a 757 from Gatwick one starry night carrying a defect which would normally be acceptable at most other airports (Inoperative APU) there was a serious issue. We had to keep the right engine running at idle power on that tiny apron while we offloaded passengers and boarded the new ones again on the left side of the aircraft. When that was complete, we closed up the left doors, removed steps, started the left engine and then shutdown the right engine to change the baggage over and refuel... It all seemed to take hours and by the time we were airborne again on our way home, the crew was exhausted.

*

The advent of TCAS and perhaps more importantly Secondary Radar with ground based controllers providing separation based upon transponder information has been a great step towards improved flight safety. These days it is almost impossible to recognise 'Old Greece' in regular airline operations. Operational Risk Areas such as lack of aircraft handling equipment, poor airfield lighting maintenance, inadequate paved surfaces and sub-standard ATC are things of the past. It is reassuring to note that commercial air operations throughout Greek airspace are at the same level as the most developed nations of Europe. Precision airfield approach systems (ILS) are commonplace, although it is fair to say that the advances in GPS based LNAV precision approaches for use in IMC have also been beneficial in providing a greater level of safety margin.

Summer 2016 is bringing new operators, travellers and holidaymakers to Greece. Despite all the economic ordeals which this incredible "country of a thousand islands" has had to face, it is still optimistic about the future and tourism. Most of that holiday trade will be arriving and departing by air of course in a huge aerial industry which is safer than ever. Even in the middle of a busy summer schedule it is apparent that hard working colleagues can keep their sense of humour. One of my favourite anecdotes was when I heard a UK bound charter flight on the ramp at Heraklion Airport in the old days; call the tower on the radio for engine start clearance. "Heraklion Tower, *Calamari*, this is Dan-Air 123 requesting start for London Gatwick..." In our cockpit we stopped what we were doing and listened intently as we realised he had just mistakenly used the Greek word for Squid! (What he meant to say was *Kalimera* - Good day). With hardly any hesitation and without any hint of a smile in his voice, the controller replied with "*Calamari* Dan-Air 123! Clear to start engines, call ready for taxi". We were still chuckling about this over an hour later as we passed the FIR boundary at cruise altitude on our way home.

*

PS. *Rhodos Paradisi airport became Rhodos Diagoras. He was an ancient, famous Greek boxer from 5th Century BC.*

Ultramodern 'new' Athens International Airport opened 2001

--0--

31 - APPROXIMATIONS AND ABBREVIATIONS

It is strange that a field as scientific and precise as aviation should be treated so casually by some of its proponents – perhaps I should explain. An example is when learning to fly as a pilot in the very early days and it is not easy for the instructor to convey how much to deflect the flying controls. In fact the very first lesson of the pilot's syllabus is 'Effects of Controls'.

"How far do I move it?" asks the student referring to the control column and looking for guidance to how much deflection is required. The response from the instructor is often, "...well, not a lot... Just a *Bit*. Think of light pressures on the stick..."

Then when trying to fly straight and level the student queries "...how much lower the nose of the aircraft has to be, compared to the horizon to maintain level flight at this power setting and speed?"

"Well – just a *Tad*" replies the instructor.

"A 'Tad'? What's a 'Tad'?" I remember asking in my own case while trying to fly a Cessna 152 all those years ago. To which the response from the other seat was,

"Well you know... it's in-between a *'Bit'* and a *'Smidgeon'*..." he thought for a moment and then said "...in fact it is almost exactly *half a 'Smidgeon'!"* he pronounced and sat there with a huge grin, very pleased with himself. I remember shaking my head, confused and thinking, there's more to this flying lark than I thought....

*

Later, much later, in my career I was still coming across these wonderful approximations and vague descriptions in abundance.

In fact I was often using them myself for example trying to describe to a trainee how much rudder application to use in the case of an engine failure on takeoff on a large twin-jet airliner. "Well just stick a *bootful* of rudder in..." I caught myself saying on one occasion. "Try a *handful* of throttle...", "...yes, think in terms of *big-handfuls*..." (of whatever is necessary to get the desired response from the aircraft) In reality of course these vague descriptions and casual expressions are helpful to the student when trying to master the art of aviation because they tend to de-mystify the science, making it less intimidating and easier to grasp.

What it says to the trainee, is that 'really anybody can do it, (fly planes) have *confidence*; be *diligent* in your studies; *practice* profusely and you will perfect it'. It is a form of dumbing down and a good one, because some of the stuff which you have to learn is quite daunting and not a little stressful. Too much stress is an acknowledged barrier to learning, so the addition of humorous phrases and expressions helps to take the tension out of the situation.

Flying Instructors / Training Captains will suggest using "a *couple* of percent" of power on the N1 gauge or "a *few* more Revs" on the RPM gauge and what they are effectively teaching the student to do here is to find the exact power setting needed by trial and error. Interestingly "A couple" is quite well defined as being an expression for the number two, but a few is less exact, "A small number" is how the dictionary describes it. In my mind it equates to around 3. I suppose "a handful" would be 5 – as in fingers and thumb, but I digress...

Of course as we know, errors are an important part of the learning process. We have to be able to allow the trainee to make their own errors, encourage them to recognise and correct them so that they can perfect the required technique for whatever it is they are trying to achieve. Of course of all this 'casual-professionalism', has a time and a place. I recall some illustrative anecdotes from the early days when under training in the Royal Navy. No better place to learn the finer points of professional aviation.

You can imagine the scene on an exercise out at sea and a naval fighter jet shot over the bows of a warship in a crescendo of jet noise The First Lieutenant leaning from the bridge wing, shouted down to the young Midshipman on the foredeck, "MISTER _____WHAT THE FUCK WAS THAT!?" to which came the almost immediate shout from the quick thinking junior;

"IT WAS...... T.F.F.T.B.R. SIR!" to which the senior officer, looking puzzled hailed back, "WHAAAT...?" and the Midshipman explained *Too Fucking Fast To Be Recognised Sir!"* much to the appreciation of the watching sailors, however the First Lieutenant was less amused.

"MISTER _____ REPORT TO THE BRIDGE IMMEDIATELY!"

*

Similarly another junior officer under-training made a miscalculation regarding the appropriate time and place for a humorous response during the anchoring of a warship in a remote bay. Needless to say the Navy takes these things rather seriously; in fact almost without fail any Captain whose ship runs aground loses their Command with immediate effect. They can be tense times as the depth of water reduces in the shallows and without exception the Master and Commander will be on the bridge.

Of course in the days before GPS, navigating was quite a tricky business and the Junior Officers would be tasked with taking sighting bearings from the large compasses on the bridge wings of landmarks, then transferring those bearings onto the chart to fix the position of the anchorage exactly.

Pity the poor Midshipman who misjudged the seriousness of the situation when asked by his Captain, "How would you describe the position Mister _____, shall we drop anchor?" to which he replied brightly, "BHD SIR!" The Captain, unfamiliar with the three letter abbreviation asked for clarification, to which the hapless Mid responded cheerily, "'Bout Here'll Do...!" There was complete silence from the other officers and ratings, before the furious Captain ordered him "......*OFF THE BRIDGE SIR!*"

*

In flying we need to focus on what is important - hence the use of 'big-handfuls' etc to make sure that we "do not sweat the small stuff". In armed forces flying training especially they are experts at verbalising the philosophy when describing "Flight Lieutenant X has a good grip on the trivia!" or "Flying Officer Y is too focussed on the niff-naff!"

Of course there are times when precision is essential and part of the rules of the game is learning which pieces of information are vital to the operation. Prioritising and Airmanship are very valuable skills to learn as a pilot and they do not come easily. With experience and the positive development of your professional Situational Awareness (SA) the whole thing starts to come naturally.

I recall when I was a junior First Officer. I used to be a little bit in awe of the Airline Captains I flew with who would breeze into crew briefing only a few minutes before 'Report Time' for duty, have a quick scan of the weather / Notams, then after deciding on the fuel to be carried look at me and smile, with "Shall We... go and *commit aviation* then?"

There was something so immensely reassuring about flying with an experienced Captain whose demeanour was completely unruffled by all of the scientific processes involved in getting a large jet transport safely from A to B. He/she knows the key performance indicators required which assure the safety margins of the operation and they communicate that confidence in their abilities to the rest of the crew in subtle ways.

Military pilots soon learn to use approximations and simple maths to perform Gross Error Checks on all that comes their way. For example 420 knots at low level becomes "7 miles a minute". They use "Maximum Drift" method to determine the required heading for each leg of the flight according to the wind blowing across the planned track.

The maximum drift is dead easy to calculate as it consists of dividing the reported windspeed by the True Air Speed (TAS) in NM/minute. So for example a 30 knot wind enroute at low level would equate to just over 4° of maximum drift at 7nm/min.

If the wind is completely across track then all of the Max Drift is applied, but if it is less than 90 degrees then an approximation is made which results in heading to apply to achieve Track Made Good (TMG). Imagine a clock face with a 60° angle as being the 12 o'clock position, so 30° becomes HALF the drift to apply, 15° a QUARTER etc.

In practice it is remarkably accurate and of course the faster the aircraft, the less the drift – brilliant! The philosophy of these low level military aviators is that they like to keep things as simple possible so they can focus on the really important parts of the task – like hitting the target for example.

I remember seeing a wall plaque on the crewroom wall of an RAF base back in the 1980s. It had been donated there as a thank-you from a USMC officer who had been posted there to learn to fly the single-seat Harrier jumpjet. The BAe Harrier was a particularly tricky fighter to master. The advice which he had inscribed on the plaque ended with the catchy slogan, "At the end of the day – just *Strap it your Ass and give it your best shot!*"

In the UK we might say something like, Aviate; Navigate; Communicate, to convey the priorities for flight. Our American cousins have a more colourful way to describe prioritising though. There is the very famous quotation which goes something like....

"However, when you are up to your ass in alligators, it is difficult to remember that your original objective was to drain the swamp."

--O--

32 - SMASHING BUGS

There is nothing worse than flying with a dirty windscreen

"I think... we killed *something* during that approach..." the First Officer's voice was hesitant, unsure as he entered the flightdeck. He had just carried out the external walkround check of the airliner and was not sure how to verbalise what he had found. It was new territory for him. I replied, "Oh really? A big *something* or a small *something*?"

"Well, I think you had better come and look at it Captain". His use of the formal address had my full attention now, not often we hear that these days to be sure, plus there was obviously something to look at. As I passed through the forward galley heading for the steps down to the ramp, the Senior Cabin Manager raised an eyebrow, perceptive as always, she knew something was up. "Shall I delay the passenger boarding Captain...?"

Hmmm... Another one? I thought to myself, how odd. They recognise and respect the 'Chain of Command' immediately when something goes awry and the mood becomes serious - testament to their quality training. I thought about it briefly and said, "No Sandra, please board the pax as normal, I'll let you know what's going on in a minute". *Why delay passenger boarding just because we have committed a small murder?* I had already reasoned that it would not have been a large murder because I would have known about it. I headed off down the steps quickly following the First Officer...

There are a few things which I am quite proud of in my three plus decades operating flying machines for a living. One of them is I can honestly say that I have never, ever, asked an engineer to clean the windscreen of an aeroplane for me. Now I know that maybe this is a small thing in many people's minds, but you would be surprised how often the windscreen needs cleaning. During the summer and/or when operating flights into and out of hot climates there are loads of bugs which get smashed to a blurry mess on the outside of the front windscreens.

Bear in mind that this piece of 4cm thick laminated, armour-plated glass is an essential piece of equipment. It is guaranteed to withstand a frozen Turkey fired directly at it at 300 plus knots... allegedly. When we make our next instrument approach in poor visibility, breaking out of cloud quite low, maybe at night, to land on a runway where the lighting is not of the best quality, then we really need every factor on our side. *Knowing* that at least the glass we are looking through is clear is a basic element and one less thing to worry about.

Naturally I do understand some of my flightdeck colleagues who might want to have the windscreen cleaned by an engineer. I appreciate the principle that it is a vital part of the airframe and therefore the onus of upkeep is on the maintainers... That being said I learned early on in my airline career that waiting for an engineer to turn up with cleaning kit for the windscreen can take a long time. Of course when they do arrive, they will need the pilot to get out of his/her seat anyway to access the side DV (Direct Vision) window and then lean out round the front of the nose of the aircraft to perform the washing.

Indeed it can be a bit of palaver. Many years ago I flew with an ex-Military pilot; (John Knowles) at that time one of the youngest B757 Captains in our airline, possibly the UK. He was a smart guy and I observed his Modus Operandi like the proverbial Hawk. One day I would be like him, I thought...

It was during the pre-flight checks when we readying the ship for flight and suddenly he looked up – his windscreen was dirty - a combination of flying insect debris and accumulated sand/dust. "Hang on a minute..." he said as he left the flightdeck and went to the forward Lav. He came back with two hands full of paper towels, one wet with liquid soap on it and the other dry. With a practised movement, he slid the heavy DV window back and extended his upper body out of it.

Now leaning right round the outside of the cockpit windows, with what my father would have described as "a boarding house reach" he washed and dried every square centimetre of glass. Returning inside he did the same. He had the DV window closed and the job done in less than 60 seconds – I was very impressed and remember it still.

In my own case I have to be careful not to look down when I lean out of the DV window of the airliner to reach the front corner of the windscreen – I can't stand heights you see. This is not uncommon among pilots although not a factor when flying. However if I'm on the top of a tall building, tower, cliff or just leaning out of a window 10m above the ground... Yuk! So in the jet I hang on to the interior handle and I never let go while I wash off the bugs.

Suffice to say I always fly with a clean windscreen. One of the reasons for this is to ensure that everything is visible from the flightdeck during the *Takeoff* roll, so that you can decide whether to stop or continue. Rejected takeoffs are not common, however the actual decision to abandon the takeoff and stop on the runway before V1* (speed) is a very serious one. The reasoning is that at some moment in time during every airliner takeoff, there is a point at which we are committed to fly - that is at (or beyond) V1.

In fact every airline company has a pre-takeoff emergency briefing between the flightdeck crew, just to ensure that they/we are all of the same mind when it comes to making the decision to stop. Not only does the brief consider all the possible reasons for stopping, but it is even specific regarding the precise actions for the pilot responsible for stopping the jet.

*

In various parts of the world the takeoff emergency briefing incorporates local threats. For example at many coastal or island airports there are often large concentrations of birds which can be a real hazard to fast moving aircraft, landing or taking off. I recall being briefed by my Captain many years ago for a night takeoff from Cairo where we had refuelled enroute from Africa heading back to the UK. He said "During the takeoff roll, IF, before V1, we see a CAMEL on the runway, we will stop, but if it's something as small as a dog we will keep going!" At that time the perimeter fence for the airport was not secure and there had been instances of stray Camels wandering on to the airfield manoeuvring area...

Naturally to hit half a tonne of Camel at speed with a jet airliner could cause a lot of damage — and not just to the poor beast! I've never forgotten that one and even now at certain minor airfields on Greek islands I include Donkeys and Dogs in my brief of threats. I have witnessed many dogs on taxiways and even crossing runways, but no Donkeys yet. We did see a Fox quite recently at Athens International, he/she was on the Alpha taxiway, and it was shortly after dawn. The other Captain I was flying with said, "Shall we report it to ATC on the radio?" I replied, "It's up to you mate. There is not much of a safety issue considering our gross weight is 65 tonnes and it's one small animal..."

He thought for a moment, and then said, "No you're right. If we tell Air Traffic Control 'there is a fox', they will come and shoot it won't they...?"

I continued taxying the airliner for takeoff and we were both quiet for a few seconds, then I said;

"What fox...?"

But there are some incidents which really are unavoidable and these are usually Birdstrikes. Similar to how it is when you drive your car and you see an animal, cat, bird, rabbit crossing the road in front of you, it is often impossible to take avoiding action quick enough to prevent the collision. In reality we rarely see the things we hit anyway, although sometimes we see near misses. Like the very lucky seagull which went past the flightdeck windows on my side very recently while we doing around 200 knots coming on to final approach at 3000 feet above the ground.

I just had a fleeting glimpse as it wheeled away from us to the left and shot past the windscreen. "Stupid bird!" I said, "there's no food up here what on earth is it doing flying THIS high?" To which my First Officer said , "It's probably Jonathan Livingston... doing a flight-test!" we laughed at the absurdity and continued with an uneventful approach and landing.

This brings us back to the witness mark under the starboard wing, on the Krueger flap just inboard of the right engine, which was discovered by the FO. We had landed at close to dusk, neither of us had seen or felt anything, but there it was, definitely a Birdstrike.

From what I could see, there was no damage and no other marks to indicate that this was anything other than a single bird. Also from the angle of the deployed flap during approach, the bird remains would have bounced over the top of the wing and away into the slipstream.

Birdstrike witness mark under starboard wing

"Call the engineers please and board the passengers for the return flight" I said to the handling agent and Sandra.

I reasoned that the engineering inspection would not take long and once complete and the Techlog signed off we would be on our way again pronto. There was nil damage and the paintwork was cleaned, very shortly afterwards we were airborne and back on schedule.

*V1 - The speed beyond which the takeoff should no longer be aborted.

--0—

33 - PERIPHERAL VISION

"Those old guys... they don't miss a trick!"   ;-)

I suppose it is a given that pilots should have good eyesight. In fact not so long ago, any applicant for a pilot role in military aviation with anything less than 20/20 vision would have been rejected. Nowadays things have changed a lot and provided corrective lenses are worn while flying, certain visual defects are accepted.

A part of the optical function which is regularly checked at recurrent medicals is peripheral vision. Often we take this for granted – after all it's not much use to us while flying on instruments or searching for conflicting traffic in the skies. In these situations we are utilising core vision which is based upon the macula part of the retina.

Recently I have been thinking that we should pay more attention to the benefits which our peripheral vision gives us. How many times have we heard "He must have eyes in the back of his head..." or, "...that one doesn't miss a trick..."?

Bear in mind that for most of our working life we are sat alongside our working partner such that actual eye to eye contact is brief and infrequent. It is not surprising then that we should receive a higher percentage of information through our peripheral vision than in other occupations.

On more than one occasion in my career have I noted that my co-pilot has placed his/her hands on the control column wheel on their side while I have been 'Pilot Flying' – this is a real no-no because the role of PF and PM (Pilot Monitoring) are very clearly defined. When this happens I usually say to them very clearly, using their name and in a loud voice such that I am not misunderstood "_____take your hands OFF THE CONTROLS!"

On the modern airliner only one pilot shall have their hands on the flying controls at any one time – if it's not you, then keep them away. A good place is on your knees during times of high workload or a critical flight phase such as takeoff or landing. That way the other pilot can 'see' them easily and is in no doubt about where they are. In extremis and if PF were to suffer a sudden collapse during takeoff for example (we train for this eventuality in the Simulator), then having your hands close to the controls will reduce the time it takes to get on them.

From the new First Officer's point of view it can also be quite distracting if the Captain has their hands 'hovering' over the control wheel on their side while the FO is doing the landing or takeoff. Again the proper place for the Captain's hands is on their knees, (palms down) unless they are required to move switches and/or levers as PM. At the direction of the PF they will need to raise the landing gear and flaps just after takeoff.

My reference to 'the modern airliner' above confirms that in olden days, things may indeed have been different. Fortunately for me I did not have the opportunity (?) to experience flying an airliner with controls so heavy that the combined force of both pilots was required to operate the aircraft in certain situations – hydraulic failure for example where manual reversion (mechanical control) is possible. I have trained pilots whose previous type was like this – usually Russian aircraft like the Tupolev 154.

These guys were amazed when they got on the Boeing 757 and 767 because all of a sudden they found that it was possible for the aircraft to be flown by 'just one pilot' at all times. In fact, the whole philosophy of the Boeing is that it can be flown by one pilot because now there are only two people in the flightdeck. In the TU154 there used to be a flightdeck crew of 5... Can you imagine it?

There were the two pilots of course (Captain and FO), the Flight

Engineer, the Navigator AND the Radio Operator. No wonder that when these former Tupolev aviators came on to the Boeing it was an uphill struggle for them to cast off their previous routines and responses.

There were many times when I had to 'freeze' the simulator and say "STOP GUYS! Wait a minute. *WHAT* are you doing...?" and this was because PM would inadvertently be trying to fly the aircraft on their side also! Both of them would look back at me sheepishly and very slowly the PM would take his hands off the controls nodding as he understood my words;

"GUYS! This AIRPLANE was *DESIGNED* to be simple enough for ONE pilot to operate... Remember, it was built for *AMERICANS* to fly!" This would always produce huge guffaws of laughter from both of my Russian trainees and they would learn the lesson well.

Not just in the cockpit of course, but also outside while doing the refuelling or external inspection of the aircraft on the ramp, peripheral vision can be extremely useful.

Several times I have avoided being in collision with a moving object outside the aircraft – either a moving baggage truck, ramp tractor or even a suitcase dropping from the baggage belt going into the hold.

Each time I have noted the movement out of 'the corner of my eye' and my resultant physical reaction saved me from injury. These days of course there is less chance of being hit by a baggage truck because of the high-vis waistcoats which we are required to wear.

A fact worth bearing in mind is that although focus and detail are largely irrelevant when talking about peripheral vision, it is movement which is picked up most easily. This would explain how an experienced Captain sitting quietly in his/her seat on the left-hand side of the cockpit can almost sense what is going through the mind of their much junior trainee on the right. Just by being aware of the First Officer's body language and movements they can predict with confidence what they are likely to do next.

For example there have been occasions when I have been acting as PM and noted that the PF is operating the aircraft through the autopilot, but NOT following through on the flying controls on their side. This is not a good practice as in the (rare) event that the automatics should fail, they (as PF) need to be able to take control of the flightpath immediately.

In fact there have been a few times when the FO has been sat there, turning on to final approach with their feet flat on the floor... Again I have picked this up out of the corner of my eye.

If we suffer an engine failure, one of the first indicators could be that the rudder pedals will move independently as the automatics try to compensate for the asymmetric thrust. Not to have this possible alert is simple ignorance, notwithstanding the fact that the PF should at all times be ready to take over rudder inputs in the case of AP failure.

*

Recently I had a flight where there was a technical failure which alerted us via the 'Master Caution' system – it was in the cruise at 34,000 feet, just before the 'top of descent' point. When we looked up at the overhead panel we could see the 'WING-BODY OVERHEAT' caption illuminated on the right-hand side – implying that there was some form of hot air duct leak from the right engine bleed system.

As PF I said to my colleague, "Okay, I have the radio – action the QRH Non-normal checklist please".

He opened the pages of the Quick Reference Handbook and started to read aloud in a steady, clear, measured voice – just as he had been taught. "Switch OFF the associated Pack Switch" he said, and although I was looking forward, flying the jet, I peripherally saw his hand moving upwards... "WAIT PLEASE!" I called to him just as he got to the Air-conditioning Pack Switch – he stopped.

"CONFIRM the RIGHT Pack Switch...?"

I continued, "...let us VERIFY before you move it..." and he nodded, saying "CONFIRM right Pack Switch...?" I turned and smiled at him, "Yes. CONFIRMED!" and he proceeded to carry out the remainder of the non-normal checklist faultlessly. We reviewed the situation using the company recommended decision making protocol and determined that we would be best continuing to land at planned destination.

*

The rest of the flight was uneventful and as we taxied in after landing we debated whether the engineers would be able to fix the problem during our turnround; or not.... which might.... *just might*, result in our being 'out of hours' to fly the next two sectors of our duty to Rome and back. It was possible we could get an early dart... excellent!

One phonecall to Maintrol however was enough to convince me that we had been wishful thinking. "No problem Captain. We will defer it and according to the MEL we can file you a flightplan at Flight Level 250 for Rome and back!" the voice on the other end of the phone said brightly. Out of the corner of my eye I saw the FO looking at me with his head inclined interested to know if we were going home now (peripheral vision again).

His face fell as I shook my head and said, "No mate. The show must go on I'm afraid. Start the refuelling, but HOLD the fuel truck; we will need more gas to fly the route at FL250".

*

1) Peripheral Vision definition – "all that is visible to the eye outside the central area of focus; side vision"
2) MEL = Minimum Equipment List – refers to all items of the aircraft which are necessary for flight. Some defects can be deferred to a later time to be fixed...WING-BODY OVHT is one of them!

--0--

34 - **S**ELLING **O**URSELVES **S**HORT

An SOS for airline pilots?

It is true that we live in an ever changing world. One where the assumptions of the past, fail to live up to the reality of today. Take pilotless planes for example. It seems like only yesterday that some pundits in the aviation industry were predicting that the continuing development of unmanned air vehicles (UAVs) would lead the way to airliners which could fly their passengers across great distances without any pilots being onboard at all. There were some of us sceptics who would respond, "Yes, it is technically possible to build and operate a large four engined UAV with 500+ seats onboard which could fly from A to B without a human hand to guide it – but you try selling the tickets!?"

*

Now however, the world has moved on. We are into the era of pilotless road vehicles already. In the USA (it happens there first and the rest of the developed world follows suit), they have been road-testing on a grand scale. Trucks for starters. Not just one or two vehicles, but literally dozens of them are out there on the highways trucking up and down the blacktop. America does have a vast number of truck drivers and they are an expensive resource which the industry would love to reduce.

You see much of the country's commercial goods travel by road and to operate each truck requires manpower. If you talk to any HR person they will tell you that when a company or enterprise employs a person they are not just paying for that person's time, but also take on the liability for their sickness, holidays, absences and their dependents' welfare. It doesn't take a large cognitive leap to see that computers and machines do not need vacations, nor pensions, or dependency leave, not even a dental appointment...

Computer guided machines which operate other machines, do not go absent from their duties in the same way as us 'Carbon life-forms'. This is why on paper you can see that the principle of driverless machines has such great potential. As a professional aviator I have been aware of the often voiced opinion of many colleagues from an early stage in my own career that we are viewed as an expensive inconvenience to many airline Financial Directors.

The Bean Counters have had a good run in recent years with being able to drive down the costs of providing pilots. Firstly the raising of the retirement age to 65 meant that suddenly there was a surfeit of qualified, experienced professional aviators and consequently there were fewer new entrants required. This in turn had the effect of reduced terms and conditions for pilots – the law of supply and demand.

Then the Low Cost Airlines (LCAs) managed to introduce self-funded training systems for junior pilots such that the expense of type-rating training was transferred from the company to the individual. Also the introduction of 'Pay to Fly' schemes – whereby the new entrant First Officer in the airlines actually pays for their own Line Training, meant that the airline business model changed significantly.

Finally reduced salary for junior FOs meant another benefit to airlines balance sheets. Very recently however (the last two years) it has become apparent that there is a shortage of airline pilots. Fewer ex-military pilots are available and the temporary glut of pilots in their early sixties has finished. More significantly perhaps there are fewer volunteers willing to make that six figure investment in a career which now has much less potential financial return. Finally some youngsters are dissuaded by the often rumoured future prospect of pilotless cockpits.

On this last point, I do not think they should worry. Although there is now accelerated development towards pilotless flightdecks for future airliners, the designers are heading up the proverbial blind alley. With the advent of Artificial Intelligence and computer systems so advanced that intelligent robotic vehicles are In use – driverless shuttle trains at airports for example – it is an easy step to visualise a future which include airliners with no flightdeck crew onboard.

Selling the tickets? That would be an easy one, simply give away the tickets at first. There would be no shortage of passengers willing to fly for free from London to Sydney for example. Once the first few weeks of scheduled operations proved 'trouble-free', people would start to pay.

The technology is already available to fly airliners automatically from airport to airport, so you have to ask the question, "What's stopping us?" The answer is simple – the problem is the operational environment. To enable pilotless airline traffic to operate safely the whole air traffic system and ground operations systems would need to change; radically. Recently I experienced a couple of busy multi-sector flying days as an airliner Captain with a huge number of challenges. These ranged from operating to/from small island airports with significant performance limitations and non-standard ATC, (short, narrow runways with reduced margin for error).

Then we had another sector with passengers not arriving at the airport gate despite having checked in with hold baggage - "Find those bags, offload them and let's go!" I even went down to the cargo hold to assist in the timely locating of the bags myself – we got away on schedule, but only just... Complex ground traffic situations with difficult to interpret R/T instructions at strangely designed airports. Last, but not least we had an in-flight medical emergency in which we had to consider the possibility of an enroute diversion. It is true to say that we as a crew expended considerable intellectual energy on all of this and by the time we had finished this demanding series of flights I was glad to rest on my days off.

*

Pilotless airliners will only be able to operate safely to and from specially adapted/designed airports where the infrastructure has been completely modified to facilitate them. To change the airport infrastructure worldwide is going to be too big an ask. A perfect example of what I'm talking about occurred only last week with one of the Google self-drive cars. There have been a few accidents with the fleet during the testing, but this one was significant, because it was an event which could not be explained away as a human factor error.

The excerpt from the Google accident report states that '...the car **ASSUMED** that the bus would yield when it attempted to merge back into the traffic lane...' This is supportive evidence of the proposal that a computer is "only an imperfect human brain". **

The question the industry experts need to ask now is, *"do we WANT imperfect human brains flying our airliners?"*

** Professor Katherine Fenton OBE

--0--

35 - SULLY

It is fair to say that the water 'ditching drills' in the Boeing QRH (Quick Reference Handbook) checklists for airliners used to be treated with a fair amount of scepticism by those of us in the industry. Of course one should bear in mind that realistically the most likely place for a large aircraft to ditch would be in an ocean.

Oceans are not calm, gentle, flat landing areas, so the likelihood was high that the eventual water landing would end catastrophically. In the early days of ETOPS (Extended range Twin-Engined Operations) across the Atlantic Ocean, the common story was that statistically it was all based around the probability of losing one complete aircraft every 7 years. In millions of transatlantic flying hours, that didn't happen, but it does give you a perspective on the way in which strategic planners think. As part of our preparations for transatlantic flights, both the aircraft required special modifications and the crews' special training. Large liferafts were fitted which would be able to accommodate more than the plane's occupants, with long term survival equipment, food and water rations etc. Hydraulic motor generators were installed to enable flight without electrical power from the engines and many other improvements fitted.

Overall it is testament to the engine manufacturers that the power units on these early aircraft had performed so reliably over such an extended period. For example on the Boeing 757s we had fitted Rolls Royce RB211 motors and in years and years of use you hardly ever saw one so much as cough... Okay, anecdotal evidence, but you get the picture. Not just Rolls; but General Electric, Pratt and Whitney and Snecma (CFM) were and still are, producing quality products with huge reliability records.

It was on the reputation of these engines that ETOPS was conceived and allowed to continue. The probability of a single engine failing inflight was so small as to be considered infinitesimal, while the notion of a double-engine flameout was unthinkable. Still the airframe maker had to cover that remote possibility, hence the 'Ditching Drills' incorporated into the QRH. These contained instructions/guidance such as "...try to touchdown along the line of the swell..." In the Atlantic Ocean...? At night? *Really?* You can imagine how we thought.

In our own minds as professional aviators, we believed that there would be little chance of the airliner staying in one piece. Probably the fuselage would be in three pieces, subsequent survival after our ditching would be a lottery with very slim odds.

*

Then in November 1996, an Ethiopian Airlines B767 was hijacked and attempted a water landing after running out of fuel. Although the actual ditching was unsuccessful, (the airliner broke up on impact) the fact that nearly a third of those onboard survived was very good news indeed. From the accident report, the left wing and engine hit the water first as the aircraft had about 10 degrees of bank at that time. Unfortunately this had the effect of huge drag forces on that side which spun the rest of the airframe and lead to catastrophic damage.

In the investigation later the pilot stated that he was attempting to land along the line of the waves... Another sad fact about this accident was that it was reported many passengers died "...because they had inflated their lifejackets inside the cabin of the aircraft which then prevented them from rapid egress..." Clearly the inclusion of instructions in airline safety demonstrations the world over regarding specifically NOT doing this, are for good reason.

*

Let us focus on the positive however, in that so many people survived what could have been a complete hull loss with all lives. The video film of the event was broadcast worldwide – it had been taken by a holidaymaker on the beach who thought the aerial stunt had been arranged as part of an airshow. We in the industry at that time, all noted the importance of being exactly wings level at the touchdown point. One of those observers was a US Airways Senior Captain called Chesley (Sully) Sullenberger. Little did he realise that 13 years later he would be required to put this knowledge into practice himself.

*

On February 15th 2009, a cold day in New York City, the Airbus A320 which was under the command of Captain Sully got airborne from La Guardia airport for a domestic flight to Charlotte in North Carolina. At a relatively low altitude and only about 90 seconds after takeoff the airliner ran into a large flock of Canadian Geese which caused catastrophic damage to both engines. The unprecedented had occurred. As Sully (played by Tom Hanks) says in the film, "...everything is unprecedented until it happens for the first time". The resulting '70 tonne glider' flight and successful water landing with all 155 lives saved are a matter of record of course.

Moving on from this single event the wider consequences were huge. An industry which had up to that time been sceptical about the chances of successfully landing a large passenger jet on water had a big wake-up call. In fact the airline world had been so pessimistic about the chances that the airlines themselves never actually trained their pilots for this eventuality. It was just assumed that a) "it ain't gonna happen", and b) "if it did, there's no chance of survival anyway..."

*

Simulator scenarios are now practiced with loss of all engines landings on water and they are successful. We have Captain Sully to thank for this and the demonstration of his exemplary flying skills on that day, have made a major contribution to flight safety in a global sense. While recognising the quality of Captain Sully's flying, we should also acknowledge the incredible contribution made by many other people to the saving of life on that day in what has become to be known as "The Miracle on the Hudson".

From the co-pilot Jeff Skiles, through ATC controllers, to the cabin crew onboard, to the crews on the ferryboats and the men and women of the NY Police and Fire departments – they all joined together without any warning to mount a huge lifesaving operation which was a total success.

I think it was only 24 minutes after touchdown that everyone was off the aircraft – amazing. In the all American tradition of catchy sayings, the outcome of this event proved that *"Teamwork makes the dream work!"*

*

Having just seen the film, my friends and colleagues have asked me what I thought of it. My reply is that apart from being a very moving piece of cinema drama, it is also a brilliant advertisement for our profession as aviators. Captain Sullenberger comes across throughout the film as a thoroughly nice gentleman who was placed in an impossible situation.

Without any warning he was forced to make a decision which would affect the lives of thousands, not just those onboard his stricken airliner. Many would say that he was just doing his job of getting the folks home safely - if he was just doing his job, he did it superbly!

--0--

36 - A BUSMAN'S HOLIDAY

"Where do airline pilots go on holiday?" I have heard this question many times over the years and at first it is not an easy one to answer. Of course by and large we go to the same places everyone else goes to – why shouldn't we? Although this can be a slightly disconcerting experience for a pilot, when sat in the back of an airliner during the approach to land; knowing that the remote Mediterranean Island has a short, narrow runway; the weather forecast was poor and there is a strong crosswind blowing...

*

I well recall in my early career when I was doing a lot of flying to the Greek islands of the eastern Med saying that *"...when I retire I will get a boat and spend time visiting them properly"*. All that exposure to stunning scenery during approaches and departures took its toll I suppose. The problem which all of us faced as UK based airline crew is that we would drop in to some piece of paradise for just long enough to feel the heat of summer, smell the exotic fragrances of a foreign country, refuel the jet and board the homebound passengers. Traditionally this was the hour-long turnround with the charter companies, but now with the low-cost operators it is usually under 30 minutes... Truly not enough time to do any sightseeing.

It is to my eternal shame that in those early days as a young co-pilot on the Boeing 757 based in Manchester, my geography was so sketchy that I did not know that the airport of Heraklion was actually on an island called Crete - fifth largest in the Mediterranean. Part of my lack of situational awareness was due to the fact that it was a nightflight (of course). I knew that the airport was near the coast however, because the sea and cliffs showed up in the landing lights as we came on to short finals for the landing on Runway 27. Seriously I thought it was on mainland Greece – what a newbie!

Fast forward three decades and I can now tell where THIS pilot goes on holiday... Having just spent a whole month sailing round the Greek islands with various friends and family, I am much more aware of the geography than ever before. Not only that, but I also managed to tick a few boxes on my own personal bucket-list. You see I have developed a curious fascination with underwater airplane wrecks. Having first started scuba diving back in the Middle East in '96, while flying for a Far East Airline, it has long been a favourite hobby of mine.

More recently I have had the geographical advantage to indulge my passion more frequently in the warm waters of the Aegean. Idly browsing the internet some five or six years ago, I searched for 'Mediterranean aircraft wrecks' and came up with lots of results. One of them which attracted me was an ex-WW2 RAF Beaufighter which was described as being remarkably intact, having ditched in November 1943. This was after being shotdown by anti-aircraft fire while 'the Beau' was attacking an Axis Naval flotilla in the channel between the islands of Naxos and Paros in the Cyclades.

Rather fortunately the crew of two (RAF Pilot and Navigator) managed to escape from the ditched aircraft and get into their survival dinghy. When you think about the age of the airmen (early 20s), the shock of being shotdown; the emergency ditching far from home - the fact that they carried out their escape drills so successfully is itself great testament to the rigorous training of the Royal Air Force. From there they paddled their way to the shores of beautiful Naxos where they were taken in by local Greeks who sheltered them from the occupying German forces. After some time, legend has it that the two aircrew were secretly smuggled to another island which was not occupied and survived the war. I use the term 'legend' because currently the full story of this particular wreck and details of the crew is uncertain. Discovered in 2007 and lying on sand at 30 metres down, this WW2 relic is not giving up its identity easily. There have been a few conflicting tales over the years and local folklore has not helped.

Not everybody's idea of fun

*

Needless to say the mystery regarding the details only makes this aircraft wreck all the more attractive and I have spent the past five years wishing to visit it in person. To do so is not an easy task of course. Firstly the remains are situated at a depth of 30 metres, which is beyond the scope of the majority of recreational divers with an 'Open Water Diver' certificate – their limit is 18. To achieve 30m depth requires the completion of the 'Advanced Open Water' scuba diving course to attain the necessary qualification. During early summer 2016, I did my Advanced course at the local dive club here in Athens in preparation. I had already booked a month's leave in October and arranged to hire a suitable sailing yacht, although bearing in mind the time of year – I realised the weather could prevent me achieving my objective.

As the weeks passed I was most excited at the prospect of realising a dream – if you look on the internet, the photos are amazing. The aircraft is upright, lying on the sandy seabed and it is clear from the bent back propeller blades of the port engine, this one was certainly turning at the moment of impact with the sea.

Previous divers have described bullet/shrapnel holes in the fuselage and evidence of starboard engine damage. The hatch above the pilot's seat is wide open, thrown back against the stops by the vacating occupant – he certainly wouldn't have had either the time or the inclination to close it again. Also the Navigator's hatch is missing and the emergency dinghy with survival pack was removed from its stowage in the top of the fuselage.

If all the above sounds a bit 'anorak', then it should be borne in mind that it is a very rare event, when you can visit a Second World War warbird wreck site which has been largely untouched in the intervening 70 odd years. Time has stood still. The only other Beaufighter I have seen in real life was preserved in a museum and appeared in mint condition. To see one up close which has not been restored, though virtually intact is a privilege.

*

Perhaps the easiest part of the whole preparation process for the event was deciding who to dive with. To that end, I made contact with Blue Fin Divers, the local diving centre on Naxos. The owner of the company and professional Dive Master is called Panos and he knew exactly what I wanted when I told him that it had been a long held dream to dive on the Beaufighter. Clearly there had been many others with similar ambition before me. He cautioned that the sea and weather conditions might prevent the dive taking place, especially as October is not the best month. There needs to be a very calm sea state, with nil current, little wind and good visibility at the dive site.

Two days later and we were good to go. There were a total of 8 divers on the boat when we set off from the beach near Blue Fin Divers for the 20 minute high speed run to the Beaufighter location. It was very reassuring to be in the company of such a group of well experienced scuba divers. The planning and briefing were comprehensive and clear, which fitted in well with what I expected from them.

Panos as dive leader was extraordinarily calm and detailed in his approach to the event. We would all have approximately 15 minutes at 30m with the wreck, before we had to commence our slow ascent to the surface with 3 decompression stops planned along the way. I was struck by how similar it is to flying in many ways, whereas we pilots are dealing with altitude from above the surface, they deal with depths below it. We would be flying beneath the waves...

Finally the coxswain dropped the lead-weighted line with confidence after consulting the GPS map – his stated aim was to get it to land on the cockpit seat of the Beau, much to our amusement. Imagine our admiration therefore when we found it had landed on the sand just next to the cockpit of the aircraft - we had followed the line all the way to the front door!

The dive was a huge success and it was such a wonderful feeling to be right 'there', to be able to see and touch the airframe after all this time. To see all the instruments still in the cockpit, the throttle, flap and landing gear levers, the control column, all present and correct... Incredible! I noted with interest that the thick armour plated windscreen was cracked – this might have occurred during ditching?

*

Afterwards I spoke with Panos at some length about the significance of the dive site and its relevance to Naxos. For sure, this and other sites are an important part of the island's tourism industry. He was very concerned that its location should remain a secret to prevent souvenir hunters from plundering the wreck. He even talked about the previous owners of the airframe possibly being interested in it, to which I assured him, *"Don't worry Panos, I'm pretty sure the Royal Air Force won't want it back now!"*

--O--

Thanks Panos & Team, Blue Fin Divers – Agios Prokopios, Naxos.

http://www.bluefindivers.gr/en/

The Naxos Beaufighter *(Giorgos Rigoutsos)*

Salute to the crew as I start my ascent *(Panos Blue Fin Divers)*

--0--

37 - THE UNLUCKIEST PUNTER AT THE RACES

Imagine a time before GPS... A time when 'single pilot IFR' Ops with no autopilot was not only legally acceptable, but was the norm. A time before the glass cockpit. A time when you could tell a happy Air Taxi Pilot by counting the number of flies on his teeth! *"Aye... in them days lad... me and Orville? We 'ad it tough!"*

*

I think it is fair to say that most pilots who have been trained by the military go through a sort of culture shock period as they leave and start work in the commercial world. It is often summed up as learning, 'how to stop dropping bombs on the customers'. In my case the bombs had never been very large and only for practice, however it would have caused a fair old stir if I'd inadvertently let one go down the high street of the small South Wales town which we flew overhead on our way to and from the bombing range.

It was naïve of me to think that the training which I had done in the service of Her Majesty would entitle me to pick up the ATPL just like that. No, there were a few more exams to be done first. Life is never easy, I thought to myself as I enrolled at Trent Air Training School at Cranfield, which is where I met Malcolm. He was a civilian QFI who was doing his exams on the same course and had been offered a job with an Air Taxi company based at Manchester International. It all sounded very exciting when he described the sort of flying he was going to be doing – little did I realise at that time how exciting it could be.

These were days when British Airways were advertising for Direct Entry Pilots (DEPs) for the first time in probably 20 years. This was an indicator of how short the industry was of commercially qualified professional aviators. Although flying for the airlines seemed like a relatively 'safe' option, I rather liked the way in which Malcolm portrayed the Air Taxi environment. It is a measure of how buoyant the employment market felt at the time, that I could think to make such a choice, but that's how it seemed to me and others in a similar position then. This was the end of the eighties and the supply of pilots had not kept pace with the rate of airline expansion. *Yes*, I thought to myself, I really fancy doing some Air Taxi work.

The company I joined had five aircraft, all light piston twins. Two of them were six seater PN68 Partenavias (affectionately known as Prats). The other three were PA31-350 Piper Chieftains. The latter aeroplanes were much more interesting with the capability to take nine passengers!

To me, who had never got airborne in any flying machine with more than a couple of seats, this seemed like a huge number of people. I couldn't wait to start Line Training, but first the Type Rating exams had to be passed. At least this time someone else was paying which was a novelty after my rude awakening on leaving the services where everything had been provided for us. Martin, the Chief Pilot at that time was new to the company too and he was our Line Training Captain and mentor.

I think he was trying to impress us when he said he had just returned from working for the British Antarctic Survey Team, "Flying Twin Otters *with skis on*"... but I wondered how could he have reached the rudder pedals? We seemed to get on quite well and I enjoyed flying with him on Line Training. Mind you he was quite a character and used to like to do things differently. Like his method for checking the fuel levels on the high wing Partenavia, when he would climb on top and then run along the wing with his home made dipstick in his hand!

"Don't tell the General Manager..."

This did have an air of comedy about it and the first time I saw him do it I couldn't stop laughing – *so that was why he always wore soft soled shoes for work,* I thought. "Don't tell the General Manager I do this", he hissed, grinning as he crouched down in his elevated position to check the fuel level in the port wing. He did seem to have a 'thing' about the General Manager and they never saw eye to eye.

You can imagine that in a relatively small business this is not good for working relations and eventually there came a parting of the ways. I'm not exactly sure what happened, but I think the huge telephone bill which was run up in the engineers' office out in the hangar, on the company line to a Spanish number had something to do with it. Martin's girlfriend at that time was living in Spain...

I was sorry to see him go in some ways because the flying had been excellent with Martin. He had plenty of corporate experience and ensured that I was exposed to the full range of operations which could be enjoyed flying the Partenavia. This included short field operations on grass when we dropped into Bodmin for tea one afternoon while waiting for a client pick-up from Exeter. Martin talked me through the short-field takeoff and landing technique which we then practiced – much later I was to make good use of this training.

Goodwood was another grass airfield we visited and it was fascinating to arrive there just after dawn looking down over Lord March's residence and the neighbouring motor racing circuit. The only problem we had at that time was the huge flock of birds which were present on the grass runways as there had been no aircraft movements yet. In retrospect, doing a low pass down the runway to clear them out of the way wasn't the smartest idea and we were lucky not to hit any, but then we learn by our mistakes thank heavens.

Short-field grass strip training- Bodmin Moor

Goodwood was a really interesting place with a resident Spitfire in the hangar which caught my eye. Sadly it was also the airfield where poor Norman Lees lost his life much later in a Spitfire crash during circuits and bumps, but that was a long way into the future, this was the autumn of '87 and my line training was nearly completed.

In those heady days of the eighties, remember Yuppies and the advent of 'Cell Phones'? There was plenty of work for us Air Taxi pilots and the variety was amazing. Executive Air Taxi was a large part of it, but then there were Medical Teams to be ferried around the UK, Night-mail flights for the Post Office and Freight flights across the Irish Sea and also to the continent.

Often we would be tasked to fly low level operations for British Gas in one of the Partenavias with the back door off and their photographer (Peter) sitting in a safety harness. Out over the sea, these would be VERY LOW LEVEL missions as he wanted to photograph the legs of Gas Drilling Rigs. I recall that you would be flying along with the first stage of flap, low enough to get salt spray on the windshield and the cry would come from the back – LOWER, *LOWER!*

In military low flying training we were always taught that you could visually judge your height above the ground by the legs of the animals. No don't laugh, it's true. If you could see the legs of the cows (as you sailed past in your BAe Hawk at 420 knots), then you were about 500 feet AGL. On the other hand if you could see the legs on the sheep, then you were at 250 feet which was the preferred height for low flying. Tactical considerations were paramount in that former life.

I remember scaring myself half to death once in the Hawk when it was bumpy at low level. I accidentally flipped the speedbrake button that was sited on the throttle and all of a sudden I felt a dramatic increase in vibration. *SHIT! I've taken a bird down the engine!?* Was my first thought as I pulled back gently on the stick putting vertical distance between me and the landscape. Looking down, all the engine indications were normal and then I felt foolish when I realised it was only the speedbrake – *Dullard McBride!* I chided myself. *Pay attention man!*

But in the Partenavia, there was no speedbrake. It was a

relatively simple light twin-engined aircraft to fly; I always enjoyed the excellent visibility from the front, especially during the approach and landing phase. This was an aeroplane in which you could really impress the passengers when you greased it on to the runway and in truth it wasn't that difficult to do. The only downside with the PN68 was its cruising speed. At around the 145 knots mark, you did have to be patient when travelling long distances.

I recall Scottish Control asking me for an estimate for Dean Cross (DCS) VOR beacon once and it took me a little time to answer them. "Ah, standby" I said promptly, but then the calculator slipped off my lap (no autopilot of course) and I took a few seconds to retrieve it. Once back on my clipboard, I ran the times up and replied with the ETA with very correct R/T. "Roger. You can put your shoes and socks back on now!" He replied implying that I had been a bit slow on the maths – Hah! Very funny.

Although it must be said that not all of the humour was one-way and sometimes we pilots had the last laugh. Like the night when I was coming in across the Irish Sea on my own in an empty Piper Chieftain towards Manchester having delivered nearly a ton of mail to Belfast; mission accomplished. I called up the Manchester controller with a cheery "Good evening Manchester, Grosvenor Wun Fife Charlie, descending flight level eight zero".

His relaxed transmission in reply reminded me that there were some good things about nightflying. All the controllers had more time and there were fewer aircraft movements, consequently much less radio traffic. "Pretty quiet tonight Manchester?" I said to the controller, he responded with a yawn, "Yep, not much going on One Five Charlie".

"Perhaps you've got time to answer a question on correct R/T procedures?" I queried. He came back straight away, more awake now.

"Err, go ahead One Five Charlie, I'll answer it if I can".

"Do you know the difference between *Roger* and *Wilco*?" I queried. There was a pause now as he thought about it for a second or two before his next transmission.

"Well they're nearly the same technically.... it's just that Wilco means *I understand and will comply,* whereas Roger is simply, *message understood'*.

I was enjoying myself, and timed my response accordingly;

"Nope that's not it Manch... *Apparently the real difference is... you can't Wilco a Cat!"*

He nearly choked on his coffee and he was still chuckling when he handed me over to the Tower frequency for landing – I was well pleased with myself as I sauntered into the hangar in the darkness of the South Side of the airport. Even more so when I flew the same route the next night, (same callsign) and the controller asked if it was me that had told his colleague the joke of the previous evening. I said it was and he replied that I would be glad to know it had "done the rounds of the entire Manchester ATC Sub-Centre in the past 24 hours".

*

The passengers were funny too. We always provided a complimentary bar service in the back of the aircraft so they could help themselves, which included a large coffee flask. There was one flight when I was asked if I would like a coffee and when it was passed to me in the front, it reeked of brandy. I handed it back and said that I was sorry, but could I have a normal one. This was met with a cheerful, "Oh go on. We won't tell anyone!"

Now bearing in mind I was the only pilot onboard, this demonstrated a lack of joined up thinking. The replacement coffee was acceptable – at least I couldn't smell any alcohol in it.

On another flight, one of the lady passengers on a business trip was caught short on the way home to Manchester and had to climb over the back row of seats in the Partenavia to answer an urgent call of nature... Well, when you're flying along the airway at Flight Level 90, there really was nowhere else to go. The question that was uppermost in my mind was what receptacle she would use? I just hoped it wasn't my flightbag. I was surprised when I saw her carefully carrying an upturned bowler hat into the back of the hangar as they disembarked; but not surprised at all when the owner didn't want it back!

One of the most memorable flights in the Partenavia was the day we nearly crashed. On the face of it, the job was an easy one. It was four passengers to go from Manchester to Newbury Racecourse and return. The two business partners and their wives were going for a day at the races with a champagne picnic.

One of the other pilots had been to Newbury a few years previously and gave me the full brief. This included the information that it was a grass runway that was not overly long and you could only land and takeoff in a certain direction to the west of the strip as it was not permitted to low-fly over the racetrack, so far so good. "Oh! And there are some trees on final approach..." was his parting shot. We checked with the racecourse and obtained the necessary permission and then booked the flight with the customer.

On the morning of the fateful day, the weather reports were not looking good. Low stratus with occasional rain in the area, but clearing up by lunchtime – hmm, what to do? The client arrived promptly and was very disappointed to hear the news; "This is most inconvenient". The aircraft was ready, the Manchester weather was not a problem and they were very keen to go. I patiently explained what the problem was with the weather and that we needed a certain cloudbase to make a visual approach. "Well I've just spoken to a friend of mine on his cellphone and he's landed there this morning, so it can't be that bad can it?" was his reply. I looked again at the METARs for the local area and came up with a plan. We would make an instrument approach at nearby XXX airfield then break off and fly low level visually to land at Newbury – the westerly breeze would help us achieve a nice short landing distance I thought. If it really was too bad, then they could all get a taxi from the instrument approach airfield – not quite as cool as landing in your own private aircraft, but it would have to do.

On the way down, they all seemed very cheerful in the back. The ladies were in high spirits with plenty of giggling; clearly champagne and altitude were working their magic. In the front, I was busy flying (still no autopilot in the Partenavia) and listening to the Volmet. I wondered what sort of aeroplane had managed to get in there before us – it must be small I mused. Sometime later it all went quiet in the cabin as we flew down the ILS, but we broke cloud with just enough of a base to manoeuvre visually onto final approach for Newbury. Still with flap down and flying nice and slow in a classic 'bad weather circuit' configuration I brought the light twin on to a curving approach for the strip.

Full flap on the PN68 with the engines throttled right back and the helpful westerly, gave a nice steep descent to the grass, which was just as well, because the trees at the threshold looked very tall. *Uh-oh... they must be at least fifty feet tall?*

I had a very uneasy feeling now as we taxied in. There were no other aeroplanes present at all – the bastard had lied to me. I suddenly felt icy cold. He didn't even mention the lack of other flying machines they were in a hurry and did not want to miss the first race. "See you later. About four-ish", was all I got and I was left with the Partenavia, a grass runway which looked too short, a tailwind takeoff and those bloody big trees.

Uh-oh... they must be at least fifty feet tall?

Newbury – Partenavia on the grass (the only aeroplane there)

I got the flight manual out and started calculating. After pacing out the length of the strip, right from the fence at the western end, visually assessing the tree tops, dipping the tanks to be sure of the fuel weight, and estimating the wind I could see it was very tight. Really, very tight. "Hmm not much margin for error", was the product of my analysis... "Bugger!" I even went so far as to heft the large heavy picnic basket, while working out the actual takeoff weight to go into the graphs, perhaps they wouldn't notice if we left it behind...

It was time to see the race organisers at the office. Needless to say it was mad busy with punters here, there and everywhere. Pushing my way through the crowds, I found the office and logged the landing with them, but they were really not interested in my plight. My request for a westerly departure was met with a complete negative while the horseracing was on. "Yes after the last race has finished and the crowds have all gone home. It'll be about six o'clock". My mood was fairly low as I left the office and headed back to the strip. I felt like the unluckiest punter at Newbury. I knew now how it was to feel lonely in a huge crowd of people – a very odd feeling for a gregarious type like me I thought.

Back at the runway we had a visitor. Another aircraft had arrived; it was a helicopter. There were no other fixed wing movements at Newbury that day. The Air Hanson pilot was a nice chap and I enjoyed his hospitality in the cabin of the big machine. As we drank our coffee, I could see the helicopter was brand new; very impressive with leather upholstery and all the bells and whistles in the cockpit. For me though, I thought it's most impressive feature was its' vertical takeoff capability!

As we spoke, I explained my problem and he listened with sympathy. He asked what I was going to do. "Well. It'll do it... but only just", I looked across at my high-wing twin fifty metres away on the grass. Did I sound convincing? I don't know, but I knew he also felt lucky to not require the runway to get airborne. "We'll just clear those trees with a few feet to spare I reckon". Was my final declaration and he nodded in agreement.

Partenavia instrumentation – good IFR setup (for the time)

"I'm sure you know what you're doing" he said in support, but I still had misgivings, even though according to the Flight Manual it was definitely do-able.

I had pre-flighted the Prat and the passengers arrived just before 4pm; they were anxious to get going. I suggested that it would be easier if we could wait until 6pm to takeoff in the other direction as the easterly departure had the trees on the climbout. The client looked at his watch and two hours seemed a long time. As we stood there beside the aircraft I looked down the strip. The trees seemed a long way away and not as tall from here, maybe I had overestimated their height? I had to make a decision.

"Right. Let's go then!" We boarded through the door in the fuselage and I took my position in the front seat. As I went through the starting sequence, my colleague from the helicopter gave a wave as I taxied right up to the fence at the western end of the grass. With the power checks done and complete silence from the cabin, I held her on the toebrakes as I ran the engines up to full power. A last look round and I checked once again that I really had set the takeoff flap, that would be essential. I let the brakes go.

"Ladies and Gentlemen, welcome to the FOUR FIFTEEN RACE AT NEWBURY.   They're lined up at the rail; THEY'RE UNDER STARTERS ORDERS...... AND .... THEY'RE OFF!

She surged forward and gathered speed. It seemed like a million thoughts ran through my brain during that takeoff, the first of which was; *will THIS be my last one!?* The engines felt strong; in fact I had never heard them roar as loud before as I held the throttles jammed hard against the front stops. The flying controls came alive as we gathered speed and I so wanted that nosewheel off the grass to reduce the rolling resistance – but not too early, it would be disastrous to stall on the rotation. *Is the grass too long?* Another thought flashed through as we got faster and faster. *JESUS CHRIST! THIS... IS... GOING... TO... BE... CLOSE!* This thought came through as we passed the point of no return; the trees looking bigger than ever.

Finally the mainwheels unstuck and WE WERE FLYING, but the trees were coming closer still - I could see we were way too low... But now... as the airspeed increased rapidly having left the ground, she started to accelerate, the engines at maximum power were really singing and I could feel the props biting through the air. *Fluid dynamics...* A flashback to aerodynamic theory lectures at naval flying college. I raised the nose of the Partenavia now - *we have got to CLIMB* – the stall warning horn screeched and kept screeching as I held the attitude to get the height, we were nearly there. *So close, so close! SO BLOODY CLOSE!!*

"COME ON MY GIRL!!!" My voice on the intercom sounded strangely unreal through the headphones, nearly there, you're nearly there! YOU'RE NEARLY THERE...!

"YESSSS!" I eased the back pressure and the stall warning horn fell silent as the leafy treetops dropped away behind us, with literally only feet to spare. *"For Fuck's sake...that was close*

mate!" I muttered to myself on the intercom.

Retracting the flaps and setting the climb power, I turned in my seat to look at my customers - four very white faces stared back at me. They were in shock.

"NEXT STOP MANCHESTER!" I shouted with a huge grin. Of course, I had good reason to smile; my Filly had just won the Four Fifteen at Newbury... *BY A NOSE!*

Postscript:

As soon as I returned to Manchester, I went to see both the Chief Pilot and the General Manager. I insisted that our company never operated into Newbury Racecourse again. They understood the reasons why. I also checked the landing gear to see if we'd picked up any greenery, there was nothing.

This is a story of classic "Commercial Pressure" which resulted in the pilot making the 'wrong' decision. The correct course of action would have been to wait two hours (plus) until the racecourse was empty of people and carry out a takeoff to the West, into wind, without the obstacles. Difficult to do when the charterer wants to go home.

As a relatively inexperienced pilot, I was placed in an almost impossible position, which with hindsight might have been avoided by the timely intervention of a senior manager in a supervisory capacity. However, I think it is true to say that odd practices still occur in Air Taxi Companies, when young inexperienced pilots are given challenging tasks which could potentially overwhelm their skills.

Some situations are not always easy to analyse when you are so closely involved and this tale proves that sometimes it is quite literally "difficult to see the wood for the trees!"

*

Partenavia in hangar 522 at Manchester - Grosvenor Aviation

First Air Taxi mission to Weston, Dublin – another grass strip

--0--

38 - "MY FIRST COMMERCIAL FLYING JOB"

The following is a true story as told to me by a friend of mine. It is the tale of how he got his first commercial job and the exciting events which occurred on Day One.

The small advert read;

'Pilot Wanted - busy Parachute Club

Needs commercial pilot for Para-dropping.

Suit new CPL holder'.

I had telephoned the number on the advert and made an appointment to go and see them at the airfield where they operated from.   Having been met by the Chief Parachuting Instructor and Jump Master, I eyed up the big high-wing Cessna with suspicion – it was called a Sky Wagon. For sure it did look like a wagon, but was it ready for the sky?

The ink was still wet on my licence and this was going to be my first commercial job. I wanted to make a good impression, but the size of this machine was bigger than anything I had flown previously and now that I was next to it, I was having second thoughts.

"It's...Erm... it's BIGGER than I expected..." I stammered, as I looked in the back of the aeroplane through the open doorway, inside it was like a truck, "I'm not SURE I can fly this..."

"Well you're a Pilot aren't you?" Challenged the Jump Master, "so I don't see the problem!" I took my courage in both hands.

"Yes! You're right, it'll be okay. I just need a good read through the pilot's notes and then it'll be fine", thinking to myself maybe the aeroplane would look smaller tomorrow morning. Also I was worried that they might give the job to somebody else, so I had better show enthusiasm for it.

"'Right! Well there's the Airplane Flight Manual, *you've got an hour* and I'll go and get the Freefall team geared up!"

'AN HOUR?' He stomped off towards the clubhouse without giving me a chance to reply and I was left with a tatty flight manual and an aircraft that seemed absolutely huge with the expectation that we would be airborne in one hour's time; heaven help me!? That hour was one of the busiest of my life as I speed-read through the book and wiggled and waggled all the bits of the Cessna which would move.

She was not exactly a transport of delight – that was clearly apparent. Several bits of airframe and interior trim seemed to have been taped up with what I would later learn was 'Speedtape' by the engineers who maintained this Queen of the skies. In those early days, I knew nothing of Acceptable Deferred Defects, nor would I have known what *was* acceptable and what *NOT*. It just seemed to me that G-XXXX had been having a hard life thus far.

The freefall parachute team, four of them plus the Jumpmaster came back as promised and I tried to look confident. At least we wouldn't be running out of fuel (full tanks noted) and I was confident of finding the right switches and controls to get it started, but the one thing which was really troubling me was the method for dropping the parachutists...

"WHEN YOU'RE OVERHEAD THE AIRFIELD AT EIGHT THOUSAND, JUST GO AS SLOW AS YOU CAN AND WE'LL JUMP OUT!" Shouted the Jumpmaster kneeling next to me on the floor as we taxied out in response to my query about para-dropping.

'Well if that's all there is to it, this job's going to be a doddle', I thought as I gave it full throttle down the runway. We seemed to take an age to get airborne and when we did so, the controls felt *really* heavy – many years later I realise that a proper check of the weight and balance would not have gone amiss. I had taken the verbal assurance from the Jumpmaster of "Yeah, we always go with five, don't worry" at face value, but with full fuel onboard the aircraft was probably overweight by quite a large amount.

The cabin cooled as we climbed and I could feel them all getting a bit restless in the back with the altimeter now reading 8,000 feet. I was looking for the airfield and trying to line up into the westerly wind, but flying straight into the afternoon sun made things a bit difficult. *There, that's about it,* I reckoned and started to reduce the power to get the speed back. The first jumper got out onto the footplate next to the starboard wheel and held on tight to the underwing strut. More left aileron needed now and rudder too to offset the drag on that side. *"Unnf...! hope he gets a move on!"*, I grunted heaving on the control-column with plenty of force and pushing loads of rudder pedal with my boot. A shouted instruction from the Jumpmaster reached me above the wind noise from the open door.

"SLOWER... *SLOWER!"* He motioned with his hand palm down. I checked the airspeed and throttled back more, it wasn't easy to see with the sun coming in over the glareshield, but I recall the ASI needle flickering around 60 or so and reducing...

The second jumper was now on footplate and strut, but the first was still there! *'What? I thought he would have gone by now?'* But no, they were hanging on together. Nearly full left aileron now and full left rudder too with plenty of back pressure on the stick... All of a sudden there was a brief squeal from the stall warning horn and then FLICK! A BIG ROLL! ***"SHIT! WE ARE UPSIDE DOWN!!"*** Yes the horizon had rolled all the way round in the windscreen. *"AARGH!"* I shouted as I pushed the throttle in and the engine roared, **"HANG ON EVERYBODY!"** As I recovered with the ailerons, rolling the Cessna back upright again, I was panting, sweating and swearing and '*that WAS the scariest moment of MY LIFE!'* I thought to myself. I looked over my shoulder wondering how my passengers had fared in all of that. The 'plane was empty – ***they had all gone!***

"OH BLOODY HELL! Now I'm in for it", I felt sick and miserable at the same time. 'Those guys are going to beat me up if I land back there'. At the very least I won't be flying for them anymore. 'Strewth, what a stupid thing to do. Of course the aeroplane would flick-roll in that condition, why hadn't I seen it coming?' I flew around for a bit, descending all the while and even though I thought about landing somewhere else, I decided to go and face the music. As I taxied in they were all there together waiting for me, still in their multicoloured jumpsuits; a Technicolor reception committee.

They were literally holding their sides laughing at me and plainly the experience had been an enjoyable one. I was aghast. This wasn't the reaction I had expected at all, are these guys crazy? Quite simply they thought it had been hilarious and they kept slapping me on the back and pumping my arm up and down, shaking my hand till it hurt.

Before long I was laughing too and could see the funny side of it all. No harm done, the Cessna was alright and they were all keen to go and do it again. I got the job and soon became quite adept at dropping 'chutes, but I always kept a close eye on the airspeed after that.

--O--

39 - FORMULA 1 RACER

How does it feel to fly a dedicated racing aircraft? I found out how much fun it can be when I flew the Cassutt Racer back in 1994.

Short wingspan, but wide chord evident in this shot

If somebody asks you if you would like to fly their single-seat Formula 1 Racer, you don't give them the chance to ask a second time. The owner has clearly assessed you to be capable of flying the beast, and to refuse the offer would be very churlish indeed. So when Arthur White offered me the chance of a flight in his Cassutt aircraft, I readily accepted the invitation and relished the anticipation of my 'first solo on type'. And it would be very much a first solo - there's no such thing as a two-seat racer...

*

One sunny afternoon in August (you may remember the one), Arthur White and I sat in a local flying club waiting for the third musketeer, Bob Screen, to arrive. He would fly me in his vintage Cessna 140 down to Sleap Airfield in Shropshire, with Arthur in the racer keeping us company. From there, Arthur had promised to let us 'have a go'. As we flew south, Arthur came alongside in the Cassutt for a little close formation practice as we had briefed, but soon became bored by the lack of speed.

Tiny silhouette from the side – the Cassutt Racer is fast

The sleek lines of the racer were not designed for 90 knot cruising. It finds about 180mph to be more comfortable. On arrival at Sleap, Bob Screen and I underwent Arthur's Cassutt Racer conversion course over the usual cup of coffee. It didn't take long. A few helpful phrases such as "You're probably wise to takeoff in the three-point attitude — there's very little prop clearance tail-up; it's twitchy on the rudder, very responsive in roll and only just stable in pitch — keep around a hundred on finals and you'll be okay", and we had completed our course.

Arthur and I watched from the control tower as Bob taxied out for his flight. I listened to Arthur's commentary as the plane took off. "He's started to climb a little bit too early. You want to hold the nose down and accelerate to 120 before climbing, and that way it will hold the speed to give best rate of climb." I made a mental note to use this technique for my own departure.

Drag cheating frontal area of the Cassutt

The little red racer rapidly became a diminutive dot going away from us. "He's got the hang of it now" said the owner with satisfaction. Fifteen minutes later Bob was on finals for a beautiful three-pointer of a landing which looked like giving me a hard act to follow. As Arthur helped me to strap in with the four-point harness, there were yet more words of advice, "She climbs at 120, but cruises anywhere up to 200. Have fun".

Inside the cockpit, two things made an immediate impression on me. Firstly, the cockpit instrumentation was directly from the minimalist school and secondly, the wings seemed to have disappeared! I noted that the instruments given pride of place at the top of panel were those that dealt with engine health, along with the airspeed indicator — so that you can scan them quickly without taking too much of your attention away from what's going on outside.

Rare to see an ASI with 300 as the top end in a light aircraft

The less prominent situation of the altimeter showed that height information is less important. As these Formula 1 Racers are designed to whizz round 20ft pylons at 230 mph, it is more sensible to judge the altitude visually rather than spending time looking at dials. With a cry of "Contact", Arthur swung the prop and the engine burst into life.

The only way to describe the sound as the motor settled to a steady 1000rpm idle is that it was loud. As the hinged canopy lowered into position the noise dropped by a decibel or two, but as you are seated almost inside the engine compartment you are very much aware of the Continental C90 that is making all that racket only a couple of feet in front of you.

The forward view on the ground is excellent for a tailwheel aeroplane, made possible by the relatively short main undercarriage legs and the close fitting engine cowling which slopes down towards the propeller. The short, fighter-like control column is ideally placed so that you can rest your right forearm on your thigh to hold it in a fixed position, which is just as well as there is no elevator trimmer.

Short, wings with full-span ailerons give an incredible roll-rate

Needless to say I made certain to hold the stick hard back throughout the engine start and taxi out to the holding point, for the run-up and pre-takeoff checks. Unlike other taildraggers, there is no need to weave the nose while taxying and I was soon lined up on the main runway ready for departure.

As I opened the throttle the noise rose to a crescendo and the little aircraft started to move forward at a rapidly quickening pace. There was no tendency to yaw during the acceleration and tailwheel steering helped to keep the nose running straight down the centreline.

There was a real sense of urgency in the take-off which you don't normally associate with light aircraft and which reaffirmed my opinion that this one was different. As the wheels left the ground together — my first three-point takeoff — I lowered the nose to enable climb speed to be gained and the Cassutt rocketed along the runway at about thirty feet. "Ooohh! This is fun!" I thought as the upwind hedge began to bloom rapidly in my field of view. A quick glance at the ASI confirmed that we were accelerating through 160mph, and a progressive backwards pressure on the stick converted speed into height in a most dramatic fashion.

As there was no 'G' meter, I was careful not to be too enthusiastic, especially in view of the fact that it wasn't my aeroplane. Still, the owner did say to enjoy myself and the aircraft is designed for a maximum positive limit of 6.5G. I calculated the rate of climb (using the altimeter and a stopwatch) at 120mph to be around 2000fpm. This was something of a surprise because I expected the low aspect ratio wings to give a poor rate of climb, but the Cassutt does not appear to interpret the laws of aerodynamics in quite the same way as the rest of us do.

As I continued the climb, I trimmed back the power a little to be kind to the engine. Arthur once suffered a catastrophic engine failure in this aeroplane and after the subsequent forced landing referred to it as 'A Very Exciting Glider!' I had no plans to find out what he meant.

I was really beginning to get the feel of it all now and very shortly the altimeter told me that we had sufficient of the vertical element to explore a few gentle acrobatic manoeuvres. I started with a loop. This was interesting in the Cassutt, as it is one of the few aircraft I have flown that you can start the loop at cruising speed. Mind you, when you consider the racer's range of cruising speeds it's not that surprising.

Due to the low-drag wing, speed appears to be merely a function of throttle position, although directly proportional to fuel flow, and it is possible to consume the entire contents of the fuel tank (14 and a half US gallons) in approximately 50 minutes if you leave the throttle in the top left hand corner. Entering the loop from level flight, there was a rapid decay in airspeed as G loading increased and this I think may be attributable to a sharp rise in lift-induced drag as angle of attack is increased.

Whatever the reason, it was still possible to pull up into a loop from 150mph which is at the lower end of the Cassutt's cruise range. Entering loops from higher speeds is child's play, although you have to be aware that the initial speed reduction is more pronounced.

After the almost childish pleasure of `pulling the stick back to make the houses get smaller', I moved on to manoeuvres around the longitudinal axis. I had really been looking forward to this, as the full-span ailerons promised a sparkling rate of roll. I was not disappointed. The roll rate must have been somewhere in the region of 300° per second. Complete aileron rolls with full stick deflection can be carried out in under two seconds.

Add that characteristic to the ability to pull up into a loop at almost any speed and you have got one highly manoeuvrable aeroplane. Of course there is no such thing as a free lunch and there is a penalty to be paid for such high manoeuvrability — and that is a lack of stability. The aircraft is only just stable in pitch and has to be flown constantly; it will not fly 'hands off' at any speed. Mind you, the answer to that is 'who cares?' You wouldn't want a racing aeroplane that flew by itself anyway and believe me, it is fun to fly!

Barrel rolls came next, with some Immelmanns and then Cuban Lazy Eights, lightning vertical rolls and four-point and slow rolls - but not too slow as there is no inverted fuel system and it is best not to have the engine cut out on you while upside down. All too soon it was time to return to the circuit and embarrass myself with the landing.

Sleap Airfield was completely free of traffic as I dived towards the field at over 220 mph on just a whiff of throttle, not being able to resist the temptation to join with a low-level run-in and break down the runway, slowing down to 160-odd on the downwind leg, pre-landing checks which consisted of... *"Yep the engine's still running";* a fighter-like curving finals turn at 100 mph, (breathing quicker now); over the fence at a shade over 90 with a trickle of power and squeak — on she goes.

3 pointer landing yes, but also for takeoff to protect the prop!

Not quite the three-point greaser I was hoping for, but it was good enough for me. "How did it go?" Arthur asked, knowing what the answer should be. A shrug of my shoulders and, "Oh ya'know; so, so..." I replied, lying through my teeth — but the metre wide grin told the truth.

*

Postscript:

Messerschmitt ME163 Komet – WW2 Rocket Powered Fighter

Many years before, as a little boy fascinated with all aspects of aviation, there was one particular flying machine which caught my imagination. It was the tiny, single seater rocket powered fighter, the Messerschmitt ME163. This incredible aircraft built and flown by the Luftwaffe in WW2 had phenomenal performance. It was capable of 700 mph and had a recommended best climb speed of 420 mph – this was in 1944, imagine!

Anyway. I used to visualise just what it would be like to be sat in that tiny little cockpit, looking out of that Plexiglas bubble rushing around the skies at incredible speed, having the ability to turn the world upside down with just a flick of my wrist. I knew I would hardly be able to see the wings from the cockpit, just the sky... In my imagination, I would be like a Rocketman.

Well, I can tell you that in 1994, on a sunny day above a quiet little airfield in Shropshire, sat in a tiny cockpit, hunched behind a little screen of Plexiglas with huge performance available to me... a little boy's dream came true!

*

ABOUT THE AUTHOR

James McBride - born in Chester, UK, the oldest of four sons. He always wanted to fly aeroplanes for a living since he was a little boy. On leaving school he worked as a nurse, and then had a career change in his twenties...

McBride joined the Royal Navy to fly jets and flew the Harrier and helicopters before 'going civil' in the late 1980's. He has been an airline Training Captain since 1998 and wrote a book on aviation called *The Flightdeck Survival Manual* – "How to survive a career flying aeroplanes for a living" in 2014. It is available on Amazon.co.uk

As the owner of a ski chalet (Chalet Louis) in the French Alps for 10 years, from 1990 he ran skiing holidays for family and friends. In 2015 he wrote a book called *Cooking On The Piste* – "A Ski Chalet Cookbook" with his friend Mark Chetham.

He has written a regular monthly column for UK publication Flight Training News since 2006. His writing has focused on flight safety and training. He was nominated/short listed for an Aerospace Journalist of the Year Award (AJOYA) in Paris in 2007.

Married with two children (Hannah & Lawrence) plus two dogs, currently he lives in Athens, Greece. Hobbies include; Sailing, Diving, Motorcycling, Cooking, Skiing and Watersports.

*

PHOTOS – CREDITS & HISTORY

All photographic images in this book are property/copyright of the Author except where Indicated.

CHAPTER

1 – Thunder Road – p9 - Dawn Wing - Hannah McBride

2 – Seat next to window – p11 – Group – Sarah Ghidouche

6 – Class of 1990 – p53 & p58 - John Whitfield

10 – Losing your First Command – p76 - Peter Hampson

20 – 'Ebony' smiling – p146 - Dianne Worby

24 – Southern Comfort – various – Seimon Pugh-Jones

28 – Capt Eric Brown - Jeremy Pratt, Crecy publishing

John Cunningham – Ken Ellis collection

30 – TWA Constellation – p225 - First Officer Bill Wilkin

36 – Naxos Beaufighter – p262 - Giorgos Rigoutsos – p263 Panos @ Blue Fin Divers Naxos

39 – ME163 – p291 – Arthur Robinson

--0--

GLOSSARY OF TERMS AND ABBREVIATIONS.

AAIB – Air Accident Investigation Branch (of Dept for Transport UK)

ABP – Able Bodied Passenger

ACMI – Aircraft, Crew, Maintenance and Insurance – also known as "Wet Lease" (i.e. WITH crew)

ADD – Acceptable Deferred Defect (also called "Hold Item")

ADF – Auto Direction Finder unit – often associated with NDB see below

AEW – Airborne Early Warning

AFDS – Automatic Flight Director System

AGL – Above Ground Level

ANO – Air Navigation Order

APU – Auxiliary Power Unit

AOC – Air Operators Certificate

ASR – Air Safety Report

ASI – Air Speed Indicator

ASIs – Air Staff Instructions (RAF top brass)

ATA – Actual Time of Arrival

ATC – Air Traffic Control

ATC Slot – See Slot

ATD – Actual Time of Departure

ATIS – Automated Terminal Information System gives aerodrome current weather

ATL – Aircraft Technical Log or "the Techlog" (RAF Form 700)

ATO – Approved Training Organisation

Autobrake – as it says, an automatic braking system for landing

A/C – shorthand for Aircraft, can also be seen as AC or a/c

BAe – British Aerospace

Baro – Barometric Altimeter

Blocks – as in "Off Blocks" – literally means the chocks holding the wheels – same as "Off Chocks"

BER – Beyond Economic Repair

BSI – Borescope Inspection of engine

CAA – Civil Aviation Authority

CAPT – Captain or Aircraft Commander

CAS – Calibrated Air Speed = IAS corrected for instrument and position error

CAVOK – Cloud And Visibility OK – very nice weather

CBT – Computer Based Training

CDL – Configuration Deviation List

CDU – Computer Display Unit

CFP – Computer Flight Plan

CFIT – Controlled Flight Into Terrain

CGI – Chief Ground Instructor

Chocks – large blocks which are stuck next to the wheels on the ramp – stops the aircraft moving if the parking brake fails

CIP – Commercially Important Passenger – same as VIP

CLB – Climb abbreviation for FMC

Coffin Corner – as the name implies, a rather undesirable place – the small corner of the flight envelope between slow speed stalling speed and high-speed buffet speed

CONFIG – Configuration of the aircraft, flaps, gear, speedbrakes etc

Configuration Warning – warning that CONFIG incorrect for manoeuvre

CPT - Captain

CRM – Crew Resource Management

CRMI – Crew Resource Management Instructor (a facilitator really)

CRS – Certificate of Release to Service (maintenance term)

CRZ – Cruise abbreviation for FMC

CRZ ALT – Cruise Altitude abbreviation for FMC

CSI – Combat Survival Instructor

CSR – Cabin Safety Report

CTBL – Contactable – referring to a crew member being available to call by crewing

CTC – Chief Training Captain (usually Postholder for Training on behalf of CAA)

CTOT – Calculated TakeOff Time – used on Flightplans

CVR – Cockpit Voice Recorder

Cyan – Colour of blue specific to Boeing EFIS displays

Damp Lease – an ACMI agreement with cockpit crew only

DDG – Dispatch Deviation Guide

DEC – Direct Entry Captain

DFDR – Digital Flight Data Recorder

DFO – Director Flight Operations

DOB – Death On Board

DODAR – Diagnose, Options, Decision, Action, Review

DV Window – Direct Vision window in flightdeck which slides open on ground

EAT – Estimated Approach Time (normally for holding aircraft in the stack)

EADI – Electronic Attitude Director Unit (part of EFIS instrumentation in Boeings)

EET – Estimated Elapsed Time (enroute on a Flight Plan)

EFIS – Electronic Flight Instrumentation System

EFATO – Engine Failure After Takeoff

EFOTO – Engine Failure On Takeoff

EHSI – Electronic Horizontal Situation Indicator

EMA – East Midlands Airport (IATA Code)

EOBT – Estimated Off Blocks Time

EPR – Engine Pressure Ratio – an expression of how much thrust is being produced

ETA - Estimated Time of Arrival

ETOPS – Extended Range Twin Engined Operations – often over water (e.g. Atlantic)

FCOM – Flight Crew Operations Manual

FCTM – Flight Crew Training Manual

FCU - Fuel Control Unit

FDM – Flight Data Monitoring

FDR – Flight Data Recorder

FFS – Full Flight Simulator

Final Line Check – After Line Training is complete to release crew member to Line

Fire Handle – shuts off fuel, hydraulics and when rotated activates Fire Extinguisher

Flightdeck – the little room at the front where the pilots sit

Flight Level – or FL – an altimeter indication in 000's of feet referenced to 1013mb

FMC – Flight Management Computer

FO – First Officer also known as Co-Pilot

FOD – Foreign Object Debris

FOM – Flight Operations Manager – usually Postholder reporting to the CAA

FOM – Flight Operations Manual

FORM 700 – The Techlog for an RAF aircraft

FPL – Flightplan

FSTD – Flight Simulator Training Device

FSO – Flight Safety Officer

FTL – Flight Time Limitations

G/A – Go-Around, aborted landing. (Used to be known as Overshoot)

Glass Cockpit – refers to the introduction of computer screens in flightdecks EFIS

GPU – Ground Power Unit – provides electrics to run the aircraft without APU

GPWS – Ground Proximity Warning System (does what it says on the tin)

GRADE – Gather (info), Review, Analyse, Decide (& Do), Evaluate

Ground Lock Pins – heavy duty bolts with flags to lock landing gear down

HF – High Frequency – Military Radio Network for Mil A/C

HSI – Horizontal Situation Indicator (Orville and Wilbur called it a compass)

Hold Item – similar to ADD. Holding over until repair is possible

HOTAC – Airline speak for "Hotel Accommodation"

IAS – Indicated Air Speed

IFALPA = International Federation of Air Line Pilots' Associations.

IFR – Instrument Flight Rules

ILS – Instrument Landing System – for precision approaches to runway in IMC

IMC – Instrument Meteorological Conditions – cloudy outside

IR – Instrument Rating – a licence to fly aircraft on instruments alone

IRS – Inertial Reference System

IRU – Inertial Reference Unit

ITCZ – Inter Tropical Convergence Zone

LCA – Low Cost Airline

LCC – Low Cost Company

LCZR – Localizer (element of the ILS)

Line Check – annual event for all crew

Line Training – after basic/initial training in Simulator, training on the line

LLZ – Localizer (azimuth) element of the ILS

LNAV – Lateral Navigation system – part of the AFDS

LOFT – Line Oriented Flying Training

LPC – Licence Proficiency Check (for pilots)

LPC – Lemon Pie Club (an alternative meaning for the original abbreviation)

LST – Licence Skills Test (for the issue of a Type Rating)

LTN – Luton Airport (3 letter IATA code)

LVPs – Low Visibility Procedures

LVOs – Low Visibility Operations

Mach No – associated with cruise speed of airliner as percentage of Mach 1.   For example 'Mach 0.8' = 80% of Mach 1.

Magenta – purple type colour specific to Boeing EFIS system

MAN – Manchester Airport (3 letter IATA code)

MEL – Minimum Equipment List

METAR – Meteorological Actual Report – "the latest weather"

MPA – Maximum Power Assurance engine runs – Engineering Technical

MPL – Multi Pilot Licence

MOR – Mandatory Occurrence Report – to CAA (or regulating authority)

MSA – Minimum Safe Altitude

MSD – Minimum Separation Distance (used by the Military to describe closest distance to ground or other surface obstacles)

N1 – engine gauge showing speed of front fan of large bypass engines

N2 – second stage fan

N3 – third stage fan

NDB – Non Directional Beacon – used with aircraft autodirection finder

NPA – Non-Precision Approach on instruments to an airfield/aerodrome

OAT – Outside Air Temperature – also known as Ambient

OPC – Operator Proficiency Check for crew

P1 – Senior Pilot onboard – another name for Captain – refers to logging the flight-time

P1/S – First Pilot under Supervision/Training

P2 – Co-pilot

PA – Public Address system – aircraft loudspeaker system to cabin

PF – Pilot Flying (also known as the Handling Pilot – with hands on controls)

PIC – Pilot In Command

PAP – Passenger x 1

PAX – Passengers Plural

PIREP – Pilot Report – usually of meteorological phenomena

PLI – Pitch Limit Indicators

PLOC – Prolonged Loss Of Communication (on the radio) – due to losing contact with ATC

Pusser – Generic Term for Royal Naval Supply Branch

QFI – Qualified Flying Instructor

QRH – Quick Reference Handbook – with emergency & non-normal checklists

Quarter-Mil – a topographical Map with scale 1:250,000

QWI – Qualified Weapons Instructor

RA – Radio Altimeter

RADALT – Radio Altimeter

Rotate – Call by Monitoring Pilot to indicate to PF that it is speed to get airborne

RPM – Revolutions Per Minute – with reference to engine speed usually

R/T – Radio Telephony – often abbreviated – VHF in Civil World

RTO – Rejected Takeoff

SAS – Special Air Services

SBY – Standby – referring to crew usually associated with rostering/crewing dept.

SCCM – Senior Cabin Crew Member

SID – Standard Instrument Departure – defined for all flights heading that direction

Slot – An ATC timed departure restriction – usually with an allowance of -5 and +10 minutes

SMS – Safety Management System

SOP – Standard Operating Procedure

Soup Dragon – Cabin Crew in forward galley serving flightdeck

SP – Safety Pilot – qualified observer on jumpseat in flightdeck for Line Training

Speedbird – British Airways' R/T callsign

SSA – Sector Safe Altitude – usually within 25 nm

STA – Scheduled Time of Arrival

STAR – Standard Arrival Routing – defined for all flights from that direction

STD – Scheduled Time of Departure

TAS – True Air Speed = speed of a/c relative to the airmass

TCAS – Traffic Collision Avoidance System

Techlog – aircraft Technical Log; a legal document – see also ATL

Thrust Reverser – on each engine deflects exhaust forward to reduce speed on landing

Topple-Free – Gyro Attitude Indicator immune to toppling

TRE – Type Rating Examiner, check airman, usually a Training Captain

TRI – Type Rating Instructor, usually a Training Captain

TRTO – Type Rating Training Organisation

TWI – Tactical Weapons Instructor

TWU – Tactical Weapons Unit

UNMIN – Unaccompanied Minor – an escorted child passenger with a large tag on a lanyard round his/her neck

UTC – Universal Time Coordinated (used to be known correctly as GMT)

V1 – Decision Speed on takeoff roll beyond which we must fly

VFR – Visual Flight Rules

VHF – Very High Frequency radio – civil airliners use it

VIP – Very Important Person – many Bizjet pax are VIP (see CIP)

VMC – Visual Meteorological Conditions

VNAV – Vertical Navigation System of FMC for automatic flight

VNE – Velocity Never Exceed

VOLMET – VHF Met reports automatically broadcast – Originally from the French VOL = Flight & MET = Meteo

VOR – VHF Omnidirectional Radio Beacon

VSI – Vertical Speed Indicator – in feet per minute for climb or descent

VVIP – Usually applies to Head of State, President, Royalty or Head of Government (Prime Minister for example)

Wet Lease – an aircraft leased to another operator WITH crew

WTL – Worn To Limits – engineering technical

--0--

THANKS GUYS ☺

I would like to especially thank Ashley Wilkes and Arthur Robinson for their painstaking proof-reading assistance. Without their help the final publication would have been littered with all sorts of errors and typos.

Any errors in the text which remain are entirely mine alone - apologies. JMcB.

65522108R00172

Made in the USA
Charleston, SC
30 December 2016